P9-BYR-330

# Faith Precedes
the Miracle

# Faith Precedes the Miracle

Based on Discourses of

## SPENCER W. KIMBALL

Published by
Deseret Book Company
Salt Lake City, Utah
1973

Library of Congress Catalog Card No. 72-91930
ISBN No. 0-87747-490-7

Third Printing 1973

Lithographed by

DESERET PRESS

in the United States of America

# *Acknowledgment*

I gratefully acknowledge the invaluable assistance
of my son Edward L. Kimball
in the preparation of this book.

# *Contents*

Preface --------------------------------------- xi

## SECTION ONE—TESTIMONY AND REVELATION

1. *Faith*

   Faith Precedes the Miracle --------------- 3
2. *Testimony*

   "Ye Receive Not Our Witness" ----------- 13
3. *Revelation*

   Continuing Communication with God ------- 21
4. *Other Worlds*

   Voices from Space -------------------- 47
5. *Knowledge of God*

   The Weak Things of the World ---------- 59
6. *Testimony of Christ*

   My Redeemer Lives Eternally ------------ 69
7. *Manifestation of God*

   Spiritual Eyes Behold God -------------- 83
8. *Death*

   Tragedy or Destiny? ------------------- 95

## SECTION TWO—MARRIAGE AND THE FAMILY

9. *Parental Responsibility*
   Reservoirs of Righteousness --------------- 109
10. *Mother's Care*
    "Are You There, Mother?" -------------- 115
11. *Marriage*
    John and Mary, Beginning Life Together ---- 125
12. *Loyalty*
    Lines of Communication ----------------- 137
13. *Fidelity*
    "Spouses . . . and None Else" ------------ 141


## SECTION THREE—MORALITY AND REPENTANCE

14. *Chastity*
    Love Versus Lust --------------------- 151
15. *Modesty*
    A Style of Our Own ------------------- 161
16. *Repentance*
    "Be Ye Clean" ---------------------- 169
17. *Forgiveness*
    "Except Ye Repent" ------------------ 187


## SECTION FOUR—RIGHTEOUSNESS

18. *Prayer*
    "Raise Your Voice to the Heavens" --------- 199
19. *Resisting Evil*
    "Put on the Whole Armour of God" -------- 213
20. *Blessings of Righteousness*
    'Tis Not Vain to Serve the Lord ---------- 221
21. *Self-Restraint*
    The Mistletoe ---------------------- 225
22. *Integrity*
    "Temptation and a Snare" -------------- 233
23. *Preparedness*
    The Ten Virgins --------------------- 249

24. *Dedication*

    Glimpses of Heaven _____ 259

25. *Sabbath Observance*

    Honor the Sabbath Day _____ 267

26. *Word of Wisdom*

    Hidden Treasures of Knowledge _____ 273

27. *Tithing*

    "Render . . . Unto God"_____ 281

# SECTION FIVE—THE RESTORED CHURCH

28. *Tolerance*

    "What God Hath Cleansed" _____ 293

29. *Compliance*

    "To Kick Against the Pricks" _____ 305

30. *Succession in the Presidency of the Church*

    The Need for a Prophet _____ 313

31. *Restoration*

    They Named Him Joseph _____ 323

32. *Book of Mormon*

    A Book of Vital Messages _____ 329

33. *Lamanite Promise*

    The Lamanite and the Gospel _____ 339

34. *Lamanite Future*

    A Changing World for Barry Begay _____ 351

Index _____ 359

# Preface

For as many years as I can remember the question has been, "How is your father?" My response to the question most often is to detail the latest news of his health and then add, "He still works harder than anyone I know." In this often-repeated exchange I am continually reminded of three major facts about him.

First, he is a widely known and loved man. Wherever I go people tell me about encounters with him—his remembering a name after years without contact, pulling on overalls to help his host milk the cows, writing individual letters to the parents of missionaries met during mission tours, giving his overcoat to someone who needed it more, and on and on—and they sense about him a dedication to the work of the Lord and a concern about them personally, which warms their feelings toward him and their memories of him.

Second, though he is no hypochondriac and suffers stoically through it all, he has had during his amazingly active life enough illnesses to make one wince simply at the listing—typhoid fever, smallpox, Bell's palsy, years of boils and carbuncles, a major heart attack, cancer of the throat resulting in the removal of most of his vocal cords, recurrence of cancer requiring radiation treatment, heart disease requiring open-heart surgery to replace a valve and transplant an artery, and most recently Bell's palsy again. It is no wonder then that when someone asks about my father, it is typically to inquire about his health. However, considering his health history and his age—77 —he is in amazingly good condition, having over a period of months since April, 1972, largely regained his strength after heart surgery so drastic as to have significant mortality rates in men his age.

Third, his capacity for work is phenomenal. He works hard and effectively and with rare dedication. Since his acceptance of the call as a General Authority, he has not stinted in his labors. He works to the point of exhaustion, yet recuperates remarkably quickly. It can be honestly said of him that he has hidden wells of strength upon which he calls so often and so substantially that one begins to think, erroneously, that they are inexhaustible.

For those who do not know them, some basic facts of his personal history may be of interest. Spencer W. Kimball was born in Salt Lake City, March 28, 1895, to Andrew and Olive Woolley Kimball. When he was a small child his father was called to move to Arizona to preside over a stake there. The family lived in Thatcher, Arizona. Father worked on the family farm, worked in a dairy in Globe, Arizona, in summers to earn his school money, and excelled academically and athletically in high school. He served a mission in the Central States. His university work was ended by a call to military service in World War I, but the war ended while he was still waiting for induction.

In 1918 he married Camilla Eyring, whose family had been driven from the Mormon colonies in Mexico during the Mexican Revolution in 1912; they lived in Pima, Arizona, a few miles from Thatcher. He was first employed in a bank and then helped develop an insurance and real estate partnership. He was called to serve as stake clerk under his father. Then, when his father died, he was clled to serve as a counselor to the new stake president. Io 1938 the stake was divided and he became the first stake president of the new Mount Graham Stake, with headquarters in Safford, Arizona, and a membership extending all the way to El Paso, Texas, 250 miles away.

During these years of laboriously building up a new business, attending to the leadership of a scattered stake, and running a small family acreage, he found time and energy for sports (especially handball) and community affairs. He contributed his efforts to the Boy Scout program, served on educational committees, worked in the Chamber of Commerce, and presided as a district governor of Rotary International. Though the family did not see him as much as other families might have seen their father, I felt no sense of abandonment; he was very much involved with us.

His call to the Council of the Twelve Apostles in 1943 was a soul-wrenching experience for him, as it must be for others called to that awesome responsibility. He described that climactic event in his life in his first conference address:

\*   \*   \*   \*   \*

I feel extremely humble in this calling that has come to me. Many people have asked me if I was surprised when it came. That, of course, is a very weak word for this experience. I was completely bewildered and shocked. I did have a premonition that it was coming, but very brief, however. On the eighth of July, when President J. Reuben Clark called me, I was electrified with a strong presentiment that something of this kind was going to happen. As I came home at noon, my boy was answering the telephone and he said, "Daddy, Salt Lake is calling."

I had had many calls from Salt Lake City. They hadn't ever worried me like this one. I knew that I had no unfinished business in Salt Lake City, and the thought came over me quickly, "You're going to be called to an important position." Then I hurriedly swept it from my mind, because it seemed so unworthy and so presumptuous, and I had convinced myself that such a thing was impossible by the time that I heard President Clark's voice a thousand miles away, saying: "Spencer, this is Brother Clark speaking. The brethren have just called you to fill one of the vacancies in the Quorum of the Twelve Apostles."

Like a bolt of lightning it came. I did a great deal of thinking in the brief moments that I was on the wire. There were quite a number of things said about disposing of my business, moving to headquarters, and other things to be expected of me. I couldn't repeat them all; my mind seemed to be traveling many paths all at once. I was dazed, almost numb with the shock. A picture of my life spread out before me. It seemed that I could see all of the people before me whom I had injured, or who had fancied that I had injured them, or to whom I had given offense, and all the small petty things of my life. I sensed immediately my inability and limitations and I cried back, "Not me, Brother Clark! You can't mean that!" I was virtually speechless. My heart pounded fiercely.

I recall two or three years ago, when Brother Harold B. Lee was giving his maiden address as an apostle of the Lord Jesus Christ from this stand, he told us of his experience through the night after he had been notified of his call. I think I now know something about the experience he had. I have been going through it for twelve weeks. I believe the Brethren were very kind to me in announcing my appointment when they did so that I might make the necessary adjustments in my business affairs, but perhaps they were more inspired to give me the time that I needed for a long period of purification, for in those long days and weeks I did a great deal of thinking and praying, and fasting and praying. There were conflicting thoughts that surged through my mind—seeming voices saying: "You can't do the work. You are not worthy. You have not the ability"—and always finally came the triumphant thought: "You must do the work assigned—you must make yourself able, worthy and qualified." And the battle raged on.

I remember reading that Jacob wrestled all night, "until the breaking of the day," for a blessing; and I want to tell you that for eighty-five nights I have gone through that experience, wrestling for a blessing. Eighty-five times the breaking of the day has found me on my knees praying to the Lord to help me and strengthen me and make me equal to this great responsiblity that has come to me. I have not sought positions nor have I been ambitious. Promotions have continued to come faster than I felt I was prepared for them.

I remember when I was called to be a counselor in the stake presidency. I was in my twenties. President Grant came down to help to bury my father, who was the former stake president, and reorganize the stake. I was the stake clerk. I recall that some of my relatives came to President Grant, unknown to me, after I had been chosen, and said, "President Grant, it's a mistake to call a young man like that to a position of responsibility and make an old man of him and tie him down." Finally, after some discussion, President Grant said very calmly, but firmly, "Well, Spencer has been called to this work, and he can do as he pleases about it," and, of course, when the call came, I accepted it gladly, and I have received great blessings therefrom.

A few days ago one of my well-to-do clients came to me and said, "Spencer, you're going away from us?"

"Yes," I said.

"Well, this is going to ruin you financially," he continued. "You are just getting started well; your business is prospering. You are making a lot of money now and the future looks bright yet. I don't know how you can do this. You don't have to accept the call, do you?"

And I said, "Brother, we do not have to accept any

call, but if you understand the Mormon way of life, those of us who have been reared in the Church and understand the discipline of the Church, we just always do accept such calls." And I further said to him: "Do you remember what Luke said, '. . . for a man's life consisteth not in the abundance of the things which he possesseth' (Luke 12:15), and all the bonds, lands, houses, and livestock are just things that mean so little in a person's abundant life."

It is strange how many things can go through one's mind in such a very short period when he is under strain and stress. I have heard of how people, when they were drowning, could see everything that had ever happened to them—especially the errors of their lives—and I have gone through that experience many times during these eighty-five endless days of emotional stress. Each dawn I seemed to expect this—which seemed such an impossible dream—to dissipate into vague nothingness, as my other dreams have, but reassurance came that it was real.

There are a few things that came to my attention recently that strengthen me and in which you might be interested—particularly with reference to prophecy made by my father. This was made known to me only a week ago. In preface to his statements, I will read a line or two from his patriarchal blessing given to him by Patriarch John Smith back in 1898. He said to my father: "Andrew Kimball, . . . thou shalt have the spirit of discernment to foretell future events and thy name shall be handed down with thy posterity in honorable remembrance from generation to generation." And then Brother Hatch, another patriarch, said: ". . . for thou art a prophet and came upon earth in this dispensation to be a great leader."

Just the other day Orville Allen came into the office to talk to me intimately and confidentially. After closing the door, he said, "Spencer, your father was a prophet. He made a prediction that has literally come to pass, and I want to tell you about it." He continued,

"Your father talked with me at the corral, one evening. I had brought a load of pumpkins for his pigs. You were just a little boy and you were sitting there, milking the cows, and singing to them as you milked. Your father turned to me and said, 'Brother, that boy, Spencer, is an exceptional boy. He always tries to mind me, whatever I ask him to do. I have dedicated him to be one of the mouthpieces of the Lord—the Lord willing. You will see him some day as a great leader. I have dedicated him to the service of God, and he will become a mighty man in the Church.'"

I say this, not in the sense of boasting, but in humility and appreciation. It came to me as a great surprise when first I heard of it the other day.

In these long weeks since July 8 I can tell you that I have been overwhelmed and have felt that I was unable to carry on this great work; that I was unworthy; that I was incapable because of my weaknesses and my limitations. I have felt many times that I was up against a blank wall. And in that interim I have been out in the desert and in high mountains alone, apart, and have poured out my soul to God. I have taken courage from one or two scriptures that constantly came to my mind and of which people continued to remind me. One was from Paul, and as I felt so foolish, small, and weak, I remembered that he said: "Because the foolishness of God is wiser than men; and the weakness of God is stronger than men. For ye see your calling, brethren, how that not many wise men after the flesh, not many mighty, not many noble, are called: But God hath chosen the foolish things of the world to confound the wise; and God hath chosen the weak things of the world to confound the things which are mighty. That no flesh should glory in his presence." (1 Corinthians 1:25-27, 29.)

When my feeling of incompetence wholly overwhelmed me, I remember the words of Nephi when he said: "I will go and do the things which the Lord hath commanded, for I know that the Lord giveth no commandments unto the children of men, save he shall prepare a way for them that they may accomplish the thing which he commandeth them." (1 Nephi 3:7.) I want to tell you that I lean heavily on these promises, that the Lord will strengthen and give me growth and fit and qualify me for this great work. I have seen the Lord qualify men. I shall do my utmost to show my appreciation to my Lord and my brethren by being a faithful servant. I am grateful for the opportunity of working with these honored and great men of the Authorities toward whom I have always had almost a worshipful devotion.

I know that this is the church and kingdom of God. It has been a part of me. Whenever it has prospered, I have gloried in it. When it was criticized, it has hurt me, for it seemed a part of my very being. Every fibre in my body bears witness that this is the gospel of Jesus Christ in its fullness. I testify to you that this is the work of God, that Jesus is the Christ, our Redeemer, our Master, our Lord, and I bear testimony to you in all sincerity and in deepest humility, in the name of Jesus Christ. Amen.

\*　\*　\*　\*　\*

From the beginning of his service as a General Authority, he has worked tirelessly in his assignments. For most of his nearly thirty years in the apostleship he has made up the schedules of conference assignments for action by the president of the quorum; he has been chairman of the Budget Committee, which has responsibility for allocating the financial resources of the Church among the programs; he has headed the Church Missionary Committee, with responsibility for assigning missionaries and suggesting mission presidents; he headed the Church Indian Committee for twenty-five years. Perhaps no aspect of Church work is so uniquely identified with his name as the Indian student placement program. He has been an advocate of the Indian peoples and the indefatigable promoter of Church programs designed to hasten the day when the promises to the Lamanites are wholly fulfilled.

He has not seen his role as author. As a General Authority he has devoted nearly all his time and talent to the tasks of preaching, counseling, and administering the programs of the Church. But those very tasks have in some measure compelled him to become an author.

In his responsibility to preach the gospel he has been conscientious in preparation and painstaking in formulation of his messages to the Church and to the world. As a counselor to thousands who have been burdened with sin and sorrow, he has gained an understanding of the myriad problems with which even striving Saints become burdened and has formulated responses to their earnest questions concerning the way of repentance and forgiveness. This experience led him finally to publish in book form *The Miracle of Forgiveness.*

Publication of that book was intended primarily to give him a convenient place to which to send troubled people for the answers he had thought through prayerfully and over the course of many years. The book's reception left him frankly amazed but deeply gratified that his work was responsive to a widespread interest in the overcoming of sin and the obtaining of divine forgiveness.

Even after the enthusiastic response to his book he was dubious about the wisdom of the proposal that he add one more book of sermons to those available in the stores and libraries. There was no new message he had to give the people; it was simply the gospel of Christ as explained in his words, with liberal reference to the scriptures. But the same could have been said of *The Miracle of Forgiveness,* which apparently filled a real need. He was finally persuaded that, just as he had been surprised at the number who found help in his first book, so there could be many people who would be helped by the messages in his sermons.

But having decided to make a book of sermons, it was still not enough simply to string together what had been said over the past thirty years. He decided rather to use the sermon as a resource from which to draw heavily, yet to attempt to mold them into a contemporary statement. Thus, an effort has been made to style the sermons for reading, while preserving the highly personal mode of expression.

In the many sermons he has delivered over the years there are several repeated strains. One is the Church Indian program. Another reflects his feeling of responsibility to speak forthrightly to members of the Church about sexual sins, warning of the approaches to them, emphasizing the seriousness of succumbing to the near-universal temptations, and pointing out the road back for those who have erred and yearn for reconcilation with the Lord. This is a difficult and unpleasant task, but one he has not shirked. His objective has not been to be popular, or to please the ear, but to preach repentance. It is true, however, that his directness, his earnestness, his careful statement of the problem and solution, and his obvious love and concern for those to whom he speaks have made him one of the most respected speakers of his generation. What he says is not intended to be entertaining, but almost always is worth hearing and rehearing.

This book is an effort to preserve for the benefit of those who read it the substance of his efforts to communicate to the Latter-day Saints his understanding of the gospel, his concern for the welfare of the people, and his love for the Savior. It is his hope that these efforts may help guide men to that faith in Christ which leads to the miracle of spiritual rebirth.

Edward L. Kimball

# SECTION ONE

*Testimony
and Revelation*

# Chapter One

*Faith*

# *Faith Precedes the Miracle*

Throughout the Church hundreds of thousands of faithful Saints have truly consecrated their lives and their energies to the work of the Lord, secure in the assurance that thereby they please him.

It is a disappointment, however, to find many others who are not willing to trust the Lord—or to trust in his promise when he says, "Prove me and see." I often wonder why men cannot trust their Lord. He has promised his children every blessing contingent upon their faithfulness, but fickle man places his trust in "the arm of flesh" and sets about to make his own way unaided by him who could do so much.

The Lord has challenged us:

> . . . prove me . . . if I will not open you the windows of heaven, and pour you out a blessing, that there shall not be room enough to receive it. (Malachi 3:10.)

The prophet Moroni stopped abruptly in his abridging to offer his own inspired comments concerning the matter of faith:

> I would show unto the world that faith is things which are hoped for and not seen; wherefore, dispute not because

ye see not, for ye receive no witness until after the trial of your faith. (Ether 12:6.)

## Father Adam understood this basic principle:

> . . . an angel of the Lord appeared unto Adam, saying: Why dost thou offer sacrifices unto the Lord? And Adam said unto him: I know not, save the Lord commanded me. (Moses 5:6.)

He showed his unwavering faith—and since the witness and the miracle follow rather than precede the faith, the angel then sought to enlighten him, saying:

> This thing is a similitude of the sacrifice of the Only Begotten of the Father. . . . (Moses 5:7.)

In faith we plant the seed, and soon we see the miracle of the blossoming. Men have often misunderstood and have reversed the process. They would have the harvest before the planting, the reward before the service, the miracle before the faith. Even the most demanding labor unions would hardly ask the wages before the labor. But many of us would have the vigor without the observance of the health laws, prosperity through the opened windows of heaven without the payment of our tithes. We would have the close communion with our Father without fasting and praying; we would have rain in due season and peace in the land without observing the Sabbath and keeping the other commandments of the Lord. We would pluck the rose before planting the roots; we would harvest the grain before sowing and cultivating.

If we could only realize, as Moroni writes:

> For if there be no faith among the children of men God can do no miracle among them. . . .

> And neither at any time hath any wrought miracles until after their faith; wherefore they first believed in the Son of God. (Ether 12:12, 18.)

## John said:

> But though [Jesus] had done so many miracles before them, yet they believed not on him. (John 12:37.)

The Lord made it clear that faith is not developed by miracles.

> But, behold, faith cometh not by signs, but signs follow those that believe. (D&C 63:9.)

To the scribes and Pharisees who demanded signs without the preliminary faith and works the Lord said:

> An evil and adulterous generation seeketh after a sign. . . . (Matthew 12:39.)

In our own modern times we have eloquent evidence. Sidney Rigdon did not retain his membership in the kingdom even though he had, with Joseph Smith, witnessed marvelous signs. Had he not participated in the great vision and had he not been the recipient of many revelations? And in spite of all these manifestations from our Heavenly Father, he did not remain in the kingdom.

Oliver Cowdery saw many signs. He handled the sacred plates; saw John the Baptist; received the higher priesthood from Peter, James, and John; and was the recipient of many great miracles, and yet they could not hold him to the faith.

Amassed evidence in signs and works and miracles failed to touch the stony hearts of the Galilean cities:

> Then began he to upbraid the cities wherein most of his mighty works were done, because they repented not:
>
> Woe unto thee, Chorazin! woe unto thee, Bethsaida! . . .
>
> And thou, Capernaum, which art exalted unto heaven, shalt be brought down to hell: for if the mighty works, which have been done in thee, had been done in Sodom, it would have remained until this day. (Matthew 11:20-21, 23.)

Paul, speaking to the Hebrews, said: .

> By faith Noah, being warned of God of things not seen as yet, moved with fear, prepared an ark to the saving of his house. . . . (Hebrews 11:7.)

As yet there was no evidence of rain and flood. His people mocked and called him a fool. His preaching fell on deaf ears. His warnings were considered irrational.

There was no precedent; never had it been known that
a deluge could cover the earth. How foolish to build an
ark on dry ground with the sun shining and life moving
forward as usual! But time ran out. The ark was finished.
The floods came. The disobedient and rebellious were
drowned. The miracle of the ark followed the faith manifested in its building.

Paul said again:

> Through faith also Sara herself received strength to con-
> ceive seed, and was delivered of a child when she was past
> age, because she judged him faithful who had promised.
>
> Therefore sprang there even of one, and him as good as
> dead, so many as the stars of the sky in multitude, and as the
> sand which is by the sea shore innumerable. (Hebrews 11:11-
> 12.)

So absurd it was to be told that children could be
born of centenarians that even Sarah doubted at first.
But the faith of a noble pair prevailed, and the miracle
son was born to father multitudes of nations.

Exceeding faith was shown by Abraham when the
superhuman test was applied to him. His young "child
of promise" must now be offered upon the sacrificial altar.
It was God's command, but it seemed so contradictory!
How could his son, Isaac, be the father of an uncountable
posterity if in his youth his mortal life was to be terminated? Why should he, Abraham, be called upon to do
this revolting deed? It was irreconcilable, impossible!
And yet he believed God. His undaunted faith carried
him with breaking heart toward Mount Moriah with this
young son who little suspected the agonies through which
his father must have been passing. Saddled asses took
the party and supplies. The father and the son, carrying
the fire and the wood, mounted to the place of sacrifice.

"Behold the fire and the wood," said Isaac, "but
where is the lamb for a burnt offering?" What a heavy
heart and sad voice it must have been which replied:
"My son, God will provide himself a lamb for a burnt
offering. . . ." (Genesis 22:7-8.)

The place was reached, the altar built, the fire kindled, and the lad, now surely knowing, but trusting and believing, was upon the altar. The father's raised hand was stopped in mid-air by a commanding voice:

> Lay not thine hand upon the lad. . . . now I know that thou fearest God, seeing thou hast not withheld thy son, thine only son from me. (Genesis 22:12.)

And as the near perfect prophet found the ram in the thicket and offered it upon the altar, he heard the voice of God again speaking:

> And in thy seed shall all the nations of the earth be blessed; because thou hast obeyed my voice. (Genesis 22:18.)

This great and noble Abraham—

> Who against hope believed in hope, that he might become the father of many nations. . . .
>
> And being not weak in faith, he considered not his own body now dead, when he was about an hundred years old, neither yet the deadness of Sarah's womb:
>
> He staggered not at the promise of God through unbelief; but was strong in faith, giving glory to God;
>
> And being fully persuaded that, what he had promised, he was able also to perform. (Romans 4:18-21.)

Father Abraham and Mother Sarah knew—knew the promise would be fulfilled. How? They did not know and did not demand to know. Isaac positively would live to be the father of a numerous posterity. They knew he would, even though he might need to die. They knew he could still be raised from the dead to fulfill the promise, and faith here preceded the miracle.

Paul again said to the Hebrews:

> By faith they [the children of Israel] passed through the Red sea as by dry land. . . . (Hebrews 11:29.)

The Israelites knew, as did Pharaoh and his hosts, that "they are entangled in the land, the wilderness hath shut them in." (Exodus 14:3.)

And as Pharaoh's trained army approached with all the horses and chariots of Egypt, the escaping multitudes knew full well that they were hemmed in by the marshes, the deserts, and the sea. There was no earthly chance for them to escape the wrath of their pursuers. And in their terror they indicted Moses:

> Because there were no graves in Egypt, hast thou taken us away to die in the wilderness? . . .
>
> . . . it had been better for us to serve the Egyptians, than that we should die in the wilderness. (Exodus 14:11-12.)

No hope on earth for their liberation! What could save them now? The gloating armed forces of Egypt knew that Israel was trapped. Israel knew it only too well. But Moses, their inspired leader with supreme faith, knew that God would not have called them on this exodus only to have them destroyed. He knew God would provide the escape. He may not at this moment have known just how, but he trusted.

Moses commanded his people:

> Fear ye not, stand still, and see the salvation of the Lord, which he will shew to you to day: for the Egyptians whom ye have seen to day, ye shall see them again no more for ever.
>
> The Lord shall fight for you. . . . (Exodus 14:13-14.)

The mighty warriors pressed on. Hope must have long since died in the breasts of the timid Israelites who knew not faith. Deserts and wilderness and the sea—the uncrossable sea! No boats, no rafts, no bridges, nor time to construct them! Hopelessness, fear, despair must have gripped their hearts.

And then the miracle came. It was born of the faith of their indomitable leader. A cloud hid them from the view of their enemies. A strong east wind blew all the night; the waters were parted; the bed of the sea was dry; and Israel crossed to another world and saw the returning sea envelop and destroy their pursuers. Israel was safe. Faith had been rewarded, and Moses was vindicated. The impossible had happened. An almost superhuman faith had given birth to an unaccountable and mysterious miracle that was to be the theme of the sermons and warnings of Israel and their prophets for centuries.

Israel was later ready to cross into the Promised Land, the productivity and beauty of which could probably be seen from the higher hills. But how to get there? There were no bridges nor ferries across the flooding Jordan. A great prophet, Joshua, received the mind of the Lord and commanded, and another miracle was born of faith.

> . . . and [as] the feet of the priests that bare the ark were dipped in the brim of the water. . . .
>
> . . . the waters which came down from above stood and rose up upon an heap . . . and those that came down . . . failed, and were cut off: . . .
>
> . . . and all the Israelites passed over on dry ground, until all the people were passed clean over Jordan. (Joshua 3:15-17.)
>
> . . . the soles of the priests' feet were lifted up unto the dry land, that the waters of Jordan returned unto their place, and flowed over all his banks, as they did before. (Joshua 4:18.)

The elements find control through faith. The wind, the clouds, the heavens obey the voice of faith. It was by and through the faith of Elijah that the drouth, which devastated Israel, prolonged for three interminable years, was finally ended when repentance had come to Israel.

> . . . Ahab did more to provoke the Lord God of Israel to anger than all the kings of Israel that were before him. (1 Kings 16:33.)

And Elijah the prophet declared:

> . . . there shall not be dew nor rain these years, but according to my word. (1 Kings 17:1.)

The brooks dried up; rivers ceased to run; forage was scarce; famine was upon the land; and a king and his people were begging for relief—a people who had lost themselves in the worship of Baal. At Mount Carmel came the contest of power. At Elijah's command, fire came down from heaven and ignited the sacrifice and shocked the Baal worshipers once more into repentant submission.

Miracle followed faith again, and though the heavens were still clear and there was no indication of rain on the parched land, the prophet warned King Ahab:

> . . . Prepare thy chariot, and get thee down, that the rain stop thee not. (1 Kings 18:44.)

With his face between his knees, as he sat on Carmel, Elijah sent his servant seven times to look toward the sea. Six times there were cloudless skies and calm sea, but on the seventh he reported: "Behold, there ariseth a little cloud out of the sea, like a man's hand. . . ." (1 Kings 18:44.)

Soon the heavens were black with clouds, and the wind was carrying them to Palestine, and "there was a great rain" and a dry, parched land was drenched in moisture, and the miracle of faith had again made good the promises of the Lord.

It was by the supreme faith of the three Hebrews that they were delivered from the fiery furnace of their king, Nebuchadnezzar. And the king asked:

> Did not we cast three men bound into the midst of the fire? They answered and said unto the king, True, O king.
>
> He answered and said, Lo, I see four men loose, walking in the midst of the fire, and they have no hurt; and the form of the fourth is like the Son of God.
>
> . . . these men, upon whose bodies the fire had no power, nor was an hair of their head singed, neither were their coats changed, nor the smell of fire had passed on them. (Daniel 3:24-26, 27.)

Now, if you would discount these miracles of the Old Testament, how can you accept the New Testament? You would also have difficulty in accepting Paul and his associate apostles, and the Lord Jesus Christ, for they have verified and documented those miraculous events.

How can these stories of faith be brought into our own lives? Faith is needed as much as ever before. Little can we see. We know not what the morrow will bring. Accidents, sickness, even death seem to hover over us continually. Little do we know when they might strike.

It takes faith—unseeing faith—for young people to proceed immediately with their family responsibilities in the face of financial uncertainties. It takes faith for the young woman to bear her family instead of accepting employment, especially when schooling for the young husband is to be finished. It takes faith to observe the Sabbath when "time and a half" can be had working, when profit can be made, when merchandise can be sold. It takes a great faith to pay tithes when funds are scarce and demands are great. It takes faith to fast and have family prayers and to observe the Word of Wisdom. It takes faith to do home teaching, stake missionary work, and other service, when sacrifice is required. It takes faith to fill full-time missions. But know this—that all these are of the planting, while faithful, devout families, spiritual security, peace, and eternal life are the harvest.

Remember that Abraham, Moses, Elijah, and others could not see clearly the end from the beginning. They also walked by faith and without sight.

Remember again that no gates were open; Laban was not drunk; and no earthly hope was justified at the moment Nephi exercised his faith and set out finally to get the plates.

Remember that there were no clouds in the sky nor any hygrometer in his hand when Elijah promised an immediate break in the long extended drouth. Though Joshua may have witnessed the miracle of the Red Sea, yet he could not by mortal means perceive that the flooding Jordan would back up for the exact time needed for the crossing, and then flow again on its way to the Dead Sea.

Remember that there were no clouds in the sky, no evidence of rain, and no precedent for the deluge when Noah built the ark according to commandment. There was no ram in the thicket when Isaac and his father left for Moriah for the sacrifice. Remember there were no towns and cities, no farms and gardens, no homes and storehouses, no blossoming desert in Utah when the persecuted pioneers crossed the plains.

And remember that there were no heavenly beings in Palmyra, on the Susquehanna, or on Cumorah when the soul-hungry Joseph slipped quietly into the grove, knelt in prayer on the river bank, and climbed the slopes of the sacred hill.

But know this, that just as undaunted faith has stopped the mouths of lions, made ineffective fiery flames, opened dry corridors through rivers and seas, protected against deluge and drouth, and brought heavenly manifestations at the instance of prophets, so in each of our lives faith can heal the sick, bring comfort to those who mourn, strengthen resolve against temptation, relieve from the bondage of harmful habits, lend the strength to repent and change our lives, and lead to a sure knowledge of the divinity of Jesus Christ. Indomitable faith can help us live the commandments with a willing heart and thereby bring blessings unnumbered, with peace, perfection, and exaltation in the kingdom of God.

# Chapter Two

# "Ye Receive Not Our Witness"

Many persons have experienced the glow, the warmth, the peace that comes to those who see the eternal path clearly and know positively of its correctness, and who are courageously toiling toward eternal goals. Others are doubtful that anyone can "know" any such thing, but the Lord has repeated numerous times the definite promise.

> If any man will do his will, he shall know of the doctrine, whether it be of God, or whether I speak of myself. (John 7:17.)

In courts of law the witness is asked to take an oath that the information he is about to give is "the truth, the whole truth, and nothing but the truth," and the statements made are called his "testimony."

In spiritual matters, we may likewise give testimony. We can have positive certainty of the reality of a personal God; the continued active life of the Christ, separate from but like his Father; the divinity of the restoration through Joseph Smith and other prophets of the organization and doctrines of God's church on earth; and the power of the divine, authoritative priesthood given to men through revelations from God. These can be known by every responsible person as surely as the knowledge that the sun shines. To fail to attain this knowledge is to admit that one has not paid the price. Like academic degrees, it is obtained by intense strivings. That soul who is clean through repentance and the ordinances receives it if he desires and reaches for it, investigates conscientiously, studies, and prays faithfully.

A sure knowledge of the spiritual is an open door to great rewards and joys unspeakable. To ignore the testimony is to grope in caves of impenetrable darkness, to creep along in fog over hazardous highways. That person is to be pitied who may still be walking in darkness at noonday, who is tripping over obstacles that can be removed, and who dwells in the dim flickering candlelight of insecurity and skepticism when he need not. The spiritual knowledge of truth is the electric light illuminating the cavern; the wind and sun dissipating the fog; the power equipment removing boulders from the road. It is the mansion on the hill replacing the shack in the marshes; the harvester shelving the sickle and cradle; the tractor, train, automobile, and plane displacing the ox team. It is the rich nourishing kernels of corn instead of the husks in the trough. It is much more than all else, for—

> . . . this is life eternal, that they might know thee the only true God, and Jesus Christ, whom thou hast sent. (John 17:3.)

Eternal life is the prize of greatest value. To obtain it is not easy. The price is high.

Nicodemus of old inquired concerning the price. The answer perplexed him. Let us interview that good man who came so near and yet evidently missed the mark.

Your name is Nicodemus? You are a member of the powerful sect of the Pharisees? You are a member of the Jewish Sanhedrin? You knew the person from Nazareth called Jesus Christ? You heard his sermons and witnessed his miracles? You looked into his eyes and heard his voice?

You are a good man, Nicodemus, honorable and just, for you will yet defend our Lord before your colleagues, asking he be not condemned without a hearing. You are also generous, for you will yet bring one hundred weight of aloes and myrrh to his burial. You have at least some faith, but have you courage enough to face criticism? You come under cover of darkness because of your position. You have not been seen. You are addressing our Lord:

> Rabbi, we know that thou art a teacher come from God: for no man can do these miracles that thou doest, except God be with him. (John 3:2.)

His ready answer to your unspoken question wrinkles your brow. It is the simple total answer to the weightiest of all questions.

> Verily, verily I say unto thee, Except a man be born again, he cannot see the kingdom of God. (John 3:3.)

You are well versed in the law, Nicodemus, but what of the gospel? To gain eternal life, there must be a rebirth, a transformation, and an unburdening oneself of pride, weaknesses, and prejudice. You must be as a little child, clean, teachable. You seem not to understand.

"How can a man be born when he is old?" (John 3:4.) Your question is strange for a learned man. Must you reduce all to human logic? Must everything be rational to your finite, materialistic mind?

Is it so complex? Are you afraid of what your brother Pharisees may think of you, fearful of losing your exalted place in the Sanhedrin? Or do you not see? Certainly a little glimpse has been given you. You acknowledged the miracle worker must be sent from God, but the curtain so slightly opened will close again if you do not act upon the new knowledge being offered you.

You are highly educated, my good man. Many sit at your feet to learn. Does your superior training blind you? Must a prophet or a God be measured in the test tubes of a physical laboratory? Can you not accept anything you cannot prove by the rules of the schools in which you studied?

You are not accepting it. Is it frustrating in its simplicity? You are rationalizing, sir. You cannot weigh this on the scales of your secular knowledge and training. They are too crude, mundane. You need some finer mechanism.

> Verily, verily, I say unto thee, Except a man be born of water and of the Spirit, he cannot enter into the kingdom of God.
>
> That which is born of the flesh is flesh; and that which is born of the Spirit is spirit.
>
> Marvel not that I said unto thee, Ye must be born again.
>
> The wind bloweth where it listeth, and thou hearest the sound thereof, but canst not tell whence it cometh, and whither it goeth; so is every one that is born of the Spirit. (John 3:5-8.)

How beautiful—how forceful—how positive! Is there excuse to question, to hesitate, to reject? O Nicodemus, this moment of crisis cannot last long. You are on a perilous summit. Your decision can mean the difference between exaltation and a deprivation greater than you know. You had a spark of desire. Would you extinguish it?

What made you refer to our Master as "a teacher come from God"? Do you not believe in prophets? Have you not all your life waited for a Redeemer? After all his sermons, testimonies, and miracles, is he still only an inspired teacher to you? Could he not be the long-awaited Christ? Have you tried to believe and accept, or are you bound down with fetters of tradition, chains of materialism, and handcuffs of prestige?

O timid one, awaken, exert yourself, draw back the curtains your training and background have hung over the windows of your soul. You are speaking to no ordinary man, no common philosopher, no mere teacher. You are in the presence of the real Messiah, the great physician, the master psychiatrist, the very Christ. You are questioning the maker of heaven and earth, the Son of God.

Open the curtains, my skeptic brother. Rid yourself of your intellectual conservatism. This is a crucial moment. You are being offered a gift priceless beyond your imagination. Will you let it pass? Talking with Christ, you should be awed to a tremble, quaking in shoeless feet on such holy ground, and on your knees in reverent humility. This is your Lord, your Savior, your Redeemer. Can't you understand, O ye of little faith? Can't you feel his love and kindness and see the sadness and disappointment in those penetrating eyes as he notes your withdrawal? He is saying, in effect, "Set aside your pride and arrogance. Cast from you all worldly burdens. Repent of your transgressions; purify your hands, and mind, and heart, believing that I am the bread of life, the waters from the pure spring. Accept me and my gospel. Go down into the waters in proper baptism."

Can you envision the cleanliness as one emerges from the watery grave, washed, and the freedom and joy and glory of it? But after all this you still ask, "How can these things be?" Your question brings from the Master this chastisement: "Art thou a master of Israel, and knowest not these things?" (John 3:10.)

O my brother, opportunity's doors are closing. Why can't you understand? Too many materialistic obstacles? He knows your influence, wealth, erudition, your exalted place in community, in government, in the powerful church group.

He offers you not a dependent, decadent kingdom like your doomed and dying Judah. He invites you to rule, not as emperor of a temporary world power like Rome, which is destined to crumble as clay, but citizenship in the kingdom of heaven, eventually to rise in stature and authority until you are a king in your own right with a dominion greater than the combined empires of all the earth.

Your decision seems burdened with concern for earthly treasures and the plaudits of men and the conveniences of affluence. Our heart weeps for you, friend Nicodemus. You seem such a good man, philanthropic, kind, generous. You could have been such a power in the Lord's kingdom. You had a spark of desire. It could have been kindled into a living flame. You might have been one of his seventies, to proselyte as an advance agent, or an apostle, or even to be the president of his church. You might have filled the vacancy when Matthias was called or have been an apostle to the gentiles with Paul. How little we realize the doors of opportunity that we oft close with one wrong decision. But the price was too high.

Unwilling that you slip back in your darkness without having every opportunity, Christ will bear you his testimony again. He will not leave you guiltless. You cannot escape the condemnation of this testimony, Mr. Rationalizer. Hear him:

> If I have told you earthly things, and ye believe not, how shall ye believe, if I tell you of heavenly things?
>
> For God sent not his Son into the world to condemn the world; but that the world through him might be saved.
>
> Verily, verily, I say unto thee, We speak that we do know, and testify that we have seen; and ye receive not our witness. (John 3:12, 17, 11)

O Nicodemus, why did you receive not his witness? Why did you not open your heart to understanding? Why did you hestitate when the Redeemer of the world so condescended? Had you humbly taken the first steps of repentance and proper baptism, then would have come to you the Holy Ghost through the laying on of hands by one of his apostles, or he himself might have done it.

The Holy Ghost would have abided with you so long as you merited and would have whispered to you so that you too could have exclaimed with your Redeemer:

> We speak that [which] we do know, and testify that [which] we have seen. (John 3:11.)
>
> You might have walked where Jesus walked and stayed where he was staying;
> You might have eaten bread and sop and knelt where he was praying;

He might have washed your weary feet and wiped them with
his dryer;
He might have laid his precious hands upon your head with
fire.

You might have eased his weary way and wiped away his
bleeding;
You might have helped in his defense when he was sorely
needing;
Most disappointing words are oft expressed by tongue and
writing;
The saddest words, "It might have been," are always the most
biting.

Now, my beloved friends, you too are generous and
kind. You too are prayerful and religious. But are you
also like Nicodemus, burdened down with preconceived
and prejudiced notions? Are you too wealthy and fettered
with the cares of this world to accept the difficult demands
of Christ's church? Are you so influential as to fear prejudice to your position or local influence? Are you too weak
to accept and carry a load of service? Are you too busy to
study and pray and learn of Christ and his program? Are
you too materialistically trained to accept the miracles,
visions, prophets, and revelations?

If any of you is a modern Nicodemus, I beg of you to
grasp the new world of truths. Your Lord Jesus Christ
pleads with you:

My true church is restored to earth with my saving doctrines.

I have placed in authoritative positions apostles and others
divinely called, and in leadership a prophet who today receives
my divine revelations.

Churches are many, but they are churches of men, not
mine.

Creeds are numerous, but they are not of my authorship.

Organizations are everywhere, but they are not organized
nor accepted by me.

Pretended and usurping representatives are legion, but I
called them not; nor do I recognize their ordinances.

My second coming is near at hand.

\* \* \* \* \*

. . . I stand at the door, and knock: if any man hear my voice, and open the door, I will come in to him, and will sup with him, and he with me.

To him that overcometh will I grant to sit with me in my throne. . . .

He that hath an ear, let him hear. . . . (Revelation 3:20-22.)

# Chapter Three

*Revelation*

# Continuing Communication with God

$\mathcal{I}$ received a letter of inquiry from a missionary in Germany, in which he said: "We speak continually . . . of the necessity of living prophets upon the earth and base our case on the testimony of a young man who saw and spoke with the Father and the Son, and recorded his experiences. . . . However, . . . *we have no record of a continuation of revelation. . . .*"

My first reaction was shock—shock to think that a young person twenty years old could be conscientious in making the statement that "we have no record of a continuation of revelation."

Millions feel that what is written in the Bible is the total of the revelations of the Lord, in spite of John's statement that if all that Jesus did were recorded, there would be numerous books. Some Latter-day Saints also make a similar error and feel that what is written in the standard works constitutes the sum total of the revelations in this dispensation. To this error George Q. Cannon, a member of the First Presidency, speaks:

> Some have deceived themselves with the idea that because revelations have not been written and published, therefore,

there has been a lessening of power in the Church of Christ.
This is a very great mistake.

. . . the servants of the Lord *do* receive revelations, and
they are as binding upon the people as though they were
printed and published throughout all the Stakes of Zion. The
oracles of God are here, and He speaks through His servant
whom He has chosen to hold the keys. . . . We have been blessed
as a people with an abundance of revelation.

Have this people ever seen the day when the counsel of
God's servants has not been sufficient to guide them in the
midst of difficulties? No. We never have. There has not been
a single minute that this people has been left without the voice
of God; there has not been a single minute since this church
was founded to this time that the power of God has not been
plainly manifested in our midst. . . . (*Gospel Truth,* p. 332.)

The day of revelation has never passed; the Lord continues to communicate with his servants in our own day
*as always.*

If revelations cease, either men are unresponsive and
in the darkness of apostasy or God is dead. Since we know
positively that God lives and is the same "yesterday, today
and forever," we can gauge the faithfulness and spirituality
of men by the degree and intensity of the communication between them and God.

Revelation is the process whereby God makes himself
known to men. . . . Revelation presupposes on the part of
men a capacity of response. . . . Response calls for faith. . . .
The scriptures are the record of God's self-revelation and its
results. . . . Revelation is therefore inseparable from faith, and
unless a faith response is evoked, there is no proper revelation.
(*Harper's Bible Dictionary,* p. 614.)

If the gifts are rejected, that does not end the existence
of the gift. If the diamond ring offered is not accepted,
the ring itself is not destroyed. President George Q. Cannon
says:

Their reception or non-reception [of revelations] would not
affect in the least the divine authenticity. But it would be for
the people to accept them after God had revealed them. In
this way, they have been submitted to the Church to see
whether the members would accept them as binding upon them

or not. Joseph himself had too high a sense of his prophetic office and the authority he had received from the Lord to ever submit the revelations which he had received from the Lord to any individual or to any body, however numerous, to have them pronounce upon their validity. (*Gospel Truth,* p. 332.)

It is worth emphasizing that there are many kinds of revelations; some are awesome and world-transforming while others are less spectacular, involving inspiration in carrying out the details of the Lord's work. The vision in which the Prophet Joseph Smith saw the Father and Son is one of the greatest of all revelations, ancient or modern. It is not inferior even to the vision to Peter, James, and John, the Presidency of the early church on the Mount of Transfiguration. They followed Jesus into the high mountain, where "his face did shine as the sun and his raiment was white as the light." Here they saw Moses and Elias, long since dead, and were with the transfigured Christ and heard the voice of Elohim introducing his Beloved Son, Jehovah.

Another spectacular vision was that of Saul of Tarsus, who saw and heard the resurrected Lord, Jesus Christ. Apparently he did not see Elohim at this time.

Enoch's vision was awesome. He says:

> . . . I stood upon the mount, I beheld the heavens open, and I was clothed upon with glory;

> And I saw the Lord; and he stood before my face, and he talked with me, even as a man talketh one with another, face to face; and he said unto me: Look, and I will show unto thee the world for the space of many generations. (Moses 7:3-4.)

Abraham was known as "the friend of God" and he said:

> . . . I, Abraham, talked with the Lord, face to face, as one man talketh with another; and he told me of the works which his hands had made. (Abraham 3:11.)

And through Aaron and Miriam the Lord described his revelations to Moses:

> If there be a prophet among you, I the Lord will make myself known unto him in a vision, and will speak unto him in a dream.

> My servant Moses is not so, who is faithful in all mine house.
>
> With him will I speak mouth to mouth, even apparently, and not in dark speeches; and the similitude of the Lord shall he behold: wherefore then were ye not afraid to speak against my servant Moses. (Numbers 12:6-8.)

These tremendously important experiences are so uncommon that in all of recorded history there is only a small number that are comparable. Few revelations, whether to Moses or Abraham or Joseph Smith, were so spectacular.

I would not minimize the importance of any of the revelations in the Doctrine and Covenants, but only a few of the 136 sections reveal the appearance of heavenly beings. Most of the revelations came as did the countless revelations to the prophets throughout the centuries: by vision, by dream, and by deep impressions. This is illustrated by the words of Enos:

> And while I was thus struggling in the spirit, behold, the voice of the Lord came into my mind again, saying: I will visit thy brethren according to their diligence in keeping my commandments. . . . (Enos 10.)

It must be remembered, too, that not all the revelations that came to the Prophet are printed in the Doctrine and Covenants. These he chose as being more helpful and more greatly needed by the people. Many of his revelations applied only to the moment and to the problem at hand.

There were others of our brethren in the days past who had spectacular visions or spiritual experiences. There were Adam, Lehi, Nephi, the brother of Jared, and many others.

Revelations often come in dreams, also, and who is there to say when a dream ends and a vision begins? President Wilford Woodruff made this statement in the general conference, October 10, 1900:

After the death of Joseph Smith, I saw and conversed with him many times in my dreams in the night season. On one occasion he and his brother Hyrum met me when on the sea going on a mission to England. I had Dan Jones with me. He received his mission from Joseph Smith before his death; and the Prophet talked freely to me about the mission I was then going to perform. And he also talked to me with regard to the mission of the Twelve Apostles in the flesh, and he laid before me the work they had to perform; and he also spoke of the reward they would receive after death. And there were many other things he laid before me in his interview on that occasion. And when I awoke many of the things he had told me were taken from me, I could not comprehend them. I have had many interviews with Brother Joseph until the last fifteen or twenty years of my life; I have not seen him for that length of time. But during my travels in the southern country last winter I had many interviews with President Young, and with Heber C. Kimball, and George A. Smith, and Jedediah M. Grant, and many others who are dead. They attended our conference, they attended our meetings. And on one occasion, I saw Brother Brigham and Brother Heber ride in a carriage ahead of the carriage in which I rode when I was on my way to attend conference; and they were dressed in most priestly robes. When we arrived at our destination I asked President Young if he would preach to us. He said, "No, I have finished my testimony in the flesh, I shall not talk to this people any more. But (said he) I have come to see you; I have come to watch over you, and to see what the people are doing. Then (said he) I want you to teach the people—and I want you to follow this counsel yourself—that they must labor and so live as to obtain the Holy Spirit, for without this you cannot build up the kingdom: without the spirit of God you are in danger of walking in the dark, and in danger of failing to accomplish your calling as apostles and as elders in the Church and Kingdom of God. And, said he, Brother Joseph taught me this principle." And I will here say, that I have heard him refer to that while he was living. But what I was going to say is this: The thought came to me that Brother Joseph had left the work of watching over this Church and Kingdom to others, and that he had gone ahead, and that he had left this work to men who have lived and labored with us since he left us. This idea manifested itself to me, that such men advance in the spirit world. And I believe myself that these men who have died and gone into the spirit world had this mission left with them, that is, a certain portion of them, to watch over the Latter-day Saints. (*Journal of Discourses*, volume 21, pp. 317-18.)

Would not these modern visions and dreams rate fully with the dreams of Joseph, son of Jacob, when the sheaf of Joseph stood upright in the field surrounded by the sheaves of his brethren, all of which bent toward his and made obeisance to Joseph's sheaf? (See Genesis 37:7.)

And his dream in prison revealing the seven years of plenty and the seven years of famine? (See Genesis 41: 26-30.)

Are not the visions of President Woodruff and President Joseph F. Smith on the redemption of the dead on a par with the vision of Lehi of the tree of life; and that of Nephi with his similar dream; and that of Jacob when he saw the ladder set up on the earth and angels of God ascending and descending on it?

Again, you will recall the vision of the Prophet Joseph and Sidney Rigdon, when they saw the Redeemer on the right hand of the Father. Would those visions not be comparable to the experience of Daniel when he also saw the great vision and described the heavenly being who came to him? And also like the vision of John the Revelator who similarly described the person and being of Jesus Christ whom he saw and heard?

There must be innumerable experiences that the Brethren have had which are considered too sacred to relate or publish. But we have the published experience of Orson F. Whitney. Though serving on a mission he was spending much of his time as a correspondent for the *Salt Lake Herald.*

> Then came a marvelous manifestation, an admonition from a higher source, one impossible to ignore. It was a dream, or a vision in a dream, as I lay upon my bed in the little town of Columbia, Lancaster County, Pennsylvania. I seemed to be in the Garden of Gethsemane, a witness of the Savior's agony. I saw Him as plainly as ever I have seen anyone. Standing behind a tree in the foreground, I beheld Jesus, with Peter, James and John, as they came through a little wicket gate at my right. Leaving the three Apostles there, after telling them to kneel and pray, the Son of God passed over to the

other side, where He also knelt and prayed. It was the same prayer with which all Bible readers are familiar: "Oh my Father, if it be possible, let this cup pass from me; nevertheless not as I will, but as thou wilt."

As He prayed the tears streamed down his face, which was toward me. I was so moved at the sight that I also wept, out of pure sympathy. My whole heart went out to him; I loved him with all my soul, and longed to be with him as I longed for nothing else.

Presently He arose and walked to where those Apostles were kneeling—fast asleep! He shook them gently, awoke them, and in a tone of tender reproach, untinctured by the least show of anger or impatience, asked them plaintively if they could not watch with him one hour. There He was, with the awful weight of the world's sin upon his shoulders, with the pangs of every man, woman and child shooting through his sensitive soul—and they could not watch with him one poor hour! . . .

All at once the circumstances seemed to change, the scene remaining just the same. Instead of before, it was after the crucifixion, and the Savior, with the three Apostles, now stood together in a group at my left. They were about to depart and ascend into Heaven. I could endure it no longer. I ran from behind the tree, fell at his feet, clasped Him around the knees, and begged Him to take me with Him.

I shall never forget the kind and gentle manner in which He stopped, raised me up, and embraced me. It was so vivid, so real. I felt the very warmth of his body, as He held me in His arms and said in tenderest tones: "No, my son; those have finished their work; they can go with me; but you must stay and finish yours." Still I clung to Him. Gazing up into His face—for He was taller than I—I besought him fervently: "Well, promise me that I will come to you at the last." Smiling sweetly, He said: "That will depend entirely upon yourself." I awoke with a sob in my throat, and it was morning.

"That's from God," said Elder Musser, when I related to him what I had seen and heard. "I do not need to be told that," was my reply. I saw the moral clearly. I had never thought of being an Apostle, nor of holding any other office in the Church, and it did not occur to me even then. Yet I know that those sleeping Apostles meant me. I was asleep at my post—as any man is who, having been divinely appointed to do one thing, does another.

But from that hour, all was changed. I was never the
same man again. I did not give up writing; for President
Young, having noticed some of my contributions to the home
papers, advised me to cultivate what he called my "gift for
writing." "So that you can use it," said he, "for the establish-
ment of truth and righteousness." I therefore continued to write
but not to the neglect of the Lord's work. I held that first and
foremost; all else was secondary. (*Through Memory's Halls, Life
Story of Orson F. Whitney,* pp. 81-83.)

Why are we mortals so prone to garnish the sepulchers
of the dead and stone the living, or give great credence to
the past and deny the present, or to assume that only
what is written has happened?

Let us consider for a moment some revealed movements and colonization programs, ancient and modern.

Since Adam there have been many exoduses and
promised lands: Abraham, Jared, Moses, Lehi, and others
led groups. How easy it is to accept those distant in time
as directed by the Lord, yet the ones near at hand as
human calculations and decisions. Let us consider for a
moment the great trek of the Mormon refugees from Illinois to Salt Lake Valley. Few, if any, great movements
equal it. We frequently hear that Brigham Young led the
people to make new tracks in a desert and to climb over
mountains seldom scaled and to ford and wade unbridged
rivers and to traverse a hostile Indian country; and while
Brigham Young was the instrument of the Lord, it was not
he but the Lord of heaven who led modern Israel across
the plains to their promised land.

Again, the numerous colonization efforts in Nevada,
on the Muddy River, in Idaho, in the Indian Territory,
at Moab, in Canada, in Mexico, in Arizona, and in Colo-
rado. These minor treks must have seemed to those who
made them quite equal to the trek of Lehi across the
deserts.

How easy it would be for a thoughtless person to say
that all these later exoduses were human calculations but
that similar movements in earlier history were inspired

and directed of the Lord. The motion picture *Brigham Young* pictured President Young wondering if he were called of God. The picture showed him vacillating, unsure, and questioning his calling. In the climax of the play he is shown wavering, ready to admit to his people that he had no divine calling, that he had not been inspired, that he had lied to them and had misled them. The movie showed him about to make a sweeping admission of his guilt and misrepresentation when the seagulls came to save the day for him. But there was nothing vacillating or weak or wavering about Brigham Young. He knew he was God's leader; he knew that the Lord was revealing to him the things to do. And he went vigorously and courageously into his program of bringing the Saints west and then colonizing the valleys of the mountain. Listen to Brigham Young:

> I know that there are those in our midst who will seek the lives of the Twelve as they did the lives of Joseph and Hyrum. We shall ordain others and give the fulness of the Priesthood so that if we are killed, the fulness of the Priesthood may remain.
>
> Joseph conferred on our heads all the keys and powers belonging to the Apostleship which he himself held before he was taken away and no man or set of men can get between Joseph and the Twelve in this world or in the world to come.
>
> How often has Joseph said to the Twelve, "I have laid the foundation and you must build thereon. For upon your shoulders, the Kingdom rests."
>
> I have the keys and the means of obtaining the word of God on the subject.

Brigham Young knew the Lord was the leader of the exodus across the plains:

> I do not wish men to understand I had anything to do with our being moved here, that was the providence of the Almighty; it was the power of God that wrought out salvation for this people, I never could have devised such a plan. . . .
>
> We came to these mountains by faith. . . .
>
> There never has been a land, from the days of Adam until now that has been blessed more than this land has been blessed by our Father in Heaven; and it will still be blessed more

and more, if we are faithful and humble, and thankful to God. . . .

Most recorded revelations in the Doctrine and Covenants and in the Bible were deep feelings and an impressive consciousness of direction from above. This is the sort of revelation individuals often have for their own needs. I have in mind the experience of a young soldier who died in Europe and who, prior to his death, was led to make friends with a family in England who gave to him great quantities of family history and genealogy. I believe this was no coincidence.

I have often told the story of a young man who was promised safe return from World War II but who found himself in a terrifying and hazardous situation on the beach-heads of Italy. After three strong impressions came to him, he moved from the spot where he was looking at his map to deploy his soldiers, and immediately after his moving, a bomb came from the skies and blew up everything in the area where he had stood.

Wilford Woodruff tells of an unusual experience.

> While on the road there, I drove my carriage one evening into the yard of Brother Williams. Brother Orson Hyde drove a wagon by the side of mine. I had my wife and children in the carriage. I had not been there but a few minutes when the spirit said to me, "Get up and move that carriage." I told my wife I had to get up and move the carriage. She said, "What for?" and I said, "I don't know." That's all she asked me on such occasions. When I told her I did not know, that was enough. I got up and moved my carriage four or five rods and put the off fore wheel against the corner of the house. I then looked around me and went to bed. The same spirit said, "Go and move your animals from that oak tree." They were two hundred yards from where my carriage was. I went and moved my horses and put them in a little hickory grove. I again went to bed.

> In thirty minutes a whirlwind came up and broke that oak tree off within two feet from the ground. It swept over three or four fences and fell square in that dooryard near Brother Orson Hyde's wagon and right where mine had stood. What would have been the consequences if I had not listened

to that spirit? Why, myself, wife and children doubtless would have been killed. That was the still small voice to me. No earthquake, no thunder, no lightning but the still small voice of the Spirit of God. It saved my life. It was a spirit of revelation to me. (*Discourses of Wilford Woodruff*, pp. 295-96.)

He could never have become President of the Church, his destiny, if he had not been responsive.

I suspect there are people in the Church today who believe in the written revelations but think calls to missionary work are a result solely of deliberation and cold calculation and that the opening of missions and the calling of mission presidents and the assignment of missionaries are just a matter of routine. That same person might believe in the words recorded in Alma 17:11 wherein the Lord said to the missionaries:

Go forth among the Lamanites, thy brethren, and establish my word; yet ye shall be patient in long-suffering and afflictions, that ye may show forth good examples unto them in me, and I will make an instrument of thee in my hands unto the salvation of many souls.

Or he might believe in the call of Enoch to preach repentance to the antediluvians. After he heard a voice, Enoch bowed himself to the earth and said:

Why is it that I have found favor in thy sight, and am but a lad, and all the people hate me; for I am slow of speech; wherefore am I thy servant? (Moses 6:31.)

We find a great similarity between the work of modern missionaries and those of ancient days.

Is there any difference between Paul's giving leadership to the missionary work in Asia Minor, Greece, Rome, and Spain and the many mission presidents now who give leadership to the proselyting program all over the world?

Is there a difference between the call of over a hundred missionaries a week and their being assigned to places all over the world to preach to all nations and the call through the Prophet Joseph in 1830 to Ziba Peterson, Oliver Cowdery, Peter Whitmer, and Parley P. Pratt to proselyte the Indians? The Lord said:

> . . . and I myself will go with them and be in their midst; and I am their advocate with the Father, and nothing shall prevail against them. (D&C 32:3.)

Let us speak of structures, edifices, temples, and tabernacles.

Moses built a tabernacle in the wilderness for the children of Israel. Solomon built a most magnificent temple in Jerusalem, and after that plan the Nephites built their temples. Joseph Smith built houses of the Lord in Kirtland and Nauvoo; Brigham Young built temples in Salt Lake City, St. George, Logan, and Manti; President Joseph F. Smith built temples in Hawaii and Canada; President Heber J. Grant built a temple in Arizona; President George Albert Smith built a temple in Idaho Falls; President David O. McKay built temples in Switzerland, New Zealand, England, Los Angeles, and Oakland; President Joseph Fielding Smith completed temples in Ogden and Provo.

These have been initiated and built under the same spirit and from the same revelation from the same God. Remember, he is the same today, tomorrow, and forever. Or do the people feel that the temples built in our own day might be the mere planning calculation of human beings? Having been fairly close to all of them since the Arizona Temple in 1927, I personally regard all of the houses of the Lord as the work of Jehovah, initiated by him, built by him, designed by him, and dedicated to him and his program.

In our own day, the Lord said:

> . . . how shall your washings be acceptable unto me, except ye perform them in a house which you have built to my name?
>
> For, for this cause I commanded Moses that he should build a tabernacle, that they should bear it with them in the wilderness, and to build a house in the land of promise, that those ordinances might be revealed which had been hid from before the world was. (D&C 124:37-38.)

And then, in Kirtland, the Lord in our own day commanded:

> Verily I say unto you, that it is my will that a house should be built unto me in the land of Zion, like unto the pattern which I have given you. Yea, let it be built speedily. . . . (D&C 97:10-11.)

Again, in Nauvoo came the command from the Lord to gather together the gold and silver and precious stones and other valuables and "come . . . and build a house to my name, for the Most High to dwell therein." (D&C 124:26-27.)

Is it so different when, on July 28, 1847, the Prophet Brigham Young in the new unbroken land of Salt Lake Valley, "walking over the ground with associates, suddenly stopped and striking the point of his cane into the parched soil exclaimed: 'Here we will build the temple of our God.' " Wilford Woodruff drove a stake into the small hole made. That day the temple block was selected in the center of the city.

Is there a difference between those early commands and the later ones when the several Presidents of the Church set apart land, planned buildings, constructed these holy edifices, and dedicated them unto the Lord? Will there be any difference between those of the past and those of today, and those hundreds of temples that are yet to be located and built?

President Joseph F. Smith, on August 19, 1906, said:

> But the time will come, perhaps not in my days nor in this generation, when temples of God, which are dedicated to the holy ordinances of the Gospel, and not to the worship of idols, will be erected in the divers countries of the earth. For this Gospel must be spread over all the world, until the knowledge of God covers the earth as the waters.

Is there a difference between the organization of the Church today and anciently?

Since I was ordained an apostle on October 7, 1943, I have participated and assisted in the call of a great many General Authorities. How were they called? May I assure you that every one of those men was called by God, by prophecy and by revelation. There was a process of elimination through much fasting and prayer. Many people may have been considered, but finally, one man from the entire Church was nominated by the Prophet of the Lord, approved by his counselors and by the members of the Council of the Twelve, sustained by the people, and ordained by the Prophet of the Lord. This is comparable to the same operation in the days of Peter following the ascension of the Christ, when the remaining apostles, with Peter presiding as the prophet of God, combed the area for great men and by the process of elimination brought it down to two: Joseph called Barsabas, who was surnamed Justus, and Matthias. Peter took leadership and explained the qualifications necessary, stating that the appointee must have been associated with them during the entire ministry of the Christ from his baptism to his ascension, thus being a special witness of the Christ.

> And they prayed, and said, Thou, Lord, which knowest the hearts of all men, shew whether of these two thou hast chosen. (Acts 1:24.)

And Matthias was called and was numbered with the eleven apostles.

John Taylor recorded a revelation calling George Teasdale and Heber J. Grant to the apostleship:

> Thus saith the Lord, to the Twelve, and to the Priesthood and people of my Church: Let my servant George Teasdale and Heber J. Grant be appointed to fill the vacancies in the Twelve . . . and then proceed to fill up the presiding Quorum of Seventies . . . you may appoint Seymour B. Young to fill up the vacancy.

It has likewise been my privilege, through twenty-nine years, to assist in calling many scores of men to positions of responsibility in stake presidencies and ordaining many hundreds of bishops, and I am convinced that the calls of these hundreds of stake presidents and bishops and other leaders, as well as the General Authorities, come as they came in the beginning of the early-day church when

> as they ministered to the Lord, and fasted, the Holy Ghost said, Separate me Barnabas and Saul for the work whereunto I have called them.

And when they had fasted and prayed, and laid their hands on them, they sent them away. (Acts 13:2-3.)

Section 124 of the Doctrine and Covenants describes the quorum and ecclesiastical organization of the Church as outlined by the Lord.

The Lord was setting up an organization among men who were not acquainted with his great church, and he gave explicit details how to organize the Presidency, the Twelve, the Seventies, the Patriarch, the stake leaders, the ward leaders, and the quorum leaders, even down to the deacons quorum. It was necessary for this to come by revelation, since no one on the earth at that time knew the perfect plan. But once having delivered the program, it will never be necessary for the Lord to reveal again those details.

I suppose there are those who think of the organization of a stake presidency as a matter of mere human calculations. George Q. Cannon said:

Brother Brigham Young used to say—and I always have appreciated his remark—that he did not want to write revelations because the people would be held to stricter accountability than they were.

What written revelation is there concerning the organization of these stakes as we see them? Here is this Davis stake with a Presidency and High Council; what is there written in the Book of Doctrine and Covenants to sustain this? In the 102 Section, we find a plan given for the organization of the High Council and over that High Council the Presidency of the Church presided. But as we are now organized there is nothing specially written concerning it. How then have these stakes been organized? Did President Young organize them out of his own mind? or did he organize these stakes according to the revelation of God? He organized them by revelation just as much so as if he had written the revelation. God did not require him to write it, and yet the stakes are organized. And Zion is now as perfectly organized as circumstances will admit.

We have our ward organizations and our stake organizations, and they extend throughout the length and breadth of Zion, and everybody is brought within their compass. These ward organizations have become quite perfect. How has this been done? Has it been done by written revelation to the Church? Has it been done by anything that is written in the Book of Doctrine and Covenants? No. There is scarcely anything in that book that gives any clear idea of the ward organizations that at the present exist. How have they been organized? By the spirit of revelation in and through the man whom God chose to hold the keys. (*Gospel Truth,* pp. 325-26.)

Those people who ask "Why do not we have revelations today?" are in the same category with the numerous who ask "Why do we not have spiritual gifts and manifestations?"

I have often said that if all of the spectacular manifestations and visions and pertinent dreams and healings and other miracles were written in books, it would take a great library to hold them. Let me give a few examples to illustrate that the Lord is actively working with his faithful followers as much today as ever.

President Wilford Woodruff tells of dreams or visions, including the experience of my grandfather, Heber C. Kimball, Brother Russell, and Brother Hyde when evil spirits tried hard to destroy Heber C. Kimball who "held the Priesthood and held the keys of the Priesthood so far as England was concerned. Those spirits had not therefore the power to destroy them." He tells of an experience that Heber C. Kimball, George A. Smith, and he had in London when the powers of darkness would have destroyed their lives. Three holy messengers, dressed in temple clothing, came into the room and filled the room with light. They laid their hands upon the heads of the brethren and they were delivered from that terrible power which would have destroyed them. He tells of the visit of Joseph Smith and Hyrum Smith after their death when they visited him on a ship at sea. The ship had been traveling backwards three days and nights in a heavy gale. After the brethren had a special prayer, they stepped on the deck and in less than a minute,

it was as though a man had taken a sword and cut that gale through, and you might have thrown a muslin handkerchief out and it would not have moved it.

The night following this, Joseph and Hyrum visited me and the Prophet laid before me a great many things.

President Woodruff tells of another experience when the Prophet Joseph came to him and explained why they were always in such a hurry in heaven. Joseph said:

I will tell you, Brother Woodruff, every dispensation that has had the Priesthood on the earth and has gone into the celestial kingdom has had a certain amount of work to do to prepare to go to the earth with the Savior when he goes to reign on the earth. Each dispensation has had ample time to do this work. We have not. We are the last dispensation and so much work has to be done and we need to be in a hurry in order to accomplish it. (*Discourses of Wilford Woodruff*, p. 289.)

Leaders of our day, including George Q. Cannon, saw heavenly beings. Wilford Woodruff said:

I have had the administration of angels in my day and time, though I never prayed for an angel. I have had, in several instances, the administration of holy messengers. (*Discourses of Wilford Woodruff*, p. 286.)

There is the notable experience of the young apostle, Heber J. Grant, when in Arizona he had a dream or vision of councils in heaven explaining his call to the Twelve.

There are two spirits striving with us always, one telling us to continue our labor for good, and one telling us that with the faults and failings of our nature we are unworthy. I can truthfully say that from October, 1882, until February, 1883, that spirit followed me day and night telling me that I was unworthy to be an Apostle of the Church, and that I ought to resign. When I would testify of my knowledge that Jesus is the Christ, the Son of the Living God, the Redeemer of mankind, it seemed as though a voice would say to me: "You lie! You lie! You have never seen Him."

While on the Navajo Indian reservation with Brigham Young, Jr., and a number of others, six or eight, on horseback, and several others in "white tops"—riding along with Lot Smith at the rear of that procession, suddenly the road veered to the left almost straight, but there was a well beaten path leading ahead. I said: "Stop, Lot, stop. Where does this trail lead? There are plenty of foot marks and plenty of horses' hoof marks here." He said, "It leads to an immense gulley just a short distance ahead, that it is impossible to cross with a wagon. We have made a regular 'Muleshoe' of miles here to get on the other side of the gulley."

I had visited the day before the spot where a Navajo Indian had asked George A. Smith, Jr., to let him look at his pistol. George A. handed it to him, and the Navajo shot him.

I said, "Lot, is there any danger from Indians?"

"None at all."

"I want to be all alone. Go ahead and follow the crowd." I first asked him if I allowed the animal I was riding to walk if I would reach the road on the other side of the gulley before the horsemen and the wagons, and he said, "Yes."

As I was riding along to meet them on the other side I seemed to see, and I seemed to hear, what to me is one of the most real things in all my life, I seemed to see a Council in Heaven. I seemed to hear the words that were spoken. I listened to the discussion with a great deal of interest. The First Presidency and the Council of the Twelve Apostles had not been able to agree on two men to fill the vacancies in the Quorum of the Twelve. There had been a vacancy of one for two years, and a vacancy of two for one year, and the Conference had adjourned without the vacancies being filled. In this Council the Savior was present, my father was there, and the Prophet Joseph Smith was there. They discussed the question that a mistake had been made in not filling those two vacancies and that in all probability it would be another six months before the Quorum would be completed, and they discussed as to whom they wanted to occupy those positions, and decided that the way to remedy the mistake that had been made in not filling these vacancies was to send a revelation. It was given to me that I had done nothing to entitle me to that exalted position, except that I had lived a clean, sweet life. It was given to me that because of my father having practically sacrificed his life in what was known as the great Reformation, so to speak, of the people in early days, having been practically a martyr, that the Prophet Joseph and my father desired me to have that position, and it was because of their faithful labors that I was called, and not because of anything I had done of myself or any great thing that I had accomplished. It was also given to me that that was all these men, the Prophet and my father, could do for me; from that day it depended upon me and upon me alone as to whether I made a success of my life or a failure. . . .

It was given to me, as I say, that it now depended upon me. No man could have been more unhappy than I was from October 1882, until February, 1883, but from that day I have never been bothered, night or day, with the idea that I was not worthy to stand as an Apostle, and I have not been worried since the last words uttered by Joseph F. Smith to me: "The Lord bless you, my boy, the Lord bless you; you have got a great responsibility. Always remember this is the Lord's work and not man's. The Lord is greater than any man. He knows whom He wants to lead His Church, and never makes any mistake. The Lord bless you."

I have been happy during the twenty years that it has fallen my lot to stand at the head of this Church. I have felt the inspiration of the Living God directing me in my labors. From the day that I chose a comparative stranger to be one of the Apostles, instead of my lifelong and dearest living friend, I have known as I know that I live, that I am entitled to the light and the inspiration and the guidance of God in directing his work here upon this earth; and I know, as I know that I live, that it is God's work, and that Jesus Christ is the Son of the Living God, the Redeemer of the world, and that he came to this earth with a divine mission to die upon the cross as the Redeemer of mankind, atoning for the sins of the world. (*Conference Report*, April 1941, pp. 4-6.)

We have the remarkable experience when Bishop Wells' son, who had been killed by a train, returned to his unconsoled mother to assure her that all was well and that she should not mourn longer.

We have the unusual experience told by President David O. McKay in Hawaii when a native Hawaiian brother reported that while the prayer was being offered at the spot where the first baptism had occurred, he saw George Q. Cannon and President Joseph F. Smith stand in the circle. They had long been dead.

There are so many such heavenly manifestations in our own modern days that we have neither time nor space to mention them all.

President George F. Richards had a heavenly experience that was printed in the *Church News:*

More than forty years ago I had a dream, which I am sure was from the Lord. In this dream I was in the presence of my Savior as he stood in mid-air. He spoke no word to me, but my love for him was such that I have not words to explain. I know that no mortal man can love the Lord as I experienced that love for the Savior unless God reveals it to him. I would have remained in His presence but there was a power drawing me away from him, and as a result of that dream I had this feeling, that no matter what might be required at my hands, what the

Gospel might entail unto me, I would do what I should be asked to do, even to the laying down of my life.

And so when we read in the scriptures what the Savior said to his disciples:

"In my Father's house are many mansions. . . . I go to prepare a place for you . . . that where I am, there ye may be also. (John 14:2-3.)" I think that is where I want to be. If only I can be with my Savior and have that same sense of love that I had in that dream, it will be the goal of my existence, the desire of my life.

Elder Melvin J. Ballard wrote of a manifestation to himself. He said:

> I lost a son six years of age and I saw him a man in the spirit world after his death, and I saw how he had exercised his own freedom of choice and would obtain of his own will and volition a companionship, and in due time to him and all those who are worthy of it, shall come all of the blessings and sealing privileges of the House of the Lord. (*Three Degrees of Glory,* p. 31.)

Another experience described by Brother Ballard indicates that the heavens and the earth are close and there has continued to be spiritual manifestations.

> I recall an incident in my own father's experience. How we looked forward to the completion of the Logan Temple. It was about to be dedicated. My father had labored on that house from its very beginning and my earliest recollection was carrying his dinner each day as he brought the rock down from the quarry. How we looked forward to that great event! I remember how in the meantime, father made every effort to obtain all the data and information he could concerning his relatives. It was the theme of his prayer night and morning that the Lord would open up the way whereby he could get information concerning his dead.
>
> The day before the dedication while writing recommends to the members of his ward who were to be present at the first service, two elderly gentlemen walked down the streets of Logan, approached my two young sisters, and, coming to the older one of the two placed in her hands a newspaper and said:
>
> "Take this to your father. Give it to no one else. Go quickly. Don't lose it."
>
> The child responded and when she met her mother, her mother wanted the paper. The child said, "No. I must give it

to father and to no one else." She was admitted into the room and told her story. We looked in vain for these travelers. They were not to be seen. No one else saw them. Then we turned to the paper.

The newspaper, *The Newbury Weekly News*, was printed in my father's old English home, Thursday, May 15, 1884, and reached our hands May 18, 1884, three days after its publication. We were astonished, for by no earthly means could it have reached us, so that our curiosity increased as we examined it. Then we noticed one page devoted to the writings of a reporter of the paper, who had gone on his vacation, and among other places had visited an old cemetery. The curious inscriptions led him to write what he found on the tombstones, including the verses. He also added the names, date of birth, death, etc., filling nearly an entire page.

It was the old cemetery where the Ballard family had been buried for generations and very many of my father's immediate relatives and other intimate friends were mentioned.

When the matter was presented to President Merrill of the Logan Temple he said, "You are authorized to do the work for those because you received it through messengers of the Lord."

There is no doubt that the dead who had received the Gospel in the spirit world had put it into the heart of the reporter to write these things and thus the way was prepared for my father to obtain the information he sought. (*Three Degrees of Glory*, pp. 21-22.)

A statement of basic importance on the subject of revelation is a sermon by Wilford Woodruff in 1890:

Read the life of Brigham Young and you can hardly find a revelation that he had wherein he said, "Thus saith the Lord." But the Holy Ghost was with him; he taught by inspiration and revelation; but with one exception, he did not give those revelations in the form that Joseph did; for they were not written and given as revelations and commandments to the Church in the words and name of the Savior. Joseph said, "Thus saith the Lord" almost every day of his life, in laying the foundation of this work. But those who followed him have not deemed it always necessary to say, "Thus saith the Lord." Yet they have led the people by the power of the Holy Ghost and if you want to know what that is, read the first six verses of the 68th Section of the Book of the Doctrine and Covenants where the Lord told Orson Hyde, Luke Johnson, Lyman Johnson and William E. McClellan to go out and preach the gospel to people as they were moved upon by the Holy Ghost. "And whatsoever they shall speak when moved upon by the Holy Ghost shall be scripture, shall be the will of the Lord, shall be the mind of the Lord, shall be the word of the Lord, shall be the voice of the Lord and the power of God unto salvation."

It is by that power that we have led Israel; by that power President Young presided over and led the Church. By the same power, President John Taylor presided over and led the Church. And that is the way I have acted according to the best of my ability in that capacity. I do not want the Latter-day Saints to understand that the Lord is not with us, and that he is not giving revelations to us; for He is giving us revelation, and will give us revelation until the scene is wound up.

I have had some revelations of late and very important ones to me and I will tell you what the Lord has said to me. Let me bring your minds to what is termed the Manifesto. . . .

Since I received that revelation, I have heard of many who are tried in these things. . . . the Lord showed me by a vision and revelation exactly what would take place if we did not stop this practice. . . . the Lord is with him [Wilford Woodruff] and with this people. He has told me exactly what to do and what the result would be if we did not do it. . . . I went before the Lord, and I wrote what the Lord told me to write. I laid it before my brethren, such strong men as George Q. Cannon, Brother Joseph F. Smith and the Twelve Apostles . . . these men agreed with me and ten thousand Latter-day Saints agreed with me. Why? Because they were moved upon by the spirit of God and by the revelations of Jesus Christ to do it. . . . (*Deseret News,* November 7, 1891.)

No matter how important an individual, the time comes for him to turn over the reins to his successor. When Joshua succeeded Moses the Lord said:

There shall not any man be able to stand before thee all the days of thy life: as I was with Moses, so I will be with thee: I will not fail thee, nor forsake thee. (Joshua 1:5.)

And likewise the mantle of Joseph Smith fell on Brigham Young. Some present when Brigham rose to speak in Nauvoo after the martyrdom seemed to hear the voice of Joseph and see the person of Joseph. It was a most remarkable miracle.

The mantle of leadership has fallen in turn on each successive President of the Church. And each successor has carried forth the work, and the revelations have continued unabated. Plural marriage was discontinued through revelation; tithing was given new power and brought the Church out of debt; temples have been erected and missionary work expanded; the welfare program has been reintroduced. And through and under these prophets, revelations have continued.

Elder Marriner W. Merrill was shown that his son passed through the veil of death in order to labor with his kindred dead:

> On one occasion soon after the death of his son, as he was returning to his home, he was in his carriage so deeply lost in thought about his son that he was quite oblivious to things about him. He suddenly came into a state of awareness when his horse stopped in the road. As he looked up, his son stood in the road beside him. His son spoke to him and said, "Father, you are mourning my departure unduly. You are over concerned about my family (his son left a large family of small children) and their welfare. *I have much work to do* and your grieving gives me much concern. *I am in a position to render effective service to my family. You should take comfort, for you know there is much work to be done here and it was necessary for me to be called. You know that the Lord doeth all things well."* So saying, the son departed. (Bryant S. Hinckley, *The Faith of Our Pioneer Fathers,* pp. 182-83.)

During the years he was a member of the Council of the Twelve, President Heber J. Grant often recommended names of brethren to the First Presidency for consideration as apostles. Frequently he thought that if he ever were President of the Church he would appoint his lifelong friend, General Richard W. Young, a grandson of President Brigham Young, to the apostleship. However, when he did become President he chose instead, under the inspiration of the Lord, a relative stranger to him, Elder Melvin J. Ballard.

In 1918 President Joseph F. Smith had a vision shortly before his death:

> . . . the eyes of my understanding were opened, and the spirit of the Lord rested upon me and I saw the hosts of the dead. . . .

In the dramatic and comprehensive vision that followed, he saw multitudes of those who had lived faithful lives and was impressed by their joy and gladness as they anticipated their deliverance, as the Son of God was coming into the spirit world to redeem them. In the darkness were the hosts who had rejected him and his program. He went not to these unfaithful persons, but organized his forces who did go to the unfaithful to give them the gospel. This was the work of the Savior in the hours his body lay in the tomb at Jerusalem.

Among the faithful he saw were Adam and the great souls down through the centuries, in both hemispheres. Then he saw Joseph Smith and Brigham Young and many of the great ones of our dispensation. He saw that the faithful elders of this dispensation continue their work when they depart from this mortal life. President Smith later bore testimony that this vision was true.

Another revelation of great import to Latter-day Saints was the appearance of the signers of the Declaration of Independence and Presidents of the United States to President Wilford Woodruff in the St. George Temple. President Woodruff later reported in general conference, on April 10, 1898:

> I am going to bear my testimony to this assembly, if I never do it again in my life, that those men who laid the foundation of this American Government and signed the Declaration of Independence were the best spirits the God of Heaven could find on the face of the earth. They were choice spirits, not wicked men. George Washington and all the men that labored for the purpose were inspired of the Lord. Another thing I am going to say here, because I have a right to say it. Every one of those men that signed the Declaration of Independence with General Washington called upon me, as an Apostle of the Lord Jesus Christ, in the Temple at St. George two consecutive nights, and demanded at my hands that I should go forth and attend to the ordinances of the house of God for them. Men are here, I believe, that know of this—Brothers J. D. T. McAllister, David H. Cannon and James C. Bleak. Brother McAllister baptized me for all these men, and I then told these brethren that it was their duty to go into the Temple and labor

until they got endowments for all of them. They did it. Would those spirits have called upon me, as an Elder in Israel, to perform that work if they had not been noble spirits before God? They would not. I bear this testimony because it is true. The spirit of God bore record to myself and the brethren while we were laboring in that way. (*Temples of the Most High,* p. 87.)

On September 16, 1877, President Woodruff reported the following in general conference:

We have labored in the St. George Temple since January, and we have done all we could there; and the Lord has stirred up our minds, and many things have been revealed to us concerning the dead. President Young has said to us, and it is verily so, if the dead could they would speak in language loud as ten thousand thunders, calling upon the servants of God to rise up and build Temples, magnify their calling and redeem their dead. This doubtless sounds strange to those present who believe not the faith and doctrine of the Latter-day Saints; but when we get to the spirit world we will find out that all that God has revealed is true. We will find, too, that everything there is reality, and that God has a body, parts and passions, and the erroneous ideas that exist now with regard to him will have passed away. I feel to say little else to the Latter-day Saints wherever and whenever I have the opportunity of speaking to them, than to call upon them to build these Temples now under way, to hurry them up to completion. The dead will be after you, they will seek after you as they have after us in St. George. They called upon us, knowing that we held the keys and power to redeem them.

I will here say, before closing, that two weeks before I left St. George, the spirits of the dead gathered around me, wanting to know why we did not redeem them. Said they: "You have had the use of the Endowment House for a number of years and yet nothing has ever been done for us. We laid the foundation of the government you now enjoy, and we never apostatized from it, but we remained true to it and were faithful to God." These were the signers of the Declaration of Independence, and they waited on me for two days and two nights. I thought it very singular that notwithstanding so much work had been done, and yet nothing had been done for them. The thought never entered my heart, from the fact, I suppose, that heretofore our minds were reaching after our more immediate friends and relatives. I straightway went into the baptismal font and called upon Brother McAllister to baptize me for the signers of the Declara-

tion of Independence, and fifty other eminent men, making one
hundred in all, including John Wesley, Columbus, and others;
I then baptized him for every President of the United States
except three; and when their cause is just, somebody will do
the work for them. (*Journal of Discourses,* vol. 19, p. 229.)

One of the many stories coming down from our fore-
fathers relates this experience: Heber C. Kimball was
taking a company through the Endowment House and
felt a depressed spirit. He said to them, "There is someone
in this group unworthy to participate in these sacred ordinances. They may be excused." No one moved. A second time he repeated that the unworthy ones could now
be excused. No one moved. A third time he said, "There
is a couple in this group who are adulterers, and if they
do not leave immediately, I shall call out their names."
A couple arose and left the room, and the company proceeded through the ordinances.

These and numerous experiences of the living authorities are all testimony that, as George Q. Cannon has
said, there has never been a single minute since 1830 when
the people were left without the revealed guidance of the
Lord. As I hear the Prophet each week in the temple,
making decisions that are heaven-inspired, developing new
programs that are revealed, my testimony grows as to the
inspired leadership and the divinity of this great work,
which can never be stopped nor terminated.

When after deliberation and prayer on certain matters he says solemnly, "Brethren, the Lord has spoken," or
"Brethren, that is right; that is the way the Lord wants
it," or "We have expressed the will of the Lord here today," there is assurance in my heart that he speaks for the
Lord.

I bear witness that the Church moves on through
the revelations of God to its divinely called leaders. The
Almighty is with this people. We shall have all the revelations we need if we will do our duty and keep the
commandments of God.

# Chapter Four

# Voices from Space

We live in a marvelous age with developments far beyond the most fantastic prognostications of a quarter century ago. Our communication lines have been extended from pony express to fast air service; transportation has been speeded from horse and buggy to globe-encircling jets for the masses and speeds running into thousands of miles per hour for the explorers. From the Vikings and Columbus, we come to the astronauts. Persistent scientists continue to explore land and sea, and now they are out in space. Man has learned much by his intellect, and has pride in his accomplishments. But little does he realize how relatively elementary are these movements and discoveries and knowledge. There is another way to discovery. Scientists have sought their knowledge through study, but prophets through faith. Astronomers have developed powerful telescopes through which they have seen much, but prophets and seers have had clearer vision at greater distances with precision instruments such as the Liahona and the Urim and Thummim, which have far exceeded the most advanced radar, radio, television, or telescopic equipment.

An article by a German astronomer reports that radio

astronomers today discuss as a distinct possibility inter-planetary conversation between earth-bound men and creatures on other planets; he "demonstrates" with intricate mathematical logic that planets suitable for life may be fairly common among the stars, and that there are "perhaps ten civilized communities within 1,000 light years of the earth," and "there may well be creatures intelligent enough on some of those planets to transmit radio messages across the enormous distances of inter-stellar space."

He seems convinced that earth's astronomers may eventually detect and interpret incoming messages that highly cultured creatures from those intelligent communities might send. He says the galactic history of such planets "might take billions of years to evolve, but their flowering might well last only a few thousand years, so their brief moments of glory would seldom coincide." He reasons that "some extra-terrestrial civilizations may have destroyed themselves completely, while others may have killed off only the higher types of life, permitting new and later civilizations to evolve from the humble creatures that managed to survive."

Since no mention is made of a controlling power, we fear that there is the assumption that planets build themselves and that inhabitants create themselves. We honor and congratulate the scientists for their intensive research and some of their conclusions. But if we add to their assumptions and findings the knowledge we have acquired through the scriptures and then acknowledge an omnipotent God in the center of all things, the picture becomes clearer and the purpose we see in existence gives it meaning and color.

The Gospel writer, John, gave us these precious words:

In the beginning was the Word, and the Word was with God, and the Word was God.

The same was in the beginning with God.

All things were made by him; and without him was not any thing made that was made. (John 1:1-3.)

And modern revelation confirms:

The worlds were made by him; men were made by him; all things were made by him, and through him, and of him.

And thus he was called the Son of God. . . . (D&C 93: 10, 14.)

The Lord himself testifies: "Behold, I am Jesus Christ, the Son of the living God, who created the heavens and the earth. . . ." (D&C 14:9.) ". . .[They] are in mine hands. . . ." (D&C 67:2.)

Students of the universe might be amazed to know how much Adam knew about astronomy; how much Enoch and Moses had of accumulated knowledge of this world in its beginnings, its history, and its projected end. Many would wonder at the great Abraham, living nearly forty centuries ago, who was such an authority, not only on the earth, its movements, and conditions, but on the universe itself, extending to the very center of it.

His supernatural knowledge was probably supplemented by research and observation in the clear starry nights in the plains of Mesopotamia. Could there possibly have been observatories on the tops of the ancient ziggurats pyramiding into the sky? The Lord commands, "Seek knowledge through study and through faith." Abraham must have received the major part through the Urim and Thummim, which could have been far more revealing than the most powerful telescope in the most modern observatory. In his 175 brilliant years of life he accumulated knowledge in many fields, but especially astronomy, in which field he seems to have excelled and was perhaps equal or superior to even the highly trained Egyptian astronomers. At the altar near Bethel, close to Jerusalem, came his greatest scientific knowledge.

As he sat in Egypt and wrote his treatise on papyrus, probably to present to Pharaoh and his eminent court, he wrote:

And I, Abraham, had the Urim and Thummim, which the Lord my God had given unto me, in Ur of the Chaldees;

And I saw the stars, that they were very great, and that one of them was nearest unto the throne of God; and there were many great ones which were near unto it;

And the Lord said unto me: These are the governing ones; and the name of the great one is Kolob, because it is near unto me, for I am the Lord thy God: I have set this one to govern all those which belong to the same order as that upon which thou standest. (Abraham 3:1-3.)

The worlds were created, organized, and made to function by Jesus Christ our Lord, all this at the instance of and under the direction of his Father, Elohim, our Heavenly Father. Abraham knew, as we know, that the works of God in all creations were infinite, purposeful, efficient, limitless.

The Lord continues in his revelation to the prophet: "And there are many kingdoms; for there is no space in the which there is no kingdom; . . . And unto every kingdom is given a law. . . ." (D&C 88:37-38.) He knew the bounds set to heaven, earth, sun, and stars, their times, revolutions, laws, and glories—which orbs borrow their light from Kolob, the greatest of all the stars. (See Abraham 3.) He actually tells us about the throne of God and that he resides "on a globe like a sea of glass and fire, . . . a great Urim and Thummim." (D&C 130:7-8.)

He continues in his inspired treatise: "And the Lord said unto me, by the Urim and Thummim, that Kolob was after the manner of the Lord . . ." (Abraham 3:4), and that one revolution of it was equal to one thousand years on earth.

Kolob, signifying the first creation, nearest to the celestial, or the residence of God. First in government, the last pertaining to the measurement of time. (Pearl of Great Price, Facsimile 2:1.)

Other grand governing creations near to the place where God resides are pictured. This advanced knowledge was "revealed from God to Abraham, as he offered sacrifice upon an altar which he had built unto the Lord." (Pearl of Great Price, Facsimile 2:2.) He says,

> Thus I, Abraham, talked with the Lord, face to face, . . . and he told me of the works which his hands had made; . . . which were many; and they multiplied before mine eyes, and I could not see the end thereof. (Abraham 3:11-12.)

As we stretch our imaginations to absorb the limitlessness of the creations of God we turn to a favorite song:

> If you could hie to Kolob in the twinkling of an eye,
> And then continue onward with that same speed to fly,
> D'ye think that you could ever, through all eternity,
> Find out the generation where Gods began to be?
> Or see the grand beginning, where space did not extend?
> Or view the last creation where Gods and matter end?
> Methinks the Spirit whispers, "No man has found 'pure space,'"
> Nor seen the outside curtains, where nothing has a place.
> The works of God continue, and worlds and lives abound;
> Improvement and progression have one eternal round.
> There is no end to matter; there is no end to space;
> There is no end to spirit; there is no end to race.
> —Hymns, No. 257

The noted scientist speaks of other planets and suggests civilized space communities. Time was when most people thought the earth was the major unit of creation and that the sun, the moon, and the stars were earth's inferior appendages, existing merely to give light like lanterns hanging in the sky. But now the people generally know, as prophets knew long before them, that the earth is but one minor unit of numerous creations in space, illuminated by the presence of God, "who is in the midst of all things." (D&C 88:13.) "And so great shall be the glory of his presence that the sun shall hide his face in shame. . . ." (D&C 133:49.)

Our friend astronomer speaks of interstellar civilizations, probably experiencing turbulent history such as our own earth has had with the rise and fall of great civilizations, such as Babylon, Ninevah, Jerusalem, Egypt, Greece, Rome, and numerous others that have flared like an arc

light, then dimmed to candlelight proportions or even
expired. The prophets knew through the centuries that
not only civilizations come and go, but worlds are born,
mature, and die. The Lord said,

> And the end shall come, and the heaven and the earth
> shall be consumed and pass away. . . . it is the workmanship
> of mine hand. (D&C 29:23, 25.)

> . . . the earth abideth the law of a celestial kingdom,
> for it filleth the measure of its creation, . . . notwithstanding it
> shall die, it shall be quickened again, . . . and the righteous
> shall inherit it. (D&C 88:25-26.)

### The Prophet Joseph writes:

> The earth rolls upon her wings, and the sun giveth his
> light by day, and the moon giveth her light by night, and the
> stars also give their light, as they roll upon their wings in their
> glory, in the midst of the power of God.

> . . . and any man who hath seen any of the least of these
> hath seen God moving in his majesty and power. (D&C 88:45,
> 47.)

> For after it hath filled the measure of its creation, it shall
> be crowned with glory, even with the presence of God, the
> Father;

> That bodies who are of the celestial kingdom may possess
> it forever and ever; for, for this intent was it made and created,
> and for this intent are they sanctified. (D&C 88:19-20.)

To Moses, to Joseph Smith, and to others of the
great prophets came visions and revelations so clear, so
distinct, so complete that it will yet be long, if ever, when,
through observation and exploration only, men will gain
the same knowledge. "But only an account of this earth,
and the inhabitants thereof, give I unto you," said the
Lord to Moses. "For behold, there are many worlds that
have passed away by the word of my power. And there
are many that now stand, and innumerable are they unto
man; but all things are numbered unto me, for they are
mine and I know them." (Moses 1:35.)

We are awed by the perspicacity and discernment of
the scientists whose accumulated knowledge is great, but

there is still greater knowledge; there are more perfect instruments; there is much more to learn. Most of us can but imagine how the great truths have been transmitted through the ages. Exactly how this precious instrument, the Urim and Thummim, operates we can only surmise, but it seems to be infinitely superior to any mechanism ever dreamed of yet by researchers. It would seem to be a receiving set, or instrument. For a set to receive pictures and programs, there must be a broadcasting set. The scripture above quoted indicates that the abode of God is a master Urim and Thummim, and the synchronization of transmitting and receiving apparatus of this kind can have no limitation.

In a short period man has so improved his communication techniques as to hear voices around the world. A few years ago, even with earphones, we could decode only part of the static over the newborn radio. Our first television pictures were very local and very amateurish. Today, we see in our homes a fight in Madison Square Garden, a football game in the Cotton Bowl, the Tabernacle Choir in Chicago, an astronaut on his way to the moon. Is it hard to believe that with such accomplishments by puny man Omnipotent God has precision instruments with which to enlarge the knowledge of those who have the skill to use them? Is it difficult to believe that the Urim and Thummim could be such a precision instrument to transmit messages from God to his supreme creation— man? Can God have limitations? Can atmosphere or distance or space hold back his pictures? Would it be so difficult for Moses or Enoch or Abraham or Joseph to see a colorful, accurate, moving picture of all things past and present, and even future? The Creator said to Moses, ". . . look, and I will show thee the workmanship of mine hands; but not all, for my works are without end. . . ." (Moses 1:4.)

> And worlds without number have I created; and I also created them for mine own purpose; and by the Son I created them, which is mine Only Begotten. (Moses 1:33.)

> . . . the heavens, they are many, and they cannot be numbered unto man; but they are numbered unto me, for they are mine. (Moses 1:37.)

The perfected Enoch, as he saw the brilliant, awesome picture, exclaimed:

> And were it possible that man could number the particles of the earth, yea, millions of earths like this, it would not be a beginning to the number of thy creations. . . . (Moses 7:30.)

And then the Creator said:

> . . . there is no end to my works, neither to my words. For behold, this is my work and my glory—to bring to pass the immortality and eternal life of man. (Moses 1:38-39.)

The quoted doctor speaks of the flowering of the civilizations upon the various planets. The Lord told Enoch:

> Wherefore, I can stretch forth mine hands and hold all the creations which I have made; and mine eyes can pierce them also, and among all the workmanship of mine hands there has not been so great wickedness as among thy brethren. (Moses 7:36.)

The scriptures postulate that worlds have gone out of existence through self-destruction, but other worlds have gone on unto perfection, and communication between the higher and the lower is not only possible but is an actuality. At the controlling center of the universe in such a perfected world is God. He knows all things that could possibly affect us, and because of his experience in his creation of us in his image, he is eager that we become like him—perfect. Accordingly, he has continued communication with us through the millennia. Without plane or rocket, messengers have come.

Our surprise is greatest in the last conclusion made by the scientist when he expresses the belief that "the earth's young civilization is now approaching its first great crisis because of its newfound powers of self-destruction," and "man's best hope of avoiding disaster is to listen hard for radioed advice. Far out in starry space," he says, "perhaps is an old wise civilization that has survived many crises and is trying to warn the callow earth against the mistakes of its own youth." What an astute observation! Yet for thousands of years our omniscient Heavenly Father from his "wise old world" has been trying to get his children to listen hard for such radioed advice and televised wisdom, but they were blind of eyes and dull of ears. They were not connected to the power line.

Handwritten messages of warning have come. Wicked Belshazzar, with lords and ladies in ugly debauchery, drank wines from golden vessels stolen from holy temples, and while drunkenness and sensual indulgences were at their height,

> . . . came forth fingers of a man's hand, and wrote over against the candlestick upon the plaister of the wall of the king's palace: and the king saw the part of the hand that wrote.
>
> Then the king's countenance was changed, and his thoughts troubled him, so that the joints of his loins were loosed, and his knees smote one against another. (Daniel 5:5-6.)

This was a message from another world, and Daniel interpreted the solemn warning. On another continent Aminadi ". . . interpreted the writing which was upon the wall of the temple, which was written by the finger of God." (Alma 10:2.) Another message, written by the Lord on two sets of stone tables, came from Mount Sinai: ". . . And he wrote upon the tables the words of the Covenant, the ten commandments." (Exodus 34:28.)

How else except through extraplanetary messages could landlubber Nephi, without experience, have built a seaworthy ship that would safely cross an ocean? How else could Noah have known the minute specifications for an ark to successfully ride the flood? How else could Moses know the dimensions, materials, and uses of the tabernacle, and how else could Solomon know the specifications for his temple?

Communications have come in great numbers through the ages, faithfully interpreted by the Jeremiahs, the

Ezekiels, and the Daniels; by the Nephis, the Moronis, the Benjamins; by the Peters, the Pauls, and the Joseph Smiths.

Better than radio or television communications have come personal messengers without plane or rocket ship from God's abode to announce the birth of Isaac, the destruction of Sodom and Gomorrah, the coming of Saul to Damascus. Joseph saw the coming famine in Egypt so he could warn Pharaoh and save his own people. And another Joseph received a message causing him to flee to Egypt with the Christ child, and return to Nazareth. Peter saw a picture of the four-cornered sheet filled with beasts and heard voices that were to send the proselyting program not only to Jews, but also to all the world. A messenger from the Father crossed space to announce:

> For unto you is born this day in the city of David a Saviour, which is Christ the Lord.
>
> And suddenly there was with the angel a multitude of the heavenly host praising God, and saying,
>
> Glory to God in the highest, and on earth peace, good will toward men. (Luke 2:11, 13-14.)

Comforting messengers stood by the Christ in Gethsemane after his momentous decision was reached. One messenger was outside Jerusalem's wall by the empty tomb, and "rolled back the stone from the door, and sat upon it." (Matthew 28:2.) He said, "Fear not ye: for I know that ye seek Jesus, which was crucified. He is not here: for he is risen. . . ." (Matthew 28:5-6.)

And there were two undetained by space or time, standing on the Mount of Olives, who said:

> Ye men of Galilee, . . . this same Jesus, which is taken up from you into heaven, shall so come in like manner as ye have seen him go into heaven. (Acts 1:11.)

Just last century a messenger came to Joseph Smith announcing "that he was a messenger sent from the presence of God . . . that his name was Moroni; that God had a work for [Joseph] to do. . . ." (Joseph Smith 2:33.)

In a single night repeated visits and the crossing through space between earth and the abode of God seemed to be negotiated without limitation of time or space or gravity's pull!

From the center of the universe where the power, the light, the direction, and the intelligence originate came another messenger announcing himself as the resurrected John the Baptist. Anciently beheaded, now resurrected, he came to restore the keys and powers that he himself had possessed on earth. He was followed by three other messengers, Peter, James, and John, who restored the Melchizedek Priesthood with all its powers and authority.

Divine guards had sped through space to save the life of Abraham on Potiphar's Hill in the land of Ur, to save Daniel in the lions' den, to save Nephi from the bitterness and bloodthirsty anger of his brothers, to save Isaac from the knife of sacrifice.

Then there were messages so precious, so vital, that the Lord himself came. He walked with Adam in the Garden of Eden and taught him. He spoke to Enoch and showed him the millions of units in his universe. He stood on Mt. Sinai and trained his great Moses to lead Israel. He stood on the highway near Damascus and startled Paul in his marvelous transformation and ministry.

And then there were the visits of the Father himself, who came to bear witness of his Beloved Son, Jesus Christ, at the waters of Jordan, on the Mount of Transfiguration, to the Nephites on soil of the New World. He introduced his Son on these pivotal and vital visits: "Behold, my Beloved Son, in whom I am well pleased, in whom I have glorified my name."

And again, in the Sacred Grove in New York State came the Father and the Son in the restoration of great and holy things.

Is man earthbound? Largely so, and temporarily so, yet Enoch and his people were translated from the earth, and the living Christ and angels commuted.

Is there extraterrestrial conversation? Certainly. Man may speak to God, and receive answers from him.

Is there association of nonhuman beings? There is no question.

Are planets out in space inhabited by intelligent creatures? Without doubt.

Will radioed messages ever come between planets across limitless space? Indubitably, for there have already been coming for thousands of years, properly sent, interpreted and publicized messages of utmost importance to the inhabitants of this earth. Dreams and open vision, like perfected television programs, have come repeatedly. Personal representatives have brought warning messages too numerous to mention, and it is our testimony to the world that God lives and abides in his heavenly home, and the earth is his footstool and only one of his numerous creations; that Jesus Christ is the Son of that living God; that he is the Creator, Savior, and Redeemer of the people on this earth and especially to those who will listen and obey; and that these interstellar messages—call them what you will, visions, revelations, television, radio—from the abode of God to man on this earth continue now to come to the living prophet of God among us.

# Chapter Five

# The Weak Things of the World

$\mathcal{A}$ philosopher at one of our leading universities writes, "I do not understand God, nor the way in which he works. If occasionally I raise my heart in prayer, it is to no God I can see, or hear, or feel. It is to a God in as cold and obscure night as any nonbeliever has known." God seems to be to many people "everything from a celestial gas to a kind of invisible, honorary president 'out there' in space, well beyond range of the astronauts."

A scientist says, "God if anything is hydrogen and carbon or thermonuclear fission, since that is what makes life on this planet possible."

Another person says, "God is a ghost floating in space." And another, "God is an infantile fantasy which was necessary when men did not understand what lightning was. . . ."

Another says, "God is like a fiery flame so white that it can blind you."

A seminary leader says, "God is all that I cannot understand."

Since time immemorial, man has sought for a God. It is difficult to erase from the heart of man this inborn yearning, this thirst, this hunger. It is natural for him to look for a personal Creator. This spiritual heritage of man seems to have come from the beginning. He may worship gods of wood and stone or trees or animals or earth or sky or sun, but man needs and must have a deity. In ancient Babylon, there were said to be at least 700 deities.

On a cold pre-dawn January morning my wife and I sat on the great rounded, bare rock hill under the Acropolis in Athens. This was Mars Hill. And as we sat waiting for the dawn, we could imagine on this Athenian Hyde Park the Apostle Paul discoursing to the bright minds surrounding him, arguing about the power of their many gods:

> Ye men of Athens, I perceive that in all things ye are too superstitious.
>
> For as I passed by, and beheld your devotions, I found an altar with this inscription, TO THE UNKNOWN GOD. Whom therefore ye ignorantly worship, him declare I unto you.
>
> God that made the world and all things therein, seeing that he is Lord of heaven and earth, dwelleth not in temples made with hands;
>
> Neither is worshipped with men's hands, as though he needed any thing, seeing he giveth to all life, and breath, and all things. . . .
>
> For in him we live, and move, and have our being; as certain also of your own poets have said, For we are also his offspring.
>
> Forasmuch then as we are the offspring of God, we ought not to think that the Godhead is like unto gold, or silver, or stone, graven by art and man's device.
>
> And the times of this ignorance God winked at; but now commandeth all men every where to repent. (Acts 17:22-25, 28-30.)

I believe with Paul that it is central to our salvation to accept and know the true God. The diversity of views about God and the frank doubts about his very existence remind us of the prophecy of Amos:

> Behold, the days come, saith the Lord God, that I will send a famine in the land, not a famine of bread, nor a thirst for water, but of hearing the words of the Lord:
>
> And they shall wander from sea to sea, and from the north even to the east, they shall run to and fro to seek the word of the Lord, and shall not find it.
>
> In that day shall the fair virgins and the young men faint for thirst. (Amos 8:11-13.)

"That day" is our day, when man-made institutions and human philosophies leave unsatisfied spiritual hungers and choking thirsts. It is no wonder men's spirits are faint.

The present struggles and meanderings of the learned, trying to find God in a laboratory of their own making, take us back to the days of the ferment of the long-ago out of which came the unthinkable creed that was supposed to clarify religious thought but left it in darkest chaos. The records reveal that many mental giants struggled long with the same incomprehensibles and came forth with a confusion that has carried over to our day. This confusion causes brilliant men now to doubt and to try with their puny powers to unravel the mystery, always getting it more and more tangled.

All of the diverse and negative and mystical concepts could not bring any fullness of peace or hope or joy to anyone. They are but sand, and structures built upon them are in danger.

> But now, behold they are led about by Satan, even as chaff is driven before the wind, or as a vessel is tossed about upon the waves, without sail or anchor, or without anything wherewith to steer her; and even as she is, so are they. (Mormon 5:18.)

One prominent theologian says there is a growing despair over the possibility of knowing God. He says, "Now despair is found to be deepening as science and technology create a growing mountain of questions that cannot be answered scientifically. . . . Historians point out that individual men, even Saints, have felt such despair ever since men first began asking basic questions: Who are

we? Where do we come from? What is the central meaning
in our lives? Even so most theologians, including radical
ones, say that the concept of God, personal or otherwise,
is what contributes order and meaning to human existence."
It is when men lose their concept of God that they say,
"Let us eat, drink, and be merry, for tomorrow we may
die," and proceed to do just that.

Another has said, "While modern men have rejected
God as a solution to life, they cannot evade the questioning
anxiety about its meaning. The apparent eclipse of God
is merely a sign that the world is experiencing what Rahner
calls the 'the anonymous presence' of God whose word
comes to man not on tablets of stone, but in the inner
murmurings of the heart."

Again and again these basic questions arise: "Why
am I?" "What should I become and be?" "What is the
meaning of my life?"

The Apostle Paul gave the answer, but the moderns
seem reluctant to accept the direction from an ancient.
Paul found among the Ephesians men like children, "tossed
to and fro, and carried about with every wind of doctrine,
by the sleight of men, and cunning craftiness, whereby
they lie in wait to deceive," and he prescribed the cure.
He would put men at the wheel who had communication
with the Lord, in an organization with apostles, evange-
lists, pastors, and teachers. This organization had power to
perfect the Saints and to develop the ministry and edify
the people; it had as its ultimate result a unity of the faith,
a knowledge of the Son of God, and perfection of men
until they should reach the stature of Christ. (See Ephesians 4:11-14.)

In the early centuries of the Christian era, the apostasy
came not through persecution, but by relinquishment of
faith caused by the superimposing of a man-made structure
upon and over the divine program. Many men with no
pretense nor claim to revelation, speaking without divine
authority or revelation, men depending only upon their

own brilliant and inquisitive minds but claiming to represent the congregations of the Christians, in long conference and erudite council sought to make a God that all could accept.

The brilliant and educated minds with their exaggerated and developed philosophies, knowing much about the Christian traditions and the pagan philosophies, seemed to find it well to combine all these elements in an effort to please everybody. In course of time they replaced the simple ways and program of the Christ with spectacular rituals, colorful display, and impressive pageantry and dispensed it as the program of Christ and called it Christianity. At last, the prophecy had been literally fulfilled wherein Isaiah said they would have "changed the ordinance, broken the everlasting covenant." (Isaiah 24:5.) They had replaced the glorious divine plan of exaltation of Christ with an elaborate, colorful man-made system to attract the imagination of unsuspecting souls. In those days, they seemed to have little idea of totally dethroning the Christ or terminating the life of God the Father, as in our own day, but they seemed to fill the need of putting together something that would preserve the God idea but not run counter to their rational concepts.

As a result of these long and brilliant discussions, combinations of ideas, and reconciliations of concepts, they reached the point of an incomprehensible formula called "the mystery of mysteries." The creed finally decided upon ran something like this: "We believe in one God, the Father Almighty, Maker of all things, both visible and invisible: and in one Lord Jesus Christ, the Son (Word) of God, begotten of the Father, only-begotten, that is of the essence (substance) of the Father, God from God, Light from Light (Life from Life), very God from very God, begotten not made, of one essence (substance) with the Father . . . through whom all things come to be, both things in heaven and things on earth; Who for the sake of us men and for our salvation came down, and was made flesh, and became man, suffered, and rose on the third day, ascended into the heavens (to the Father), is coming to judge living and dead; and in one Holy Spirit." (James L. Barker, *The Divine Church*, vol. 2, p. 55.)

From this incomprehensible mystery came mystification. After centuries the Christians are still mystified, and this has led in no small measure to the "death of God" theorists, for as one modern thinker said, "It is easier to think of a dead God than one who is so mystified, disembodied, inactivated, powerless, unimpressive. . . . It is easier for me to think of a world without a Creator than a Creator loaded with all the contradiction of the world."

No wonder Paul says, "The wisdom of the world is foolishness with God."

Paul spoke of arrogant Romans who worshiped their own minds rather than Him who gave them their brains, saying:

> Because that, when they knew God, they glorified him not as God, neither were thankful; but became vain in their imaginations, and their foolish heart was darkened.
>
> Professing themselves to be wise, they became fools,
>
> And changed the glory of the uncorruptible God into an image made like to corruptible man, and to birds, and to four-footed beasts, and creeping things.
>
> Wherefore God also gave them up to uncleanness through the lusts of their own hearts, to dishonour their own bodies between themselves:
>
> Who changed the truth of God into a lie, and worshipped and served the creature more than the Creator, who is blessed for ever. Amen. (Romans 1:21-25.)

And the Savior asks in parabolic terms which is greater, the Creature or his Creator?

> Ye fools and blind: for whether is greater, the gold, or the temple that sanctifieth the gold?
>
> And, Whosoever shall swear by the altar, it is nothing; but whosoever sweareth by the gift that is upon it, he is guilty.
>
> Ye fools and blind: for whether is greater, the gift, or the altar that sanctifieth the gift? (Matthew 23:17-19.)

He chose Peter and the other apostles for their humility, responsiveness, and childlike faith and devotion, not for their intellectual attainments. Though Paul was not an untrained man, he was pliable and teachable, and this seemed to be his theme:

> Let no man deceive himself. If any man among you seemeth to be wise in this world, let him become a fool, that he may be wise.
>
> For the wisdom of this world is foolishness with God. For it is written, He taketh the wise in their own craftiness.
>
> And again, The Lord knoweth the thoughts of the wise, that they are vain.
>
> Therefore let no man glory in men. For all things are yours;
>
> Whether Paul, or Apollos, or Cephas, or the world, or life, or death, or things present, or things to come; all are yours;
>
> And ye are Christ's; and Christ is God's. (1 Corinthians 3: 18-23.)
>
> Beware lest any man spoil you through philosophy and vain deceit, after the tradition of men, after the rudiments of the world, and not after Christ. (Colossians 2:8.)

Why will men spend their time, energies, and life on a drifting selfmade raft in the great ocean of uncertainties, storms, waves, thirst, and sunstroke, especially when there is available a great powerful ship, equipped, safe, and sure?

The traditional Christian churches have failed.

> These are wells without water, clouds that are carried with a tempest; to whom the mist of darkness is reserved for ever.
>
> For when they speak great swelling words of vanity, they allure through the lusts of the flesh, through much wantonness, those that were clean escaped from them who live in error.
>
> While they promise them liberty, they themselves are the servants of corruption: for of whom a man is overcome, of the same is he brought in bondage. (2 Peter 2:17-19.)

Someone has said that we live in a day in which God, if there be a God, chooses to be silent, but The Church of Jesus Christ of Latter-day Saints proclaims to the world that neither the Father nor the Son is silent. They are vocal and commune as proper and necessary, and constantly express a willingness, indeed an eagerness, to maintain communication with men and to become well acquainted enough that men may know positively of the existence, personality, purposes, and work of God, all of which narrows down to one dual objective, as is said: "For behold, this is my work and my glory—to bring to pass the immortality and eternal life of man." (Moses 1:39.)

One of the theologians above quoted indicated it was impossible for man to find God or know God. This is like saying: I have never climbed Mt. Ararat—no one can climb Ararat; or, I have never bathed in the clear warm waters of the Adriatic—there is no Adriatic Sea; or, I have never hunted in Kreuger Park, nor have I seen the wildlife therein—there is no Kreuger Park; or, because I've never seen on the slopes of the Rockies or the Andes Mountains a burning bush, there was no burning bush; or, I have always had health—therefore, the pain that people claim to suffer is a figment of their imaginations. I have never rocketed into space—therefore, it is impossible. I have never heard or seen God—therefore, no man has ever seen or heard God or walked with him. How presumptuous and arrogant for any man to say God is unapproachable, unknowable, unseeable, unhearable because one himself has not prepared himself for the experience.

In his funeral sermon for King Follett, our modern prophet made some positive statements:

> There are but very few beings in the world who understand rightly the character of God. . . .
>
> If men do not comprehend the character of God, they do not comprehend themselves. . . .
>
> God himself was once as we are now, and is an exalted Man, and sits enthroned in yonder heavens! . . .
>
> [I]f you were to see Him today, you would see Him like a man in form—like yourselves in all the person, image, and very form as a man; for Adam was created in the very fashion, image

and likeness of God, and received instruction from, and walked, talked and conversed with Him, as one man talks and communes with another.

> And this is life eternal, that they might know thee, the only true God, and Jesus Christ, whom thou hast sent. (John 17:3.)

No amount of human study can find out God, but he has revealed himself to his servants the prophets, and they have taught us of his nature. We can each have a confirmation of the truth through our own fasting and prayer. The theological storms around us find us calm in the center of tempest with a simple, sure knowledge of the Father and the Son derived from the ancient and modern scriptures and affirmed by the Spirit. In this knowledge we have hope of eternal life.

# Chapter Six

# ℳy Redeemer Lives Eternally

*A*nd I, brethren, when I came to you, came not with excellency of speech or of wisdom, declaring unto you the testimony of God.

For I determined not to know any thing among you, save Jesus Christ, and him crucified. (1 Corinthians 2:1-2.)

The pastor of a church in Illinois said that he felt the same reverence for Santa Claus as he did for Jesus Christ:

> I consider both of them to be folk-tales, but in different categories. The story of Santa Claus is not so deeply tinged with religious feeling or so implanted in the culture of the people.

He finds one difference, however, in that "a man named Jesus" did exist, while Santa Claus is a "figure of the imagination."

In *Time,* a noted professor emeritus in one of our largest universities was quoted at length in his conception of Jesus and his works. He gives him human warmth, a great capacity for love, astounding understanding. He explains that Lazarus was not dead, but was merely "brought 'back to health' by Jesus, the power of mind and learning, and by the 'therapy of his own abundant vitality.' "

Many in the world share this view of Jesus of Nazareth, but I bear testimony that Jesus is not only a great teacher, a great humanist, and a great dramatist, but is in very deed the Son of the living God, the Redeemer of the world, the Savior of mankind. I want to further testify that he not only lived in the meridian of time for approximately thirty-three years, but that he lived eternities before this, and will live eternities beyond it; and I bear testimony that he was not only the organizer of the kingdom of God upon the earth, but the Creator of this world, the Redeemer of mankind.

He first comes into our knowledge when with a host of spirits he stood before his Father in solemn assembly. The vision of this primeval gathering is recorded as follows:

> Now the Lord had shown unto me, Abraham, the intelligences that were organized before the world was; and among all these there were many of the noble and great ones;
>
> . . . and he said unto me: Abraham, thou art one of them; thou wast chosen before thou wast born.
>
> And there stood one among them that was like unto God, and he said unto those who were with him: We will go down, for there is space there, and we will take of these materials, and we will make an earth whereon these may dwell;
>
> And we will prove them herewith, to see if they will do all things whatsoever the Lord their God shall command them. (Abraham 3:22-25.)

Another of the number offered to go down to the earth and, by compulsion, save all men, but the one "like unto God" came forward to support a plan of free agency by which redemption, salvation, and exaltation would be offered to the people of the earth but not forced upon them. This latter plan, urged by Jehovah, or Jesus Christ, was accepted.

The time finally came when the earth was to be created.

> And then the Lord said: Let us go down. And they went down at the beginning, and they, that is the Gods, organized and formed the heavens and the earth. (Abraham 4:1.)

And Jesus the Christ, or Jehovah, was one of the Gods who created the earth and gave it light and established upon it the plant and animal life and finally man, created in the image of God. He said long centuries later to the Nephites:

> Behold, I am Jesus Christ the Son of God. I created the heavens and the earth, and all things that in them are. . . . (3 Nephi 9:15.)

The Redeemer bore witness again to Adam and Eve, who were given dominion over this earth. They lived in the Garden of Eden from which they were expelled after partaking of the forbidden fruit. Adam and Eve, with their large family, scattered out upon the land and tilled it and tended their flocks. Having been commanded by the voice of God to offer sacrifices of the firstlings of their flocks, Adam obeyed.

> And after many days an angel of the Lord appeared unto Adam, saying: Why dost thou offer sacrifices unto the Lord? And Adam said unto him: I know not, save the Lord commanded me.
>
> And then the angel spake, saying, This thing is a similitude of the sacrifice of the Only Begotten of the Father, which is full of grace and truth.
>
> And in that day the Holy Ghost fell upon Adam, which beareth record of the Father and the Son, saying: I am the Only Begotten of the Father from the beginning, henceforth and forever, that as thou hast fallen thou mayest be redeemed, and all mankind, even as many as will. (Moses 5:6-7, 9.)

The gospel of repentance and redemption was made clear to these ancestors by the Savior himself.

After some generations the Redeemer came again to earth to visit his choice servant and mighty leader Enoch, who, because of his righteousness, was permitted to hear the voice of Jehovah, who commanded him to preach repentance to a wicked people. First he heard the voice of God calling people to repentance. Enoch bowed himself to the earth before the Lord and spake:

> Why is it that I have found favor in thy sight, and am but a lad, and all the people hate me; for I am slow of speech; wherefore am I thy servant?

> And the Lord spake unto Enoch, and said unto him: Anoint thine eyes with clay, and wash them, and thou shalt see. And he did so. (Moses 6:31, 35.)

And he beheld the spirit world and all creations not visible to the natural eye.

> . . . thenceforth came the saying abroad in the land: A seer hath the Lord raised up unto his people. (Moses 6:36.)

From hills and high places, Enoch testified against them for sin. In concluding his preaching to his people, he bore testimony:

> . . . I stood upon the mount, I beheld the heavens open, and I was clothed upon with glory;
>
> And I saw the Lord; and he stood before my face, and he talked with me, even as a man talketh one with another, face to face. . . . (Moses 7:3-4.)

The transgressions of the people of the generation of Enoch seem to have continued unabated, for Noah comes forth to continue throughout the long years of his ministry a vigorous warning and preachment against the sins of the world. The world had become ripe in iniquity. The people had attempted to take the life of the prophet Noah.

> And thus Noah found grace in the eyes of the Lord; for Noah was a just man, and perfect in his generation; and he walked with God. . . . (Moses 8:27.)

Again, at the time of the tower of Babel when the Jaredites prepared to cross the ocean for the promised land, now known as America, they went into the mountains and "did molten out of the rock, sixteen small stones" (Ether 3:1), and the prophet entreated the Lord to touch these stones that they might shine forth in the darkness of the enclosed vessels to give light while they crossed the sea. And as the Lord touched each stone,

> —the veil was taken from off the eyes of the brother of Jared, and he saw the finger of the Lord; and it was as the finger of a man, like unto flesh and blood. . . .
>
> And the Lord said unto him: Because of thy faith thou hast seen that I shall take upon me flesh and blood; and never has man come before me with such exceeding faith as thou hast; for were it not so ye could not have seen my finger. . . .

And when he had said these words, behold, the Lord showed himself unto him, and said: . . .

Behold, I am he who was prepared from the foundation of the world to redeem my people. Behold, I am Jesus Christ. . . .

. . . Seest thou that ye are created after mine own image. . . ?

Behold, this body, which ye now behold, is the body of my spirit; and man have I created after the body of my spirit; and even as I appear unto thee to be in the spirit will I appear unto my people in the flesh. (Ether 3:6, 9, 13-16.)

Some centuries later in what is known as the meridian of time, the people on the American continent were watching for the signs of the coming of the Messiah in fulfillment of prophecy. The wicked figured that the day had passed and issued ominous warnings to the believers of Samuel's prophecies concerning the birth of Christ. Nephi, being greatly concerned, prayed devoutly unto the Lord all day, at the end of which there came to him the voice of the Lord, saying:

Lift up your head and be of good cheer; for behold, the time is at hand, and on this night shall the sign be given, and on the morrow come I into the world, to show unto the world that I will fulfill all that which I have caused to be spoken by the mouth of my holy prophets. (3 Nephi 1:13.)

That night the darkness did not come, and two days and a night were as one day, and the righteous people knew that that day would see the birth of the Savior of the world. And a new star appeared as further evidence that the Christ was born.

Far across the ocean in the land of Judea this same star shone forth and led the three wise men from the East to a stable out of Bethlehem. Here they found, according to the many prophetic scriptures, "a babe wrapped in swaddling clothes and lying in a manger." Mary, a virgin, became the mother of the Son of God. Her husband, Joseph, the carpenter of Nazareth, had brought her to the city of David at tax time, and here the predictions of many centuries were fulfilled in the mortal birth of Jesus the Christ. The shepherds as well as the wise men called and paid homage, the angels sang hosannas, and the Savior came into his flesh and blood tabernacle.

Little is told of the childhood of Jesus, but it is related in Luke:

> And the child grew, and waxed strong in spirit, filled with wisdom: and the grace of God was upon him. (Luke 2:40.)

And when Jesus was a man and came up out of the waters of baptism—

> . . . the heavens were opened unto him, and he saw the Spirit of God descending like a dove, and lighting upon him:

> And lo a voice from heaven, saying, This is my beloved Son, in whom I am well pleased. (Matthew 3:16-17.)

In the wilderness the devil came to tempt the Savior, but Jesus withstood and rebuked him.

We follow our Savior down the dusty roads of Judea; over the rocky paths of the highlands and the sandy beaches of the seas; into the synagogues to reprove and rebuke the sinner; in the byways to call to repentance.

We find the Redeemer at the marriage at Cana turning water into wine; at the temple at Jerusalem where, with his handmade scourge of small cords, he drove from the temple the desecrating traders and money-changers, saying, ". . . make not my Father's house an house of merchandise." (John 2:16.)

He declared to the woman of Samaria:

> Whosoever drinketh of the water that I shall give him shall never thirst. . . . (John 4:14.)

The mortal life of the Lord was a hard one judged by the standards of the world. He said:

> Foxes have holes, and birds of the air have nests; but the Son of man hath not where to lay his head. (Luke 9:58.)

He was a man of sorrows and acquainted with grief. He walked the dusty roads of Judea followed by great multitudes of interested disciples, curious sign seekers, and critical annoyers, with always some vicious men lurking in the background, seeking his very life.

Even in his old home town he was not appreciated. At his first visit home he was thrust out of the synagogue, out of the city, and led to the brow of the hill to be killed, but he escaped. Many of his disciples "went back and walked no more with him." Though a price was on his head, his disciples urged him to make a display of his miracles, "For neither did his brethren believe in him." (John 7:5.) The hypocritical Pharisees and the chief priests took counsel to trap him that he might be put to death.

Constantly under strain from the throngs of demanding people, he frequently retired "into a mountain to pray, and continued all night in prayer to God." (Luke 6:12.)

> And Jesus, walking by the sea of Galilee, saw two brethren . . . fishers.
>
> And he saith unto them, Follow me, and I will make you fishers of men. And they straightway left their nets, and followed him. (Matthew 4:18-20.)

And he saw James and John mending their nets and likewise called them and subsequently called other eight from all walks of life to lead his church, and he "named them apostles."

The numerous miracles of the Redeemer brought him early attention. The curious followed with wonder, the believers looked on with awe, and because of his increasing popularity, his enemies followed to catch him in law-breaking that they might dispose of him.

Beginning at Cana he astounded his followers. He blessed the loaves and fishes and fed many thousands of hungry people. He placed his fingers in the ears of a deaf person, saying, "Be opened," and the man heard clearly. He "spit and touched" the tongue of one with an impediment in his speech, "and he spake plain." He touched the eyes of the blind, saying, "According to your faith be it unto you. And their eyes were opened." (Matthew 9:29-30.)

The multitudes marveled, saying, "It was never so seen in Israel" as he cast out the devil. His accusers found him healing on the Sabbath and blamed him when they heard him say to the man with a withered hand: "Stretch forth thine hand. And he stretched it forth; and it was restored whole, like as the other." (Matthew 12:13.)

"We never saw it on this fashion," the people said as they saw a sick man carry away his bed at the command: "Take up thy bed and go thy way."

He stopped a funeral procession and, touching the bier of the son of the widow of Nain, said: "Young man, I say unto thee, Arise. And he that was dead sat up and began to speak." (Luke 7:14-15.)

He astounded the people when he said to the dead daughter of Jairus, "Damsel, I say unto thee arise." (Mark 5:41.) They had laughed him to scorn, but now they were shocked when the damsel arose and walked.

The woman who for twelve years of affliction had "spent all her living upon physicians, neither could be healed of any, came behind him, and touched the border of his garment" (Luke 8:43-44) and immediately was healed. Again, he forgave the sinner, stilled the tempest, cleansed the lepers, and raised the dead, even his friend Lazarus, who was four days dead when the voice of Jehovah commanded, "Lazarus, come forth." (John 11:43.)

And toward the end of his ministry,

> Jesus taketh Peter, James, and John his brother, and bringeth them up into an high mountain apart,
>
> And was transfigured before them: and his face did shine as the sun, and his raiment was white as the light.
>
> And, behold, there appeared unto them Moses and Elias talking with him.
>
> . . . behold, a bright cloud overshadowed them: and behold a voice out of the cloud, which said, This is my beloved Son, in whom I am well pleased; hear ye him. (Matthew 17:1-3, 4.)

Knowing that his hour had come, he repaired to the room that had been prepared, and there he gave to his disciples the Last Supper, after which he retired into the Garden of Gethsemane, where he poured out his soul to his Father:

O my Father, if this cup may not pass away from me, except I drink it, thy will be done. (Matthew 26:42.)

Then came a mob headed by the betrayer, Judas. They stripped Jesus and put on a scarlet robe. They pushed down upon his head a crown of thorns and placed a reed in his right hand and bowed the knee and mocked and spit upon him and smote him on the head. Then they led him to Calvary to be crucified. Between thieves he was nailed to the cross, and the executioners divided his garments among them.

Those who loved him crouched about his feet and wept in their helplessness. As his life ebbed he called:

Father, forgive them; for they know not what they do. (Luke 23:34.)

And he cried with a loud voice,

Father, into thy hands I commend my spirit: and . . . he gave up the ghost. (Luke 23:46.)

Then they took his body carefully down, wrapped it in linen, and laid it in a sepulchre that was hewn in stone wherein never man before was laid. And the women prepared spices and ointments for the body. The three days were ended and Jesus came forth as he had promised. His disciples, both men and women, had been to the tomb and found it empty. They were surprised, still not comprehending the fact of the resurrection. He said to Mary:

Touch me not; for I am not yet ascended to my Father: but go to my brethren, and say unto them, I ascend unto my Father, and your Father; and to my God, and your God. (John 20:17.)

The same day he appeared in the locked room with his apostles and revealed himself to them, assuring them that he lived again. Many hundred were similarly convinced.

Now his church was organized, the program clarified, and leaders developed. And when his followers were gathered together in Jerusalem,

. . . he was taken up; and a cloud received him out of their sight.

And while they looked stedfastly toward heaven as he went up, behold, two men stood by them in white apparel;

Which also said, Ye men of Galilee, why stand ye gazing up into heaven? this same Jesus, which is taken up from you into heaven, shall so come in like manner as ye have seen him go into heaven. (Acts 1:9-11.)

On the Western Hemisphere also, there was at the death of Jesus darkness and destruction, cities burned, mountains leveled, and seas raised, and in the suffering and lamentations of the people a voice was heard among the inhabitants, explaining the disasters and saying:

Behold, I am Jesus Christ the Son of God. I created the heavens and the earth, and all things that in them are. . . .

I came unto my own, and my own received me not. . . .

I am the light and the life of the world. I am Alpha and Omega, the beginning and the end.

Behold, I have come unto the world to bring redemption unto the world, to save the world from sin. (3 Nephi 9:15-16, 18, 21.)

Again the Nephites were conversing about Jesus Christ, the sign of whose death had been given to them, and a small, penetrating voice came out of heaven, which pierced them to the very soul and caused their hearts to burn. The voice uttered these words:

Behold my Beloved Son, in whom I am well pleased, in whom I have glorified my name—hear ye him.

And . . . they cast their eyes up again towards heaven; and behold, they saw a Man descending out of heaven; and he was clothed in a white robe; and he came down and stood in the midst of them. . . .

And . . . he stretched forth his hand and spake unto the people, saying:

Behold, I am Jesus Christ whom the prophets testified shall come into the world.

. . . I have drunk out of that bitter cup which the Father hath given me, and have glorified the Father in taking upon me the sins of the world. . . .

. . . when Jesus had spoken these words the whole multitude fell to the earth; for they remembered that it had been prophesied among them that Christ should show himself unto them after his ascension into heaven.

And it came to pass that the Lord spake unto them saying:

Arise and come forth unto me, that ye may thrust your hands into my side, and also that ye may feel the prints of the nails in my hands and in my feet, that ye may know that I am the God of Israel, and the God of the whole earth, and have been slain for the sins of the world. (3 Nephi 11:7-14.)

And all the people felt the prints of the nails and of the spear and

. . . did know of a surety and did bear record, that it was he, of whom it was written by the prophets, that should come. (3 Nephi 11:15.)

And he organized his church and called his twelve apostles and taught them the doctrines and blessed their children. He restored sight to the blind, strength to the infirm, and wholeness to those who were ill, and after his appearances among them,

. . . there came a cloud and overshadowed the multitude that they could not see Jesus.

And while they were overshadowed he departed from them, and ascended into heaven. And the disciples saw and did bear record that he ascended again into heaven. (3 Nephi 18:38-39.)

The time passed and apostasy displaced faithfulness. But eventually the darkness of centuries was beginning to be dissipated, the new world of America had been rediscovered, and honorable, God-fearing people had settled it. War had been waged and freedom gained and religious liberty granted, and the Lord Jesus Christ appeared again to restore and reestablish his work and kingdom upon the earth. A young boy with an open and unbiased mind knelt on a beautiful spring morning in a grove and prayed for light. Though the evil power attempted to destroy him, he was relieved by the appearance of a pillar of light "above the brightness of the sun."

It no sooner appeared than I found myself delivered from the enemy which held me bound. When the light rested upon me I saw two Personages, whose brightness and glory defy all description, standing above me in the air. One of them spake unto me, calling me by name and said, pointing to the other—This is My Beloved Son. Hear Him!

. . . I asked the Personages, who stood above me in the light, which of all the sects was right—and which I should join. (Joseph Smith 2:17-18.)

Following this visit came numerous other visitations from heavenly beings in the restoration of the gospel and the establishing of the kingdom upon the earth.

The work went forward, the Church was organized, the Book of Mormon was printed, the revelations were given, twelve apostles were appointed, the temple in Kirtland was built, and during the dedication ceremonies after the administering of the sacrament on Sunday, April 3, 1836, Joseph Smith and Oliver Cowdery retired to the pulpit, the veils being dropped, and there bowed in silent prayer. After arising from their knees, they saw the Savior appear to them, standing on the breastwork of the pulpit. He blessed them and accepted the building.

And so, having traced the scripturally recorded appearances of the Lord Jesus Christ from preexistence to date, we look forward now to his second coming, as he promised, which promise will literally be fulfilled as were his many other promises. In the meantime we praise his holy name and serve him and bear testimony of the divinity of his mission, along with the prophets through the generations. We testify with John the Baptist, who, as he saw the Lord approaching him, said: "Behold the Lamb of God, which taketh away the sin of the world." (John 1:29.)

We testify again with John the Beloved, who, after fishing all night without success, and seeing Jesus on the shore, said with conviction: "It is the Lord!"

And with Simon Peter, who, when asked by the Lord, "But whom say ye that I am?" answered: "Thou art the Christ, the Son of the living God." (Matthew 16:15-16.)

And finally we bear testimony with the Prophet

Joseph Smith, who was willing to give his life for his testimony, which comes to us in his own words:

> ... I had actually seen a light, and in the midst of that light I saw two Personages, and they did in reality speak to me; and though I was hated and persecuted for saying that I had seen a vision, yet it was true; and while they were persecuting me, reviling me, and speaking all manner of evil against me falsely for so saying, I was led to say in my heart: Why persecute me for telling the truth? I have actually seen a vision; and who am I that I can withstand God, or why does the world think to make me deny what I have actually seen? For I had seen a vision; I knew it, and I knew that God knew it, and I could not deny it, neither dared I do it; at least I knew that by so doing I would offend God, and come under condemnation. (Joseph Smith 2:25.)

We too know and cannot deny that Jesus is the Christ, the Savior of all mankind, that he died for our sins, and that he lives and reigns today in the heavens, resurrected and perfect, awaiting the day of his second coming to glory.

# Chapter Seven

# Spiritual Eyes Behold God

If I were to tell you in all seriousness that in your own backyard you could find an acre of diamonds, would you ignore the suggestion and take no trouble to search? Today, I am telling you with all the fervor of my soul that in easy reach there is a prize of inestimable worth. Diamonds can buy one food and shelter. Diamonds can embellish and decorate. But the prize that is within your grasp is more brilliant than jewels. It will not lose its sparkle, nor can it be stolen by thieves. I speak of the greatest gift—the gift of eternal life. It may not be obtained through mere asking; it cannot be purchased with money; hopeful wishing will not bring it; but it is available to men and women the world over who comply with the requirements.

There have been long periods of history when the total truth of how to obtain this prize was not immediately available to the inhabitants of the earth. But in our day, the whole eternal program is here and can carry men to exaltation and eternal life, all the way to godhood. Early in man's history the full gospel was known. But, as Amos predicted:

> Behold, the days come, saith the Lord God, that I will send a famine in the land, not a famine of bread, nor a thirst for water, but of hearing the words of the Lord:
>
> And they shall wander from sea to sea, and from the north even to the east, they shall run to and fro to seek the word of the Lord, and shall not find it. (Amos 8:11-12.)

After the early Christian era there followed centuries of spiritual darkness, as described by Amos. But we solemnly announce to all the world that the spiritual famine is ended, the spiritual drought is spent, the word of the Lord in its purity and completeness is available to all men. One need no longer wander from sea to sea nor from the north to the east seeking the true gospel, for the everlasting truth is available, restored through the Prophet Joseph Smith.

To Joseph Smith the Master himself gave the basic truth: "This is eternal lives—to know the only wise and true God, and Jesus Christ, whom he hath sent. I am he." And then his command: "Receive ye, therefore, my law." (D&C 132:24.)

In spite of all the gods that men make for themselves, and the confusion incident thereto, the living and true God is in his heaven and is available to his children. If there is estrangement, it is men who have cut themselves off from God.

The most important question one can ask himself is this: Do I really know God the Father and Jesus Christ, his Son? And in the answer is the difference between floundering through indecision and having sureness and certainty.

The Lord promised:

> . . . every soul who forsaketh his sins and cometh unto me, and calleth on my name, and obeyeth my voice, and keepeth my commandments, shall see my face and know that I am. (D&C 93:1.)

The beatitudes of Christ add: "Blessed are the pure in heart: for they shall see God." (Matthew 5:8.)

Celestial life may be had by every soul who will fulfill the requirements. To know is not enough. One must do. Righteousness is vital and ordinances are necessary.

Jehovah proclaims: "But no man is possessor of all things except he be purified and cleansed from all sin." (D&C 50:28.)

And the Redeemer continues: "And surely every man must repent or suffer. . . ." (D&C 19:4.)

> . . . I, God, have suffered these things for all, that they might not suffer if they would repent;
>
> But if they would not repent they must suffer even as I;
>
> Which suffering caused myself, even God, the greatest of all, to tremble because of pain. . . ." (D&C 19:16-18.)

There are three Gods: the Eternal Father, Elohim, to whom we pray; Christ or Jehovah; and the Holy Ghost, who testifies of the others and witnesses to us the truth of all things.

Many seem to delight in confusing the matter with their rationalizations and human calculations. The Father and the Son, in whose image we are created, separate and distinct beings, as like as any father and son, have identified themselves through the ages.

The Christ has declared himself to be the Lord God Almighty, Christ the Lord, the Beginning and the End, the Redeemer of the world, Jesus the Christ, the Mighty One of Israel, the Creator, the Son of the living God, Jehovah.

The Father Elohim declares Jesus to be "Mine Only Begotten Son," "the Word of my power." And twice, at least, at baptism and on the Mount of Transfiguration, the Father declared: "This is my Beloved Son, in whom I am well pleased."

The Bible gives much secular and religious history and much in glorious teachings. But even with these scriptures, confusion continues in the Christian world.

To know God, one must be aware of the person and attributes, power and glory of God the Father and God the Christ. We learn much from the encounters prophets have had.

Moses declares "he saw God face to face, and he talked with him. . . ." (Moses 1:2.)

This experience of Moses is in harmony with the scripture that says:

> For no man has seen God at any time in the flesh, except quickened by the Spirit of God.
>
> Neither can any natural man abide the presence of God, neither after the carnal mind. (D&C 67:11-12.)

It must be obvious, then, that to endure the glory of the Father or of the glorified Christ, a mortal being must be translated or otherwise fortified.

Grease on the swimmer's body or a heavy rubber skin-diver's suit may protect one from cold and wet; an asbestos suit might protect a firefighter from flames; a bullet-proof vest may save one from assassin's bullets; one's heated home may protect from winter's chilling blasts; deep shade or smoked glass can modify the withering heat and burning rays of the midday sun. There is a protective force that God brings into play when he exposes his human servants to the glories of his person and his works.

Moses, a prophet of God, held the protecting holy priesthood:

> . . . and the glory of God was upon Moses; therefore Moses could endure his presence. (Moses 1:2.)

In heavenly glorious vision, Moses "beheld the world . . . and all the children of men. . . ." (Moses 1:8.) He was protected then, but when the protection from such transcendent glory was relaxed, Moses was left near-helpless.

> And the presence of God withdrew from Moses, that his glory was not upon Moses; and Moses was left unto himself. And . . . he fell unto the earth. (Moses 1:9.)

Many hours elapsed before he could regain his natural strength. He exclaimed:

> . . . mine own eyes have beheld God . . . my spiritual eyes, for my natural eyes could not have beheld; for I should have withered and died in his presence; but his glory was upon me; and I beheld his face, for I was transfigured before him. (Moses 1:11.)

There is another power in this world, forceful and vicious. In the wilderness of Judea, on the temple's pinnacle and on the high mountain, a momentous contest took place between two brothers, Jehovah and Lucifer, sons of Elohim. When physically weak from fasting, Christ was tempted by Lucifer: "If thou be the Son of God, command this stone that it be made bread." (Luke 4:3.)

On the temple's pinnacles, the evil one taunted again, suggesting the unwarranted use of power. Christ replied: "Thou shalt not tempt the Lord thy God." (Luke 4:12.)

On a high mountain, the devil tantalized the Christ, offering kingdoms, thrones, powers, dominions; satisfactions of urges, desires, passions; the glory of wealth, ease, comfort—all this to possess on condition that he worship Lucifer.

Jesus, in his mortality, was tempted but resisted: "Get thee hence, Satan. . . ." (Matthew 4:10.)

Similarly Satan had contended for the subservience of Moses. Satan, also a son of God, had rebelled and had been cast out of heaven and not permitted an earthly body as had his brother Jehovah. Much depended upon the outcome of this spectacular duel. Could Lucifer control and dominate this prophet Moses, who had learned so much directly from his Lord?

"Moses, son of man, worship me," the devil tempted, with promise of worlds and luxuries and power. But Moses looked upon Satan and said: "Who art thou? For behold, I am a son of God, in the similitude of his Only Begotten. . . ." (Moses 1:13.)

Moses knew well his role and was prepared for this temptation:

> . . . where is thy glory, that I should worship thee?
>
> For behold, I could not look upon God, except his glory should come upon me, and I were strengthened before him. But I can look upon thee in the natural man. Is it not so, surely?
>
> Blessed be the name of my God, for his Spirit hath not altogether withdrawn from me, or else where is thy glory, for it is darkness unto me? And I can judge between thee and God. . . . (Moses 1:13-15.)

The contrast was compelling. Moses the priesthood bearer must be protected to see Jehovah but could face this imposter with his natural eyes and without discomfort. What a contrast!

And with full knowledge now the prophet demanded: "Get thee hence, Satan. . . ." (Moses 1:16.) The liar, the tempter, the devil unwilling to give up this possible victim, now in rage and fury "cried with a loud voice, and rent upon the earth, and commanded, saying: I am the Only Begotten, worship me." (Moses 1:19.)

Moses recognized the deception and saw the power of darkness and the "bitterness of hell." Here was a force not easily reckoned with nor evicted. Terrified, he called upon God, then commanded with new power:

> I will not cease to call upon God . . . for his glory has been upon me, wherefore I can judge between him and thee. . . . In the name of the Only Begotten, depart hence, Satan. (Moses 1:18, 21.)

Not even Lucifer, the star of the morning, the archenemy of mankind, can withstand the power of the priesthood of God. Trembling, quaking, cursing, weeping, wailing, gnashing his teeth, he departed from the victorious Moses.

When properly protected with the glory of God, and when sufficiently perfected, *man can see God.*

Again the glory of the Lord was upon Moses and he heard the promise:

> . . . thou shalt deliver my people from bondage. . . .
>
> . . . and thou shalt be made stronger than many waters; for they shall obey thy command as if thou wert God. (Moses 1:26, 25.)

What a promise! What power! As one hears this promise from the God of heaven, one can envision water coming from the rock, manna from the sky, quails from the bushes, and waters of the sea rolling back to provide dry crossing for the refugee children of Israel.

A heavenly visitor identified himself to Abraham:

> I am the Lord thy God; I dwell in heaven. . . . My name is Jehovah. . . . (Abraham 2:7-8.)

And Abraham—

> talked with the Lord, face to face, as one man talketh with another. . . . And he said unto me: My son, my son. . . . And he put his hand upon mine eyes, and I saw those things which his hands had made . . . and I could not see the end thereof. (Abraham 3:11-12.)

Abraham was protected so that he could withstand the brilliance of the Lord and so that he could see and comprehend. The visions that Abraham saw at this time before his sojourn in Egypt were beyond all description. Perhaps no soul even with the strongest telescopes has ever seen the thousandth part of what Abraham saw as to this universe with all its limitless parts and functions. He also saw the creation of this earth, and the Father is quoted as telling him:

> And worlds without number have I created; and I also created them for mine own purpose; and by the Son I created them, which is mine Only Begotten. (Moses 1:33.)

How great the power of God, the majesty of God, the glory of God!

Again, as Jehovah came to call Saul of Tarsus to his mission, the vision was given to him only.

And the men which journeyed with him stood speechless, hearing a voice, but seeing no man. (Acts 9:7.)

But Saul of Tarsus saw Jehovah, the glorified Christ, and heard his voice and conversed with him. Even partially protected as he was from the brilliance of light from heaven greater than the noonday sun, Paul collapsed to the earth trembling, shocked. The voice said: "I am Jesus whom thou persecutest. . . ." (Acts 9:5.) So intense was the light that even with protection he was blinded. He said: "And when I could not see for the glory of that light, being led by the hand of them that were with me, I came into Damascus." (Acts 22:11.) A priesthood miracle restored sight to Paul after three days of total darkness.

The glory of the Lord! How great and magnificent!

Paul told Timothy:

. . . Christ . . . is the blessed and only Potentate, the King of kings, and the Lord of lords;

Who only hath immortality, dwelling in the light which no man can approach unto; whom no man hath seen, nor can see. . . . (1 Timothy 6:14-16.)

Enoch also needed protection, for the Lord speaking to Enoch said:

Anoint thine eyes with clay, and wash them, and thou shalt see. . . .

And he beheld the spirits that God had created; and he beheld also things which were not visible to the natural eye. . . . (Moses 6:35-36.)

The godless dared not touch him "for fear came on all of them that heard him; for he walked with God."

Daniel was worried so much that he mourned for three weeks and took no pleasant bread nor meat nor wine. Then came his vision, which he alone saw:

. . . there remained no strength in me . . . Yet heard I the voice of his words . . . then was I in a deep sleep on my face, and my face toward the ground.

And, behold, an hand touched me, which set me upon my knees and upon the palms of my hands.

And when he had spoken such words unto me, I set my face toward the ground, and I became dumb. (Daniel 10:8-10, 15.)

There is another world with which we mortals are little acquainted. It may not be far from us.

Peter, James, and John, the Presidency of the Church, came to know the power of God.

These three central figures climbed the high mountain with the Lord, Jehovah, while he was yet in the mortal world before his crucifixion. In the high mountain was solitude, apartness, privacy.

What a glorious experience! The Son of God, their Master, "was transfigured before them: and his face did shine as the sun, and his raiment was white as the light." Heavenly beings, Moses and Elias, appeared to them, and "a bright cloud overshadowed them: and behold a voice out of the cloud, which said, This is my beloved Son, in whom I am well pleased; hear ye him." (Matthew 17:2-3, 5.) The glory of the contact was more than they could bear and they collapsed, falling on their faces. While they were in this state, indescribable things were said and done.

The three mortals thus protected survived even this withering fiery experience.

Realizing that death by martyrdom was imminent, that a verbal witness could be forgotten, and that his important knowledge must be perpetuated down through the ages, Peter bore his solemn witness in writing. No fable was this, no conjuring of the imagination, no imagination of human minds—it was real and certain:

[We] . . . were eyewitnesses of his majesty.

For he [Christ] received from God the Father honour and glory, when there came such a voice to him from the excellent glory, This is my beloved Son, in whom I am well pleased.

And this voice which came from heaven we heard, when we were with him in the holy mount. . . . (2 Peter 1:16-18.)

The pattern was established, the chart made, the blueprint drawn. Under special need, at special times, under proper circumstances, God reveals himself to men who are prepared for such manifestations. And since God is the same yesterday, today, and forever, the heavens cannot be closed except as men lock them against themselves with disbelief.

In our own dispensation came another similar grand experience. The need was imperative; an apostasy had covered the earth and gross darkness the people, and the minds of men were clouded and light had been obscured in darkness. The time had come. Religious liberty would protect the seed until it could germinate and grow. And the individual was prepared in the person of a youth, clean and open minded, who had such implicit faith in the response of God that the heavens could not remain as iron and the earth as brass as they had been for many centuries.

This budding prophet had no preconceived false notions and beliefs. He was not steeped in the traditions and legends and superstitions and fables of the centuries. He had nothing to unlearn. He prayed for knowledge and direction. The powers of darkness preceded the light. When he knelt in solitude in the silent forest, his earnest prayer brought on a battle royal that threatened his destruction. For centuries, Lucifer with unlimited dominion had fettered men's minds and could ill-afford to lose his satanic hold. This threatened his unlimited dominion. Let Joseph Smith tell his own story:

> . . . I was seized upon by some power which entirely overcame me . . . to bind my tongue. . . . Thick darkness gathered around me, and it seemed to me for a time as if I were doomed to sudden destruction.
>
> . . . at the very moment when I was ready to . . . abandon myself to destruction—not to an imaginary ruin, but to the power of some actual being from the unseen world . . . I saw a pillar of light exactly over my head above the brightness of the sun. . . .

> . . . I found myself delivered from the enemy which held me bound. When the light rested upon me I saw two Personages, whose brightness and glory defy all description, standing above me in the air. One of them spake unto me, calling me by name and said, pointing to the other—*This is my Beloved Son. Hear Him!* (Joseph Smith 2:15-17.)

Young Joseph finally recovered his voice and asked the pertinent questions for which he had come and a conversation ensued, most of which he was forbidden to write. He continues:

> . . . When I came to myself again, I found myself lying on my back, looking up into heaven. . . . (Joseph Smith 2:20.)

Joseph had had the same general experience as Abraham and Moses and Enoch, who had seen the Lord and heard his voice. In addition, he heard the Father, bearing witness of the Son, as had Peter, James, and John on Transfiguration's mount. He had seen the person of Elohim. He had fought a desperate battle with the powers of darkness as had Moses and Abraham. And like them all, he was protected by the glory of the Lord. This young man gave a new concept to the world. Now, at least one person living knew God without question, for he had seen and heard.

And eternal life again was made available to men in the earth, for as the scripture says:

> And this is life eternal, that they might know thee the only true God, and Jesus Christ, whom thou hast sent. (John 17:3.)

In light of the testimony of Joseph Smith, the ancient scriptures take on new meaning, their literal verity confirmed by the experience of modern man who, quickened and protected by the Spirit, actually saw the Father and the Son. How great a blessing to see God and commune directly with him while yet in mortality! Though few of us will have that blessing, we can, through understanding the scriptures and by humble prayer, come in impressive measure to know God. We have the promise that if we sufficiently purify our hearts we shall surely see God and know him as he is!

# Chapter Eight

# *Tragedy or Destiny?*

The daily newspaper screamed the headlines: "Plane Crash Kills 43. No Survivors of Mountain Tragedy," and thousands of voices joined in a chorus: "Why did the Lord let this terrible thing happen?"

Two automobiles crashed when one went through a red light, and six people were killed. Why would God not prevent this?

Why should the young mother die of cancer and leave her eight children motherless? Why did not the Lord heal her?

A little child was drowned; another was run over. Why?

A man died one day suddenly of a coronary occlusion as he climbed a stairway. His body was found slumped on the floor. His wife cried out in agony, "Why? Why would the Lord do this to me? Could he not have considered my three little children who still need a father?"

A young man died in the mission field and people critically questioned: "Why did not the Lord protect this youth while he was doing proselyting work?"

I wish I could answer these questions with authority, but I cannot. I am sure that sometime we'll understand and be reconciled. But for the present we must seek understanding as best we can in the gospel principles.

Was it the Lord who directed the plane into the mountain to snuff out the lives of its occupants, or were there mechanical faults or human errors?

Did our Father in heaven cause the collision of the cars that took six people into eternity, or was it the error of the driver who ignored safety rules?

Did God take the life of the young mother or prompt the child to toddle into the canal or guide the other child into the path of the oncoming car?

Did the Lord cause the man to suffer a heart attack? Was the death of the missionary untimely? Answer, if you can. I cannot, for though I know God has a major role in our lives, I do not know how much he causes to happen and how much he merely permits. Whatever the answer to this question, there is another I feel sure about.

Could the Lord have prevented these tragedies? The answer is, Yes. The Lord is omnipotent, with all power to control our lives, save us pain, prevent all accidents, drive all planes and cars, feed us, protect us, save us from labor, effort, sickness, even from death, if he will. But he will not.

We should be able to understand this, because we can realize how unwise it would be for us to shield our children from all effort, from disappointments, temptations, sorrows, and suffering.

The basic gospel law is free agency and eternal development. To force us to be careful or righteous would be to nullify that fundamental law and make growth impossible.

> And the Lord spake unto Adam, saying: Inasmuch as thy children are conceived in sin, even so when they begin to

grow up, sin conceiveth in their hearts, and they taste the bitter, that they may know to prize the good.

And it is given unto them to know good from evil; wherefore they are agents unto themselves. . . . (Moses 6:55-56.)

. . . Satan rebelled against me, and sought to destroy the agency of man, which I, the Lord God, had given him. . . . (Moses 4:3.)

If we looked at mortality as the whole of existence, then pain, sorrow, failure, and short life would be calamity. But if we look upon life as an eternal thing stretching far into the premortal past and on into the eternal post-death future, then all happenings may be put in proper perspective.

Is there not wisdom in his giving us trials that we might rise above them, responsibilities that we might achieve, work to harden our muscles, sorrows to try our souls? Are we not exposed to temptations to test our strength, sickness that we might learn patience, death that we might be immortalized and glorified?

If all the sick for whom we pray were healed, if all the righteous were protected and the wicked destroyed, the whole program of the Father would be annulled and the basic principle of the gospel, free agency, would be ended. No man would have to live by faith.

If joy and peace and rewards were instantaneously given the doer of good, there could be no evil—all would do good but not because of the rightness of doing good. There would be no test of strength, no development of character, no growth of powers, no free agency, only satanic controls.

Should all prayers be immediately answered according to our selfish desires and our limited understanding, then there would be little or no suffering, sorrow, disappointment, or even death, and if these were not, there would also be no joy, success, resurrection, nor eternal life and godhood.

> For it must needs be, that there is an opposition in all things . . . righteousness . . . wickedness . . . holiness . . . misery . . . good . . . bad. . . . (2 Nephi 2:11.)

Being human, we would expel from our lives physical pain and mental anguish and assure ourselves of continual ease and comfort, but if we were to close the doors upon sorrow and distress, we might be excluding our greatest friends and benefactors. Suffering can make saints of people as they learn patience, long-suffering, and self-mastery. The sufferings of our Savior were part of his education.

> Though he were a Son, yet learned he obedience by the things which he suffered;
>
> And being made perfect, he became the author of eternal salvation unto all them that obey him. (Hebrews 5:8-9.)

I love the verse of "How Firm a Foundation"—

> When through the deep waters I call thee to go,
> The rivers of sorrow shall not thee o'erflow
> For I will be with thee, thy troubles to bless,
> And sanctify to thee thy deepest distress.
> —*Hymns,* No. 66

And Elder James E. Talmage wrote: "No pang that is suffered by man or woman upon the earth will be without its compensating effect . . . if it be met with patience."

On the other hand, these things can crush us with their mighty impact if we yield to weakness, complaining, and criticism.

> No pain that we suffer, no trial that we experience is wasted. It ministers to our education, to the development of such qualities as patience, faith, fortitude and humility. All that we suffer and all that we endure, especially when we endure it patiently, builds up our characters, purifies our hearts, expands our souls, and makes us more tender and charitable, more worthy to be called the children of God . . . and it is through sorrow and suffering, toil and tribulation, that we gain the education that we come here to acquire and which will make us more like our Father and Mother in heaven. . . . (Orson F. Whitney)

There are people who are bitter as they watch loved ones suffer agonies and interminable pain and physical torture. Some would charge the Lord with unkindness, indifference, and injustice. We are so incompetent to judge!

I like also the words of these verses, the author of which I do not know:

> Pain stayed so long I said to him today,
> "I will not have you with me any more."
> I stamped my foot and said, "Be on your way,"
> And paused there, startled at the look he wore.
> "I, who have been your friend," he said to me,
> "I, who have been your teacher—all you know
> Of understanding love, of sympathy,
> And patience, I have taught you. Shall I go?"
> He spoke the truth, this strange unwelcome guest;
> I watched him leave, and knew that he was wise.
> He left a heart grown tender in my breast,
> He left a far, clear vision in my eyes.
> I dried my tears, and lifted up a song—
> Even for one who'd tortured me so long.

The power of the priesthood is limitless but God has wisely placed upon each of us certain limitations. I may develop priesthood power as I perfect my life, yet I am grateful that even through the priesthood I cannot heal all the sick. I might heal people who should die. I might relieve people of suffering who should suffer. I fear I would frustrate the purposes of God.

Had I limitless power, and yet limited vision and understanding, I might have saved Abinadi from the flames of fire when he was burned at the stake, and in doing so I might have irreparably damaged him. He died a martyr and went to a martyr's reward—exaltation.

I would likely have protected Paul against his woes if my power were boundless. I would surely have healed his "thorn in the flesh." And in doing so I might have foiled the Lord's program. Thrice he offered prayers, asking the Lord to remove the "thorn" from him, but the Lord did not so answer his prayers. Paul many times could have lost himself if he had been eloquent, well, handsome, and free from the things that made him humble. Paul speaks:

> And lest I should be exalted above measure through the abundance of the revelations, there was given to me a thorn in the flesh, the messenger of Satan to buffet me, lest I should be exalted above measure.
>
> And he said unto me, My grace is sufficient for thee: for my strength is made perfect in weakness. Most gladly therefore will I rather glory in my infirmities, that the power of Christ may rest upon me.
>
> Therefore I take pleasure in infirmities, in reproaches, in necessities, in persecutions, in distresses for Christ's sake: for when I am weak, then am I strong. (2 Corinthians 12:7, 9-10.)

I fear that had I been in Carthage Jail on June 27, 1844, I might have deflected the bullets that pierced the body of the Prophet and the Patriarch. I might have saved them from the sufferings and agony, but lost to them the martyr's death and reward. I am glad I did not have to make that decision.

With such uncontrolled power, I surely would have felt to protect Christ from the agony in Gethsemane, the insults, the thorny crown, the indignities in the court, the physical injuries. I would have administered to his wounds and healed them, giving him cooling water instead of vinegar. I might have saved him from suffering and death, and lost to the world his atoning sacrifice.

I would not dare to take the responsibility of bringing back to life my loved ones. Christ himself acknowledged the difference between his will and the Father's when he prayed that the cup of suffering be taken from him; yet he added, "Nevertheless, not my will but thine be done."

For the one who dies, life goes on and his free agency continues, and death, which seems to us such a calamity, could be a blessing in disguise just as well for one who is not a martyr.

Melvin J. Ballard wrote:

I lost a son six years of age and I saw him a man in the spirit world after his death, and I saw how he had exercised his own freedom of choice and would obtain of his own will and volition a companionship, and in due time to him and all those who are worthy of it, shall come all of the blessings and sealing privileges of the house of the Lord. . . . (*Three Degrees of Glory.*)

If we say that early death is a calamity, disaster, or tragedy, would it not be saying that mortality is preferable to earlier entrance into the spirit world and to eventual salvation and exaltation? If mortality be the perfect state, then death would be a frustration, but the gospel teaches us there is no tragedy in death, but only in sin. ". . . blessed are the dead that die in the Lord. . . ." (D&C 63:49.)

We know so little. Our judgment is so limited. We judge the Lord's ways from our own narrow view.

I spoke at the funeral service of a young Brigham Young University student who died during World War II. There had been hundreds of thousands of young men rushed prematurely into eternity through the ravages of that war, and I made the statement that I believed this righteous youth had been called to the spirit world to preach the gospel to these deprived souls. This may not be true of all who die, but I felt it true of him.

In his vision of "The Redemption of the Dead" President Joseph F. Smith saw this very thing. He sat studying the scriptures on October 3, 1918, particularly the statements in Peter's epistle regarding the antediluvians. He writes:

. . . As I pondered over these things which are written, the eyes of my understanding were opened, and the Spirit of the Lord rested upon me, and I saw the hosts of the dead. . . .

While this vast multitude of the righteous waited and conversed, rejoicing in the hour of their deliverance . . . the Son of God appeared, declaring liberty to the captives who had been faithful, and there He preached to them the . . . redemption of mankind from the fall, and from individual sins on conditions of repentance. But unto the wicked he did not go, and among the ungodly and the unrepentant who had defiled themselves while in the flesh, His voice was not raised, neither did the rebellious who rejected the testimonies and the warnings of the ancient prophets behold his presence, nor look upon his face. . . .

And as I wondered . . . I perceived that the Lord went not in person among the wicked and the disobedient who had rejected the truth . . . but behold, from among the righteous He organized his forces . . . and commissioned them to go forth and carry the light of the gospel. . . .

. . . our Redeemer spent His time . . . in the world of spirits, instructing and preparing the faithful spirits . . . who had testified of Him in the flesh, that they might carry the message of redemption unto all the dead unto whom He could not go personally because of their rebellion and transgression. . . .

Among the great and mighty ones who were assembled in this vast congregation of the righteous were Father Adam . . . Eve, with many of her faithful daughters . . . Abel, the first martyr . . . Seth, . . . Noah, . . . Shem, the great High Priest; Abraham, . . . Isaac, Jacob, and Moses . . . Ezekiel, . . . Daniel. . . . All these and many more, even the prophets who dwelt among the Nephites. . . . The Prophet Joseph Smith, and my father, Hyrum S· ·ı· Brigham Young, . . . and other choice spirits . . . in the spirit world. I observed that they were also among the noble and great ones who were chosen in the beginning to be rulers in the Church of God. . . .

I beheld that the faithful elders of this dispensation, when they depart from mortal life, continue their labors in th preaching of the gospel of repentance and redemption. . . . (Joseph F. Smith, *Gospel Doctrine*, pp. 472-76.)

Death, then, may be the opening of the door to opportunities, including that of teaching the gospel of Christ. There is no greater work.

Despite the fact that death opens new doors, we do not seek it. We are admonished to pray for those who are ill and use our priesthood power to heal them.

And the elders of the church, two or more, shall be called, and shall pray for and lay their hands upon them in my name; and if they die they shall die unto me, and if they live they shall live unto me.

Thou shalt live together in love, insomuch that thou shalt weep for the loss of them that die, and more especially for those that have not hope of a glorious resurrection.

And it shall come to pass that those that die in me shall not taste of death, for it shall be sweet unto them;

And they that die not in me, wo unto them, for their death is bitter.

And again, it shall come to pass that he that hath faith in me to be healed, and is not appointed unto death, shall be healed. (D&C 42:44-48.)

We are assured by the Lord that the sick will be healed if the ordinance is performed, if there is sufficient faith, and if the ill one is "not appointed unto death." But there are three factors, all of which should be satisfied. Many do not comply with the ordinances, and great numbers are unwilling or incapable of exercising sufficient faith. But the other factor also looms important: If they are not appointed unto death.

Everyone must die. Death is an important part of life. Of course, we are never quite ready for the change. Not knowing when it should come, we properly fight to retain our life. Yet we ought not be afraid of death. We pray for the sick, we administer to the afflicted, we implore the Lord to heal and reduce pain and save life and postpone death, and properly so, but not because eternity is so frightful.

The Prophet Joseph Smith confirmed:

The Lord takes many away even in infancy, that they may escape the envy of man and the sorrows and evils of this present world; they were too pure, too lovely, to live on this earth. Therefore, if rightly considered, instead of mourning we have reason to rejoice as they are delivered from evil and we shall have them again. The only difference between the old and the young dying is, one lives longer in heaven and eternal light and glory than the other, and is freed a little sooner from this miserable world.

Just as Ecclesiastes (3:2) says, I am confident that there is a time to die, but I believe also that many people die before "their time" because they are careless, abuse their bodies, take unnecessary chances, or expose themselves to hazards, accidents, and sickness.

Of the antediluvians, we read:

> Hast thou marked the old way which wicked men have trodden?
>
> Which were cut down out of time, whose foundation was overflown with a flood. (Job 22:15-16.)

In Ecclesiastes 7:17 we find this statement:

> Be not over much wicked, neither be thou foolish: why shouldest thou die before thy time?

I believe we may die prematurely but seldom exceed our time very much. One exception was Hezekiah, 25-year-old king of Judah who was far more godly than his successors or predecessors.

> In those days was Hezekiah sick unto death. And the prophet Isaiah . . . came to him, and said unto him, Thus saith the Lord, Set thine house in order; for thou shalt die, and not live.

Hezekiah, loving life as we do, turned his face to the wall and wept bitterly, saying:

> . . . remember now how I have walked before thee in truth and with a perfect heart, and have done that which is good in thy sight. . . .

The Lord yielded unto his prayers.

> . . . I have heard thy prayer, I have seen thy tears: behold I will heal thee. . . .
>
> And I will add unto thy days fifteen years; and I will deliver thee and this city out of the hand of the king of Assyria. . . . (2 Kings 20:1, 3, 5-6.)

A modern illustration of this exceptional extension of life took place in November, 1881.

My uncle, David Patten Kimball, left his home in Arizona on a trip across the Salt River desert. He had fixed up his books and settled accounts and had told his wife of a premonition that he would not return. He was lost on the desert for two days and three nights, suffering untold agonies of thirst and pain. He passed into the spirit world and described later, in a letter of January 8, 1882, to his sister, what happened there. He had seen his parents. "My father . . . told me I could remain there if

I chose to do so, but I plead with him that I might stay with my family long enough to make them comfortable, to repent of my sins, and more fully prepare myself for the change. Had it not been for this, I never should have returned home, except as a corpse. Father finally told me I could remain two years and to do all the good I could during that time, after which he would come for me. . . . He mentioned four others that he would come for also. . . ." Two years to the day from that experience on the desert he died easily and apparently without pain. Shortly before. he died he looked up and called, "Father, Father." Within approximately a year of his death the other four men named were also dead.

God has many times preserved the lives of his servants until they could complete their work—Abinadi, Enoch, the sons of Helaman, and Paul.

And God will sometimes use his power over death to protect us. Heber C. Kimball was subjected to a test which, like the one given Abraham, was well-nigh unthinkable. Comfortless and in great perplexity he importuned the Prophet Joseph to inquire of the Lord, and the Prophet received this revelation: "Tell him to go and do as he has been commanded, and if I see that there is any danger of his apostatizing, I will take him to myself." (Orson F. Whitney, *Life of Heber C. Kimball.*)

God controls our lives, guides and blesses us, but gives us our agency. We may live our lives in accordance with his plan for us or we may foolishly shorten or terminate them.

I am positive in my mind that the Lord has planned our destiny. Sometime we'll understand fully, and when we see back from the vantage point of the future, we shall be satisfied with many of the happenings of this life that are so difficult for us to comprehend.

We sometimes think we would like to know what lies ahead, but sober thought brings us back to accepting life a day at a time and magnifying and glorifying that day. Sister Ida Allredge gave us a thought-provoking verse:

> I cannot know the future, nor the path I shall have trod,
> But by that inward vision, which points the way to God.
> I would not glimpse the beauty or joy for me in store,
> Lest patience ne'er restrain me from thrusting wide the door.
> I would not part the curtains or cast aside the veil,
> Else sorrows that await me might make my courage fail;
> I'd rather live not knowing, just doing my small mite;
> I'd rather walk by faith with God, than try alone the light.

We knew before we were born that we were coming to the earth for bodies and experience and that we would have joys and sorrows, ease and pain, comforts and hardships, health and sickness, successes and disappointments, and we knew also that after a period of life we would die. We accepted all these eventualities with a glad heart, eager to accept both the favorable and unfavorable. We eagerly accepted the chance to come earthward even though it might be for only a day or a year. Perhaps we were not so much concerned whether we should die of disease, of accident, or of senility. We were willing to take life as it came and as we might organize and control it, and this without murmur, complaint, or unreasonable demands.

In the face of apparent tragedy we must put our trust in God, knowing that despite our limited view his purposes will not fail. With all its troubles life offers us the tremendous privilege to grow in knowledge and wisdom, faith and works, preparing to return and share God's glory.

# SECTION TWO

## *Marriage and the Family*

# Chapter Nine

# Reservoirs of Righteousness

*I* grew up in a dry country. It seemed to me that hardly ever was there enough rain spread over the crop-growing period to carry us through the season—not enough water in the river to distribute among the many hungry canals and the tens of thousands of thirsty acres, not enough to irrigate all the crops.

We learned to pray for rain—we always prayed for rain.

When I was still very small, I knew that plants could not survive in a dry country more than about two or three weeks without water. I knew how to harness up the old mare to a lizard—a forked log on which a barrel was placed—and I drove her to the "big ditch," the Union Canal, which was a block below our home. With a bucket, I scooped up water from the small stream or the puddles and filled the barrel, and the horse dragged it back so I could pour buckets full of the precious liquid on the roses, the violets, and other flowers, and the small shrubs and hedges and new trees. Water was like liquid gold, so reservoirs became the warp and woof of the fabric of my life. Around the table we talked of water, irrigation, crops, floods, hot dry weeks, and cloudless skies.

We used to look for clouds somewhat as did Elijah and his people after the three-year drought.

Through the long, dry summers, we always seemed to be looking for dark, heavy clouds. And every year the clouds did gather, and the thunderstorms did come, and the dry washes did run for a few hours, and the river roared down its channel.

But the canals were often still empty, for the brush and rock dams were washed down the river by the first raging torrent. Then came the call for the able-bodied men to rush to the heads of the canals to build new dams, to get the canals full before the river water had all run down to the sea. And when working in the flood, hauling brush and trees, rocks and dirt, horses floundered and were sometimes drowned and men had narrow escapes.

Later I learned that even dependable diversion dams were not enough. A reservoir was needed—a high dam that would impound the fall, winter, and spring rains and keep them stored for the later need.

There are in our lives reservoirs of many kinds. Some reservoirs are to store water. Some are to store food, as we do in our family welfare program and as Joseph did in the land of Egypt during the seven years of plenty. There should also be reservoirs of knowledge to meet the future needs; reservoirs of courage to overcome the floods of fear that put uncertainty in lives; reservoirs of physical strength to help us meet the frequent burdens of work and illness; reservoirs of goodness; reservoirs of stamina; reservoirs of faith. Yes, especially reservoirs of faith so that when the world presses in upon us, we stand firm and strong; when the temptations of a decaying world about us draw on our energies, sap our spiritual vitality, and seek to pull us down, we need a storage of faith that can carry youth and later adults over the dull, the diffi-cult, the terrifying moments, disappointments, disillusionments, and years of adversity, want, confusion, and frustration.

And who is to build these reservoirs? Is this not the reason that God gave to every child two parents?

Who else but the forebears would clear the forests, plow the land, carve out the futures? Who else would set up the businesses, dig the canals, survey the territory? Who else would plant the orchards, start the vineyards, erect the homes?

It is those parents who sired them and bore them who are expected to lay foundations for their children and to build the barns and tanks and bins and reservoirs.

I am grateful to my parents, for they made reservoirs for my brothers, my sisters, and me. The reservoirs were filled with prayer habits, study, activities, positive services, and truth and righteousness. Every morning and every night we knelt at our chairs by the table and prayed, taking turns. When I was married, the habit persisted, and our new family continued the practice.

Lehi and Sariah built and filled reservoirs for their children. One son said:

> I, Nephi, having been born of goodly parents, therefore I was taught somewhat in all the learning of my father . . . having had a great knowledge of the goodness and the mysteries of God. (1 Nephi 1:1.)

Though two of the brothers ignored those teachings, using their own free agency, yet Nephi and others of his family were strongly fortified and all their lives could draw heavily on the reservoir built and filled by worthy parents.

Jacob, another of the sons of Lehi, drew heavily from the storage inherited from his father, and he passed the same to his son Enos, who bore testimony of it:

> . . . I, Enos, knowing my father that he was a just man— for he taught me . . . in the nurture and admonition of the Lord. . . .

> . . . went to hunt . . . and the words which I had often
> heard my father speak concerning eternal life, and the joy of
> the saints, sunk deep into my heart.
>
> And my soul hungered; and I kneeled down before my
> Maker. . . . (Enos 1, 3-4.)

Enos obtained forgiveness by drawing heavily on the
reservoir of faith his parents had set up for their children.

One day I met a delightful couple—faithful Latter-
day Saints with a splendid family and a successful life.
They told me of their family history. The husband was
one of seven children of a family of active Church members, where the Lord was central in their lives. All but
one of the seven had remained faithful, filled honorable
missions, married in the temple, and had successful, happy
families, as had their parents before them. The one had
strayed and had marital and other serious problems.

On the other hand, the wife was one of seven children in a family where the Church meant little and they
had bypassed tithing, prayers, and all church activities,
and had ignored the spiritual part of their lives. All seven
of the children had been reared in the same household,
subject to the same conditions, and all but this one
daughter ignored their spiritual obligations, as their
parents had done before them.

Both families had the same community backgrounds.
The first parents had built and filled a high, strong reservoir of habits and qualities of faith for their children.
The second family built no reservoir of spiritual strength
but depended on the runoff. Their uncertain little diversion dams, like our brush and rock ones, had washed
away when the torrents came.

The Lord has inspired his church to place increased
emphasis on building family unity and faith. Every family
is urged to engage in regular morning and night family
prayers and to devote at least one evening a week at
home in the sweet family togetherness undisturbed by the
world or any of its allurements. They will plan to turn

off the TV and radio, leave the telephone unanswered, cancel all calls or appointments, and spend a warm, homey evening together.

While one objective is reached by merely being together, yet the additional and greater value can come from the lessons of life. The father will teach the children. Here they can learn integrity, honor, dependability, sacrifice, and faith in God. Life's experiences and the scriptures are the basis of the teaching, and this, wrapped up in filial and parental love, makes an impact nothing else can make. Thus, reservoirs of righteousness are filled to carry children through the dark days of temptation and desire, of drought and skepticism. As they grow up, the children cooperate in building this storage for themselves and the family. And so we have as a basic part of the Lord's programs the home evening and the family prayers and the teaching of gospel principles in our homes.

Some years ago we visited a country where strange ideologies were taught and "pernicious doctrines" were promulgated every day in the schools and in the captive press. Every day the children listened to the doctrines, philosophies, and ideals their teachers related.

Someone said that "constant dripping will wear away the hardest stone." This I knew, so I asked about the children: "Do they retain their faith? Are they not overcome by the constant pressure of their teachers? How can you be sure they will not leave the simple faith in God?"

The answer amounted to saying "We mend the damaged reservoir each night. We teach our children positive righteousness so that the false philosophies do not take hold. Our children are growing up in faith and righteousness in spite of the almost overwhelming pressures from outside."

Even cracked dams can be mended and saved, and sandbags can hold back the flood. And reiterated truth, renewed prayer, gospel teachings, expression of love, and parental interest can save the child and keep him on the right path.

# Chapter Ten

# *"Are You There, Mother?"*

In my childhood, we had mottoes hanging on our walls, sometimes embroidered, sometimes painted, for decoration and for inspiration. One I remember read: "What is home without a mother?"

From my infancy, every time I entered the house, I called, "Mama," over and over until I found her. Totally satisfied in the security her presence afforded, I ran again to play. Just to know she was there! That was all.

When I was eleven, Mother passed away and from my aching heart came numerous times, "Mama," as I entered the house, but these were only mocking echoes of emptiness.

Later the void was filled when our stepmother gave presence to the home, and again through my youth, I called and found my security in the welcome answer, "I am here, son."

It was the same brick house through the days of security and the days of desolation, the same shelf-filled pantry, the same wood stove and water tank, the same parlor with its rag carpet, and the same old clock ticking away the hours and days and years, but stability and sureness and peace were there when Mother was there; security was there, and the house breathed belongingness.

A few years ago on Labor Day, 2,000 young people converged on the little resort town of Seaside, Oregon, smashing windows, ripping street and shop signs down, and requiring 100 policemen plus National Guardsmen to quell the rioting. I wondered if the 2,000 homes from which they came were normal ones with a mother at home who could answer, "I am here, son."

The news reported 30,000 teenagers rioting on a California beach, filling beer cans and bottles with sand and throwing them at police, boys stripping girls, and sex indulgence common and unabashed.

And I wondered how many of the 30,000 fathers were furnishing cars and money for their children to vacation at resorts for beer and brutishness. Who provided the gasoline and who paid the fines?

How many of the 30,000 mothers were making homes and how many making money?

How can mothers justify their abandonment of home when they are needed so much by their offspring? Rationalization must take over as they justify themselves in leaving home and children.

Of course, there are *some* mothers who *must* work to support their children, and they are to be praised, not criticized, but let every working mother honestly weigh the matter and be sure the Lord approves before she rushes her babies off to the nursery, her children off to school, her husband off to work, and herself off to her employment. Let her be certain that she is not rationalizing herself away from her children merely to provide for them greater material things. Let her analyze well before she permits her precious ones to come home to an empty house where their plaintive cry, "Mother," finds no loving answer.

Do not these absentee mothers and millions of approving fathers know that basic attitudes toward standards, morality, the church, and God are developed in the family circle and are quite well set while children are still small? It is said: "Give me a child until he is seven and then do with him what you will." These first years are so vital.

The Lord said: "My sheep know my voice." So do the little ones respond to their own mothers. The maid, the neighbor, the sister, the grandmother may clothe and feed and diaper the child, but no one can take the place of mother. The six-year-old who got lost from his mother in a large supermarket began to call frantically, "Martha, Martha." When the mother was found and they were reunited, she said, "Honey, you should not call me Martha; I am 'Mother' to you," to which the little fellow rejoined, "Yes, I know, but the store was full of mothers and I wanted mine."

Children need security, special love, and to be wanted.

At a distant conference, my plane brought me to the city many hours early. The stake president met me at the airport and took me to his home. Having important work to do, he excused himself and returned to his work. With the freedom of the house, I spread my papers on the kitchen table and began my work. His wife was upstairs sewing. In mid-afternoon, there came an abrupt entry through the front door and a little fellow came running in, surprised to see me. We became friends; then he ran through the rooms calling, "Mother." She answered from upstairs, "What is it, darling?" and his answer was, "Oh, nothing." He went out to play.

A little later another boy came in the front door calling, "Mother, Mother." He put his school books on the table and explored the house until the reassuring answer came from upstairs again, "Here I am, darling," and the second one was satisfied and said, "Okay," and went to play. Another half hour and the door opened again and a young teenager moved in, dropped her books, and called, "Mother." And the answer from upstairs, "Yes, darling," seemed to satisfy and the young girl began practicing her music lesson.

Still another voice later called, "Mother," as she unloaded her high school books. And again the sweet answer, "I am up here sewing, darling," seemed to reassure her. She tripped up the stairs to tell her mother the happenings of the day. Home! Mother! Security! Just to know Mother was home. All was well.

A child is happy if he feels that he is wanted and enjoyed by his parents. He needs to feel that his parents will be there, especially in a crisis.

This mother, too, could have had a job. Her children also could use more things that her wages could provide. She could have rationalized that two salaries could give her children more advantages, more outings, travel, and vacations, more clothes, gifts, and luxuries. But this mother knew well that a child needs a mother available more than all the things which money can buy.

An article in *Parents Magazine* pointed out that the feeling of security is the core and foundation for good mental health. Most of the married women over 35 in the labor force are working not because their families really "need the money," but in order to maintain a higher standard of living, get away from some housework, and lead, as they suppose, a more interesting and richer life.

Tens of millions of women in the United States now work outside the home, and the large majority of them have husbands who work, too. A large share have children still at home. There are millions and millions of children who have mothers who leave them needlessly, in order to go to work.

How nearly perfect can a mother be who rushes in the morning to get everybody off for the day, herself included, then returns weary after a hard day of employment to a tired husband and to children and youths with

problems, and then to her homemaking, cooking, cleaning, and then to a full social calendar. From such homes
come many conflicts, marital problems, and divorces and
delinquent children. Few people. in trouble ever ascribe
their marital conflicts to these first causes but rather
blame one another for the problems that were born and
nurtured in strained environments. When the relationship of father and mother is harmonious, the children can
feel secure.

General Relief Society President Belle S. Spafford has
said: "Children should be cherished with the strongest
bonds of affection. . . . No effort should be too much, no
sacrifice too great to protect them from evil and preserve
them in righteousness. . . . The love and the sanctity of
the home should be zealously safeguarded. . . ." And she
speaks of mothers' obligations "to make all else in life sub-
servient to the well-being of our homes and families."

Always in the Church, people have been admonished
to marry in the house of the Lord, to establish homes, and
bear and rear children in righteousness.

Brigham Young said: "It is the calling of the wife and
mother . . . [to tie] her offspring to herself with a love that
is stronger than death for an everlasting inheritance. . . ."
(*Discourses of Brigham Young*, p. 307.)

An authority on child rearing said: "The more the
parents approve of each other, the more the child will be
welcome—the most important single factor in the development of the child is the emotional climate prevailing between his parents."

Are music and dancing lessons and camps and clothes
justified when it may mean the sacrifice of the home and
mother on the altar of employment?

One girl said, "I really don't want to go to the girls'
camp. I'd rather stay home with Mother, but Mother is
not home to stay with." Are we glamorizing out-of-home
activities for our children when they should be home helping or off to work themselves?

Absenteeism of mothers is often linked with idle youth
—delinquent youth.

When we read of the destructive escapades by tens of
thousands of high school and college young people on their
mass invasions of resort towns, we wonder: Why are they
permitted leisure until they become sick with boredom?
Home is drab so they resort to destructiveness and immorality.

One judge said: "These mad vacations make their
biggest appeal to youngsters who have too little to do. . . .
We never have any trouble with kids who have real
interests, real hobbies, a radio ham, or a real athlete."

The idle generation! Hours each day and nothing to
do. Saturdays and nothing to do. Three long months of
school vacation and nothing to do.

No one has found a truer adage than this: "The idle
mind is the devil's workshop."

Another judge states that

too many kids are loafing. Parents do not make children get jobs.
And, this helps them into trouble. . . . there is an alarming lack
of employment among our young people . . . and [much] idleness
among those who come before me. . . .

He is not talking about the pallid, spindly urchin
working twelve hours a day in coal mines, but of the
hulking youth sitting around while his hard-working,
doting parents support him. It is foolish to expect an
energetic exuberant youth to live normally when he has
his free time largely to himself including three idle months
of summer vacation. The judge continues:

As I see young people of what I consider an employable
age sitting around drive-ins or malt shops, on park benches,
cruising around in cars or hanging around on the street corners at all hours of the day and the night, I am amazed at
their ability to stay out of trouble as well as they do. . . . idleness is a prime factor in most juvenile misbehavior. . . .

I find the average parent of the average employable but
unemployed youngster to be weak, overprotective and over-

indulgent. Both he and his wife work to afford their child the niceties of life which they now consider necessities. All the comforts of home plus car and a gasoline credit card. . . .

A woman who had not been able to hold a job in spite of the fact that she was well-trained and highly educated explained: "Oh, it's not odd at all. My parents never expected me to work and for that reason I never expected to either." She seemed to feel unabashed.

The judge proceeds:

This type of parent blindly accepts Junior's plaint: "I can't find a job."

Can't find a job! Well, Junior, I have news for you! . . . A whole generation of us grew up during the depression when there were no jobs, but we found jobs anyway. Oh, they weren't good jobs but they were jobs. There were always jobs—mean, disagreeable, back-breaking jobs. And many of these jobs didn't pay very much and they were hard. . . .

Some judges give arrested youth a choice to get a job within thirty days or be locked up. They seldom have had to lock up any. If the alternative is unpleasant enough, somehow Junior finds employment.

To this philosophy, there are rejoinders from many sources that cry there are not enough jobs to go around and that a job for a youngster means a job lost to the head of a family. And the answer of the judge to this is:

Get women out of the factories and put them back into the home where they belong . . . cooking, sewing, cleaning house, and doing the traditional woman's work. It would do both for them and their neglected youngsters a world of good.

If a few million working mothers who need not work were to go home to their families, there might be employment for men now unemployed and part and full-time work for youth who ought to help in family finances and who need occupation for their abundant energy.

The judge gave good advice in the following vein:

"Can't get a job," they say. Why, bless your souls,

the world is crying for helpers. Have we spoiled our children paying them for every effort?

They cry, "Where can we go?" Listen, youth, go home, roll up your sleeves; pick cotton, hoe the corn, thin the beets. Yes, before and after school and Saturdays and vacation days. It won't hurt you to store your ball and bat and hiking togs. Hang the storm windows, paint the fence, wash the car, pick the fruit, mow the lawn, repair the screen, plant a garden, cultivate flowers, trim the trees. A majority of youth wish responsibility and will thrive on it.

"What can we do?" they ask again.

Do the shopping, work in the hospital, help the neighbors and church custodian, wash the dishes, vacuum the floors, make the beds, get the meals, learn to sew.

Read good books, repair the furniture, make something needed in the home, clean the house, press your clothes, rake the leaves, shovel the snow, peddle papers, do baby sitting free for neighbor mothers who must work, become an apprentice.

One parent wrote to youth:

> Your parents do not owe you entertainment; your villages do not owe you recreation facilities; the world does not owe you a living; you owe the world; you owe it your time, your energy, your talents, yourself. In plain, simple words, grow up, get out of your dream world; develop your backbone, a backbone not a wishbone. . . .

Lawmakers in their eagerness to protect the child have legislated until the pendulum has swung to the other extreme. But no law prohibits most work suggested above.

President David O. McKay said:

> We are living in an age of gadgetry which threatens to produce a future generation of softness. Flabbiness of character more than flabbiness of muscle lies at the root of most of the problems facing our American youth.

Do the families of juvenile delinquents kneel in prayer night and morning before the depredations committed by their children? Do they have family home evenings, family picnics, vacations and entertainment together? Do the parents of such hoodlums exercise discipline in the home, or are the children emancipated from restraint, from duties, and from controls?

To slow down this ever-increasing rate of juvenile delinquency, there is a growing cry: We must have more detention homes and reformatories. We need more public money appropriated for better facilities, more highly trained specialists, social workers, psychologists, and psychiatrists. We need larger jails, more police.

Certainly, it must be apparent that all this is but an attempt to control the malady without dealing with causes. Isn't it time to come back to fundamentals? "We need more money," they say, but money is not the answer. Surely we must realize that an ounce of prevention is worth tons of cure.

The Lord indicated long ago the perfect pattern. He organized the family. It takes no great wisdom to know where the error lies and that the cure is prevention. With the home a religious one with discipline and love and parental bliss and sweet parent-child relationships, there would be few, if any, prodigals. Reformatories and correctional institutions could close; social agencies could lock their doors; jails would have few prisoners.

All this could come by the building of the homes of the people into spiritual fortresses. If fathers would give themselves to their families and if all mothers who can would come home from employment to be real mothers, then delinquency would be greatly reduced.

Let us organize our families properly and discipline our children wisely, thus creating the kind of homes our Heavenly Father desires for us.

# Chapter Eleven

# John and Mary, Beginning Life Together

*A*cross the desk from me sits a delightful young couple. They have come to ask me to perform the marriage ceremony for them tomorrow in the temple of the Lord. The young man has penetrating eyes, curly hair, and a captivating smile. The young woman is alert and lovely, her dark hair adding glory to her shining face, which she frequently lifts up to her companion in adoration. Here is the love of youth at its best and sweetest. And when they are comfortably seated near one another so that their hands are sometimes touching, I say to them:

And so you are going to be married, John and Mary! And tomorrow is the great day! How happy I am for you as you approach this sacred hour! Congratulations to you, John and Mary, and I wish for you eternities of happiness. This you want—this you may have—if you will do the things of which I tell you here today.

Happiness, though, is an elusive thing, John and Mary. It is a little like the pot of gold at the end of the rainbow. If you go out deliberately to find it, you may have great difficulty catching it. But if you will follow directions closely, you will not need to pursue it. It will overtake you and remain with you.

Happiness is a strange commodity. It cannot be purchased with money, and yet it is bought with a price. It is not dependent upon houses, or lands, or flocks, or degrees, or position, or comforts; for many of the most unhappy people in all the world have these. The millionaire has comforts and luxuries, but he has no happiness unless he has paid the same price for it that you can also pay. Often the rich are the most unhappy.

If you think that ease and comfort and money are necessary to your happiness, ask your parents and others whose lives are in the autumn. If they have been financially successful, they will generally tell you that the happiest days were not the ones when they were retired, with a palatial home, two cars in the garage, and money with which to travel around the world; but their joyous days were those when they, too, planned and worked for the wherewithal to make ends meet; when they had their little ones about them and were wholly absorbed in family life and Church work.

And so, Mary and John, you may live in a single room or a small cabin and be happy. You may ride the bus or walk instead of riding in a luxurious car, and still be happy. You may wear your clothes more than a single season and still be happy.

You ask, "What is the price of happiness?" You will be surprised with the simplicity of the answer. The treasure house of happiness may be unlocked and remain open to those who use the following keys: First, you must live the gospel of Jesus Christ in its purity and simplicity—not a half-hearted compliance, but hewing to the line, and this means an all-out devoted consecration to the great program of salvation and exaltation in an orthodox manner. Second, you must forget yourself and love your companion more than yourself. If you do these things, happiness will be yours in great and never failing abundance.

Now the living of the gospel is not a thing of the letter, but of the spirit, and your attitudes toward it are far more important than the mechanics of it, but a combination of doing and feeling will bring spiritual, mental, and temporal advancement and growth.

Mary and John, I congratulate you for your vision and faith and your willingness to forgo the fanfare and glamour of a worldly wedding for a simple, quiet, but beautiful marriage in the temple, a sweet eternal ceremony that will be unostentatious and sacred like your birth, blessing, baptism, or ordination.

Because your people are prosperous, Mary, I realize you could have had all that the world might offer in a glamorous wedding with candles and flowers, attendants and pageantry. But you chose the simple, sacred way— the Lord's way. I salute you!

You could have been married on a merry-go-round as a couple recently were on television, exchanging vows astride painted wooden horses, for which they were to receive all expenses for a wedding trip. You, Mary and John, would not be willing to commercialize on this sacred ordinance and sell your "birthright for a mess of pottage." You are like many other devoted Latter-day Saint people who prefer to be married in the House of the Lord. John and Mary, I commend you.

I know you plan a reception following the marriage. It offers a delightful opportunity for relatives and friends to bring gifts and wish you well, but I hope you will again avoid temptation to go to extremes in following the world in showy pageantry. There is danger that the ostentatious display may detract from and overshadow the simple wedding. With your good judgment and clear thinking, I know you can graciously entertain your guests in a wholesome, friendly, and dignified reception without the excesses so often in evidence.

Now, Mary, you must understand that John will not be able to support you as has your father, who has been accumulating for a quarter century; John is just starting.

For that matter, perhaps he never will have as much as your father.

And furthermore, Mary, with your wholesome attitude toward family life, I know you will desire to devote your life to your home and family, so when you resign your job and no longer have that income to spend upon yourself, it will mean many adjustments for you; but I understand you have considered all those things and are willing. You see, Mary, it was never intended by the Lord that married women should compete with men in employment. They have a far greater and more important service to render, and so you give up your employment and settle down to become the queen of the little new home that you will proceed to transform into a heaven for John, this man whom you adore. John will work hard and will do his best to provide you with comforts and even luxuries later, but this is the perfect way, to "start from scratch" together.

And, Mary, you have much to learn in these coming months. Perhaps you, like most of the other young women of the nation, have prepared yourself for a career that you will not follow. One college president said about ninety-two percent of all the girls in his college studied languages and mathematics and business, and then when they were married found that they not only had limited use for their specialized training, but they had also failed to train for the great career to which they were now to dedicate their lives. Mary, you are to become a career woman in the greatest career on earth—that of homemaker, wife, and mother. And so, if you failed to prepare for motherhood and homemaking when you could, you may make up somewhat devoting yourself to those subjects now. In your spare time you could now study child psychology and child discipline, the fundamentals of nursing, the art of teaching, particularly how to tell stories and teach children; and you will want to get all the theory as well as the practice now in cooking, sewing, budgeting, and buying.

John's limited income will spread far if you can learn to buy efficiently and cook expertly so that there will never be waste. And his small income can go far if you learn to make some of your own clothes and those of the children and utilize scraps and pick up bargains. And if you learn the rudiments of nursing, you may be able to save much in doctor and hospital costs by recognizing symptoms and treating minor afflictions, and you may also have the satisfaction of even saving the lives of your own precious family by your being able to do practical nursing. And so your economies will largely make up for the loss of your own income.

You wouldn't want to work outside the home anyway, Mary, for women are expected to earn the living only in emergencies, and you must know that many are the broken homes resulting when women leave their posts at home. You see, if both husband and wife are working away from home and come home tired, it is very easy for unpleasantness and misunderstandings to arise. And so, Mary, you will remain at home, making it attractive and heavenly, and when John comes home tired, you will be fresh and pleasant; the house will be orderly; the dinner will be tempting; and life will have real meaning.

And you must remember, John, that Mary's life is not always an easy one. Those months of waiting for the babies are trying ones, often associated with physical discomforts and many deprivations. You will need to be more solicitous of her comfort and more understanding if she should sometimes be irritable. You should assist her about the home and with the little ones and spend no time away from the home and family except to fulfill needed obligations imposed by church service and your occupation. You will limit your social life as she must, and to those activities in which Mary may join you.

Now, John and Mary, there may be a temptation to economize by living with the parents on either side. Do not make this serious error. You two will constitute a new family tomorrow. Well-meaning relatives have broken up many a home. Numerous divorces are attributable to the interference of parents who thought they were only protecting their loved children. Live in your own home even though it be but a modest cottage or a tent. Live your own life. Mary, you must not go home to your parents for long visits, leaving John home alone; neither will you, John, leave Mary when it can be avoided.

And John, you will, of course, do your best to provide the home and the living. But you will not take two or three jobs in order to give Mary luxuries, for Mary has already made her mental adjustments and is willing to get along on what you can reasonably produce. And you will secure employment that is compatible with good family life, John. You will not take a traveling job that will take you away from your home, except in emergencies. Both you and Mary will prefer to have a smaller salary with you at home, rather than to have greater luxuries with you away. And if your work moves you permanently to another location, Mary will go with you, even though it means being away from family and friends, and even in less desirable places and with fewer opportunities. You are being married for that reason—that you may always be together.

Your love, like a flower, must be nourished. There will come a great love and interdependence between you, for your love is a divine one. It is deep, inclusive, comprehensive. It is not like that association of the world which is misnamed love, but which is mostly physical attraction. When marriage is based on this only, the parties soon tire of one another. There is a break and a divorce, and a new, fresher physical attraction comes with another marriage which in turn may last only until it, too, becomes stale. The love of which the Lord speaks is not only physical attraction, but spiritual attraction as well. It is faith and confidence in, and understanding of, one another. It is a total partnership. It is companionship with common ideals and standards. It is unselfishness toward and sacrifice for one another. It is cleanliness of thought and action and faith in God and his program. It is parenthood in mortality ever looking toward godhood and creationship, and parenthood of spirits. It is vast, all-inclusive, and limitless. This kind of love never tires or wanes. It lives on through sickness and sorrow, through prosperity and privation, through accomplishment and disappointment, through time and eternity. John and Mary, this is the love that I feel you are bringing to one another, but even this richer, more abundant love will wilt and die if it is not given food, so you must live and treat each other in a manner that your love will grow. Today it is demonstrative love, but in the tomorrows of ten, thirty, fifty years, it will be a far greater and more intensified love, grown quieter and more dignified with the years of sacrifice, suffering, joys, and consecration to one another, to your family, and to the kingdom of God.

For your love to ripen so gloriously, there must be an increase of confidence and understanding, a frequent and sincere expression of appreciation of one another. There must be a forgetting of self and a constant concern for the other. There must be a focusing of interests and hopes and objectives into a single channel.

Now, John and Mary, many young people plan to postpone their spiritual life, church activity, and the bearing of a family, until they get their degrees or get established financially; and by the time they are prepared according to their ambitious standards, they have lost much of the inclination and powers and time.

You, John, are the head of the family. You hold the priesthood. Give this little family righteous leadership. Tomorrow at the end of your first perfect day of marriage, you two should kneel at your bedside before retiring, in your first family prayer, and thank the Lord for the love that has brought you together, and for all your rich blessings, and ask him to assist you to remain true to your covenants and keep clean and worthy and active. Then never let a day pass without your morning and evening devotion. Now is the time to chart your life's course. Determine to attend your priesthood and sacrament meetings every Sabbath, pay your tithing faithfully, sustain in very deed the authorities of the Church, support the programs of the Church, visit the temple often, give service in the organizations, and keep your actions constructive, your attitudes wholesome.

And, John and Mary, tomorrow when I repeat the phrases that will bind you for eternity, I shall say the same impressive words that the Lord said to that handsome youth and his lovely bride in the Garden of Eden: "Be fruitful and multiply and replenish the earth." The Lord does not waste words. He meant what he said. You did not come on earth just to "eat, drink, and be merry." You came knowing full well your responsibilities. You came to get for yourself a mortal body that could become perfected, immortalized, and you understood that you were to act in partnership with God in providing bodies for other spirits equally anxious to come to the earth for righteous purposes. And so you will not postpone parenthood. There will be rationalists who will name to you numerous reasons for postponement. Of course, it will be harder to get your college degrees or your financial start with a family, but strength like yours will be undaunted in the face of difficult obstacles. Have your family as the Lord intended. Of course, it is expensive, but you will find a way, and besides, it is often those children who grow up with responsibility and hardships who carry on the world's work. And, John and Mary, do not limit your family as the world does. I am wondering now where I might have been had my parents decided arbitrarily that one or two children would be enough, or that three or four would be all they could support, or that even five would be the limit; for I was the sixth of eleven children. Don't think you will love the later ones less or have fewer material things for them. Perhaps, like Jacob, you might love the eleventh one most. Young people, have your family, love them, sacrifice for them, teach them righteousness, and you will be blessed and happy all the days of your eternal lives.

Now, Mary and John, there is an indispensable element in this happiness you desire. There must be fidelity and confidence. John, you have had a legitimate and proper opportunity these past years to look the world over for a wife, to date numerous girls, and to compare and contrast them with one another, weighing their virtues and attractions, and finally, of them all you have selected Mary as the one with whom you wish to be associated forever, the one who reaches such heights of perfection in your eyes that she is worthy not only to be your helpmeet but also the mother of your posterity. You have built for Mary a pedestal, and placing her on it, will never permit any other ever to share the place with her. She is your queen, your counterpart, your love throughout the eternities.

And you, Mary, have had the same privilege of comparing all the boys who came to see you, and you have selected John as the finest specimen of young manhood, the most desirable companion, to be your husband and the father of your children; and now, having made your choice, this is final. You have built a pedestal on which you have placed John, and no one may ever share that place with him. Never again will you look upon any man as you have John, for he is now your mate and sweetheart and husband for eternities.

Henceforth, your eyes will never wander; your thoughts will never stray; in a very literal way you will keep yourselves for each other only, in mind and body and spirit. You will remember that the Lord Jesus Christ said:

> Ye have heard that it was said by them of old time, Thou shalt not commit adultery:
>
> But I say unto you, That whosoever looketh on a woman to lust after her hath committed adultery with her already in his heart. (Matthew 5:27-28.)

And it can be paraphrased also to say: ". . . she that looketh upon a man to lust after him hath committed adultery already with him in her heart." And I want to say to you, also, that flirting by married people, even though they think it innocent and limited, is a serious sin and is the approach toward eventual downfall. A very large share of all divorces have their origin in infidelity of one or both parties, so you can see how important it is to heed this warning and strictly avoid even the appearance of or approach toward evil.

Now, John and Mary, being human, you may some day have differences of opinion resulting even in little quarrels. Neither of you will be so unfaithful to the other as to go back to your parents or friends and discuss with them your little differences. That would be gross disloyalty. Your intimate life is your own and must not be shared with or confided in others. You will not go back to your people for sympathy but will thresh out your own difficulties. Suppose an injury has been inflicted; unkind words have been said; hearts are torn; and each feels that the other is wholly at fault. Nothing is done to heal the wound. The hours pass. There is a throbbing of hearts through the night, a day of sullenness and unkindness and further misunderstanding. Injury is heaped upon injury until the attorney is employed, the home broken, and the lives of parents and children blasted.

But there is a healing balm which, if applied early, in but a few minutes will return you to sane thinking; and know that, with so much at stake—your love, yourselves, your family, your ideals, your exaltation, your eternities— you cannot afford to take chances. You must swallow your pride and with courage, you, John, would say: "Mary, darling, I'm sorry. I didn't mean to hurt you. Please forgive me." And Mary, you would reply: "John, dear, it was I who was at fault more than you. Please forgive me." And you go into one another's arms and life is on an even keel again. And when you retire at night, it is forgotten, and there is no chasm between you as you have your family prayer. This time you could thank the Lord for the courage and strength he helped you muster to avert a threatened calamity. And with this fortitude and determination, you will find that the misunderstandings will reduce in numbers, and whereas they may have come at intervals of weeks, the intervals will come to be months and years, and finally you will learn wholly to enmesh your lives, forever barring the pettiness that is so disastrous.

Now, tomorrow is the glorious and eventful day. I'll meet you at the temple in the beautiful room decorated in white, typifying purity. The walls of the temple will shut out the sounds of the world below. Here in sweet composure the ceremony will be performed to unite you two for all eternity. Your immediate family and closest friends will be there and with you will rise to spiritual heights in this heaven upon earth.

And when the ceremony is completed, you two will go forth from those sacred precincts, your thoughts on a high spiritual plane a "little lower than the angels." Hand in hand, with your eyes to the light, you will go forth to conquer and build and love and exalt yourselves and your family.

Goodbye until tomorrow, John and Mary, and God bless you always.

# Chapter Twelve

# Lines of Communication

We were riding far out in the northwest of Argentina. It was cattle country. The road was straight and narrow for miles, and on either side was a four-wire barbed fence. Parallel to the fence was a series of telephone poles. Upon each pole was a crossbar, and strung from crossbar to crossbar were the communication lines.

As we traveled along where the heavy grass had recently been burned, we saw that some of the telephone poles were burned off near the ground.

Nearly all the poles for a distance were scorched or burned, but some had been burned completely off the first few feet from the ground and were hanging from the wires they were intended to support. Dangling in the air, these poles touched the ground as they were swinging in the wind on sagging wires, each time creating static on the line.

The poles had been set to hold up the lines, but they were dragging them down.

Many a time during the three years that I was in charge of the work in South America I tried to get long-distance calls through to distant places. When the connection was made, almost invariably there would be static, and the words were cut in two and grating sounds were heard. In my mind's eye I could see the telephone poles on the Salta Road swaying in the breeze, hitting the ground and occasionally breaking connection.

Telephone lines and telephone poles are a little like people. They have one purpose but sometimes serve another. They are designed to be firm and stout and to give support; but in many cases they are leaning and swaying and sagging until communications are greatly impaired, if not actually cut off.

In my experience I find that in a large number of marital cases, the problem is lack of communication; the wires are down, the poles are burned, husbands and wives are jangling, and there is static where there should be peace. There is growing disgust and hate where there should be love and harmony.

A typical young couple, only a few hectic years into their eternal marriage—only two children away from the eternal vows they had made in the holy temple of God—were each going a separate way. Their ideas of life were different as to spiritual matters (as well as many others)—one wishing to move along in a way that the other thought was fanaticism and the other moving along in a path that the first spouse thought to be almost apostasy; and both were mistaken.

They talked about it and lost their tempers and drew further and further away from their common goal. Both were good people basically, but their telephone poles were burned and the wires of communication were now sagging. Their inability to communicate in reasonableness led to anger, hard words, misunderstandings.

In time, each found another person and set up different communication lines for sympathy and understanding and comfort; and this disloyalty led to physical adventures that resulted in adulteries and two broken homes and disillusioned spouses and crushed hopes and injured children.

And all this because two basically good people let their supporting principles get down and permitted effective communication to be dragged to the ground. This is not one couple; it is tens of thousands of couples who started out in a blaze of glory, sweet felicity, and an inter-responsibility and with the highest of hopes.

In another instance two young couples from the Northwest came, bowed in sorrow. The husband of one and the wife of the other had lost themselves, disloyally finding comfort where no association should have been tolerated. The two young people, unfaithful to their spouses, had conversed and confided too much; then secret meetings followed, with disloyal disclosures concerning the spouse of each. And finally, that which at the outset surely could not have been dreamed of—the transgression.

Both couples had reduced their activity, had become casual in their churchgoing. They had joined a social group who were also turning to spiritual casualness. Their new way of living was beyond their means, and debts crowded out tithing.

They were too busy for home evenings and too rushed for family prayer, and when the great temptation came, they were not prepared. The burning grass had consumed their poles and the dangling charred stubs were hanging from the sagging wires.

Sin comes when communication lines are down—it always does, sooner or later.

We are living in a corrupt world. There has been sin since Cain yielded to Satan, but perhaps never before has the world accepted sin so completely as a way of life. We shall continue to cry repentance from thousands of pulpits. We shall continue to warn the people who are all too ready to accept the world as it pushes in upon them.

Let us fight the fire of temptation, replace the sin-

damaged supports to righteous living, and maintain
the clear communication that will keep us in harmony
with one another and with our Lord and Savior.

# Chapter Thirteen

# "*Spouses...and None Else*"

$S$atan's threat to take all those who will follow him is no idle boast. He may be depended on to engulf and capture all who will listen to him. Often we direct our warning to the young, who lack experience to know where danger lies. But Satan works not only on youth; he seeks us all. The world is ripening in iniquity, and crime and sin are rampant.

We are not unmindful of those numerous good people to whom the home life and the commands of God are still their magnificent obsession. They have their reward. But all too many are following the path of evil, and our voices must sound a warning.

The revelations say:

Wherefore the decree hath gone forth from the Father. . . .

For the hour is nigh and the day soon at hand when the earth is ripe; and all the proud and they that do wickedly shall be as stubble; and I will burn them up, saith the Lord of Hosts, that wickedness shall not be upon the earth. (D&C 29:8-9.)

Infidelity is one of the great sins of our generation. The movies, the books, the magazine stories all seem to glamorize the faithlessness of husbands and wives. To the world nothing is holy, not even marriage vows. The unfaithful woman is the heroine and is justified, and the hero is so built up that he can do no wrong; or the anti-hero is portrayed as having no control over his destiny. It reminds us of Isaiah, who said: "Woe unto them that call evil good, and good evil. . . ." (Isaiah 5:20.)

We make no apology, then, for raising our voices loud.

The adversary is subtle; he is cunning. He knows that he cannot induce good men and women immediately to do major evils, so he moves slyly, whispering half truths until he has his intended victims following him; finally he clamps his chains upon them and fetters them tight, and then he laughs at their discomfiture and their misery.

Sins cannot be forever hidden. Jacob stated:

> . . . by the help of the all-powerful Creator of heaven and earth I can tell you concerning your thoughts, how that ye are beginning to labor in sin, which sin appeareth very abominable unto me, yea, and abominable unto God. (Jacob 2:5.)

Some folks hide their guilt and will not confess, and this is what Lucifer desires. He has a greater hold on them.

In our own day the Lord promised his bishops and other appointees—

> . . . to have it given unto them to discern all those gifts lest there shall be any among you professing and yet be not of God. (D&C 46:27.)

There are those married people who permit their eyes to wander and their hearts to become vagrant, who think it is not improper to flirt a little, to share their hearts and have desire for someone other than the wife or the husband. The Lord says in no uncertain terms: "Thou shalt love thy wife with all thy heart, and shalt cleave unto her and none else." (D&C 42:22.)

And, when the Lord says *all* thy heart, it allows for no sharing nor dividing nor depriving. And, to the woman it is paraphrased: "Thou shalt love thy husband with *all* thy heart and shalt cleave unto him and none else."

The words *none else* eliminate everyone and everything. The spouse then becomes preeminent in the life of the husband or wife, and neither social life nor occupational life nor political life nor any other interest nor person nor thing shall ever take precedence over the companion spouse. We sometimes find women who absorb and hover over the children at the expense of the husband, sometimes even estranging them from him.

The Lord says to them: "Thou shalt cleave unto *him* and none else."

Marriage presupposes total allegiance and total fidelity. Each spouse takes the partner with the understanding that he or she gives totally to the spouse all the heart, strength, loyalty, honor, and affection, with all dignity. Any divergence is sin; any sharing of the heart is transgression. As we should have "an eye single to the glory of God," so should we have an eye, an ear, a heart single to the marriage and the spouse and family.

Modern revelation tells us:

> Thou shalt not commit adultery; and he that committeth adultery, and repenteth not, shall be cast out [or excommunicated]. (D&C 42:24.)

Many acknowledge the vice of physical adultery but still rationalize that anything short of that heinous sin may *not* be condemned too harshly. The Lord has said many times:

> Ye have heard that it was said by them of old time, Thou shalt not commit adultery:
>
> But I say unto you, That whosoever looketh on a woman to lust after her hath committed adultery with her already in his heart. (Matthew 5:27-28.)

The commands of the Lord apply to women with equal force, for he has but a single standard of morality. It is not always the man who is the aggressor; often it is the pursuing, coveting woman. Note that for both, *all* is lost if there is not true, sustained, and real repentance.

Home-breaking is sin, and any thought, act or association that will tend to destroy another's home is a grievous transgression. A certain young woman was single and therefore free to properly seek a mate, but she gave attention to and received attention from a married man. She was in transgression. She argued that his marriage was "already on the rocks" and that the wife of her new boy friend did not understand him and that he was most unhappy at home and did not love his wife. Regardless of the state of the married man, the young woman was in serious error to comfort him, listen to his disloyal castigation of his wife, and entertain him. The man was in deep sin. He was disloyal and unfaithful. So long as he is married to a woman, he is duty bound to protect her and defend her, and the same responsibility is with his wife. Numerous cases have come to us, such as the following one:

A husband and wife were quarreling and had reached such a degree of incompatibility that they had flung at one another the threat of divorce and had already seen attorneys. Both of them, embittered, had found companionship with other parties. This was sin. No matter how bitter were their differences, neither had any right to begin courting or looking about for friends. Any dating or such association by wedded people outside the marriage is iniquitous. Even though they proceeded with the divorce suit, to be moral and honorable they must wait until the divorce is final before either is justified in developing new romances.

So long as the marriage covenant has not been legally severed, neither spouse morally may seek new romance or open the heart to other people. After the divorce becomes final, both freed individuals may engage in proper courting activities.

There are those who look with longing eyes, who want and desire and crave these romantic associations. To so desire to possess, to inordinately want and yearn for such, is to *covet*, and the Lord in powerful terms condemns it: "And again I command thee that thou shalt not covet thy neighbor's wife; nor seek thy neighbor's life." (D&C 19:25.)

How powerful!

The seventh and tenth commandments are interwoven into one great command that is awesome in its warning.

To covet that which belongs to another is sin, and that sin begins when hearts begin to entertain a romantic interest in anyone else.

There are many tragedies affecting spouses, children, and loved ones. Even though these "affairs" begin near-innocently, like an octopus the tentacles move gradually to strangle.

When dates or dinners or rides or other contacts begin, the abyss of tragedy opens wide its mouth. And it has reached deep iniquity when physical contacts of any nature have been indulged in.

Man's desires are fed and nurtured by the food-thoughts, be they degenerate or holy.

> For as he thinketh in his heart, so is he. (Proverbs 23:7.)

Amulek, the prophet, reminded us:

> For our words will condemn us, yea, all our works will condemn us; we shall not be found spotless; and our thoughts will also condemn us; and in this awful state we shall not dare to look up to our God; and we would fain be glad if we could command the rocks and the mountains to fall upon us to hide us from his presence. (Alma 12:14.)

Nothing justifies evil. Two wrongs do not make one right. Spouses are sometimes inconsiderate, unkind, and difficult, and they must share the blame for broken homes, but this never justifies the other spouse's covetousness and unfaithfulness and infidelity.

James Allen gives us this: "The outer world of circumstance shapes itself to the inner world of thoughts."

Many super-selfish folks think only of themselves when they begin to cross the lines of propriety in their romanticizing outside their home; to them who ignore the innocent parents, the innocent spouse, and the innocent children, the scriptures are replete with warnings.

> . . . I must do according to the strict commands of God, and tell you concerning your wickedness and abominations, in the presence of the pure in heart, and the broken heart, and under the glance of the piercing eye of the Almighty God. (Jacob 2:10.)

Little do most of those who deviate think of the innocent bystanders until the heaviness of final guilt weighs down upon them. The Lord speaks again:

> For behold, I, the Lord, have seen the sorrow, and heard the mourning of the daughters of my people . . . because of the wickedness and abominations of their husbands.
>
> . . . Ye have broken the hearts of your tender wives, and lost the confidence of your children, because of your bad examples before them; and the sobbings of their hearts ascend up to God against you. . . . many hearts died, pierced with deep wounds. (Jacob 2:31, 35.)

Many women also justify themselves in irregularities; they often invite men to sensual desire by their immodest clothes, loose actions and mannerisms, their coy glances, their extreme make-up, and by their flattery.

Paul also called to repentance: "Wives, submit yourselves unto your own husbands, as unto the Lord." (Ephesians 5:22.)

And to the husbands comes the command: "Husbands, love your wives, even as Christ also loved the church, and gave himself for it." (Ephesians 5:25.)

Some who marry never cut themselves loose from the apron strings of the parents. The Lord says through his prophets: "For this cause shall a man [or a woman] leave his father and mother, and shall be joined unto his wife [or husband], and they two shall be one flesh." (Ephesians 5:31.)

Parents who hold, direct, and dictate to their married children and draw them away from their spouses are likely to regret the possible tragedy. Accordingly, when two people marry, the spouse should become the confidant, the friend, the sharer of responsibility, and they two become independent. No one should come between the husband and wife, not even parents. And Paul concludes: "Nevertheless let every one of you in particular so love his wife even as himself; and the wife see that she reverence her husband." (Ephesians 5:33.)

To those who claim their love is dead, let them return home with all their loyalty, fidelity, honor, and cleanness, and the love that has become but embers will flare up with scintillating flame again. If love wanes or dies, it is often infidelity of thought or act that gave the lethal potion.

To those who belittle marriage and its vows and responsibilities, to wives and husbands who joke with one another about possible infidelities, Paul decries jesting and joking about sacred things.

> But fornication, and all uncleanness, or covetousness, let it not be once named among you, as becometh saints;
>
> Neither filthiness, nor foolish talking, nor jesting. . . . (Ephesians 5:3-4.)

To jest with one's spouse about "affairs" could be the planting of seeds that might grow to destroy the marriage. Marriage is too holy and sacred for this.

In a restaurant four men sitting behind me were drinking. They were joking about their wives' boy friends and their own girl friends. I do not know whether they in fact were adulterers and adulteresses, but certainly no good could come from such foolish jesting, and it is an unholy way to speak of the glorious relationship of marriage.

Such light regard for marriage and becoming too familiar with someone other than one's marriage partner are dangerous waystations on the road to disaffection and infidelity.

Those who have slipped into the ugly approaches may have already silenced the still, small, pleading voice so many times that he hesitates to return, an unwelcome guest. He leaves the iniquitous one "on his own."

The Lord says: ". . . my Spirit shall not always strive with man, saith the Lord of Hosts." (D&C 1:33.)

I plead with all those bound by marriage vows and covenants to make that marriage holy, keep it fresh, express affection meaningfully and sincerely and often.

Husbands, come home—body, spirit, mind, loyalties, interests, and affections—and love your companion in an holy and unbreakable relationship.

Wives, come home with all your interests, fidelity, yearnings, loyalties, and affections—working together to make your home a blessed heaven. Thus would you greatly please your Lord and Master and guarantee yourselves happiness supreme.

# SECTION THREE

## Morality and Repentance

# Chapter Fourteen

# *Love Versus Lust*

*A*cross the desk sat a handsome nineteen-year-old and a beautiful, shy but charming, eighteen-year-old. They appeared embarrassed, apprehensive, near-terrified. He was defensive and bordering on belligerency and rebellion. There had been sexual violations throughout the summer and intermittently since school began, and as late as last week. I was not so much surprised. I have had these kinds of visits many times; but what did disturb me was that they seemed little, if any, remorseful. They admitted they had gone contrary to some social standards, but they quoted magazines and papers and speakers approving premarital sex and emphasizing that sex was a fulfillment of human existence.

Finally the boy said, "Yes, we yielded to each other, but we do not think it wrong because we love one another." I thought I had misunderstood him. Since the world began, there have been countless immoralities, but to hear them justified by Latter-day Saint youth shocked me. He repeated, "No, it is not wrong, because we love one another."

They had repeated this abominable heresy so often that they had convinced themselves, and a wall of resis-

tance had been built, and behind this wall they stubborn-
ly, almost defiantly, stood. If there had been blushes of
shame at first, such had been neutralized with their logic,
so deeply entrenched were they in this rationalization.
Had they not read in some university papers of the new
freedom where premarital sex was sanctioned, at least not
forbidden? Did they not see the looseness in every show,
on every stage, on TV screens and magazines? Had they
not discussed this in the locker room and in private conversation? Had it not been fairly well established, then, that
sex before marriage was not so wrong? Did there not need
to be a trial period? How else could they know if they
would be sexually compatible for marriage? Had they not,
like numerous others, come to regard sex as the basis for
living?

And a proverb came to my mind:

> Such is the way of an adulterous woman; she eateth, and
> wipeth her mouth, and saith, I have done no wickedness. (Prov-
> erbs 30:20.)

In their rationalization they have had much cooperation, for, as Peter said,

> . . . there shall be false teachers among you, who privily
> shall bring in damnable heresies . . . and bring upon themselves
> swift destruction.
>
> And many shall follow their pernicious ways. . . . (2 Peter
> 2:1-2.)

And here they are, false teachers everywhere, using
speech and pornographic literature, magazines, radio, TV,
street talk—spreading damnable heresies that break down
moral standards, and this to gratify the lusts of the flesh.

The Savior said that the very elect would be deceived
by Lucifer if it were possible. He will use his logic to
confuse and his rationalizations to destroy. He will shade
meanings, open doors an inch at a time, and lead from
purest white through all the shades of gray to the darkest
black.

Young people are confused by the arch deceiver, who uses every device to deceive them.

This young couple looked up rather startled when I postulated firmly and with positiveness, "No, my beloved young people, you did not love one another. Rather, you lusted for one another."

I am sure that Peter and James and Paul found it unpleasant business to constantly be calling people to repentance and warning them of dangers, but they continued unflinchingly. So we, your leaders, must be everlastingly at it; if people do not understand, then the fault may be partly ours. But if we make the true way clear to you, then we are blameless; and most want to follow if they fully understand.

> If when he [the watchman] seeth the sword come upon the land, he blow the trumpet, and warn the people;
>
> Then whosoever heareth the sound of the trumpet, and taketh not warning; if the sword come, and take him away, his blood shall be upon his own head.
>
> He heard the sound of the trumpet, and took not warning; his blood shall be upon him. But he that taketh warning shall deliver his soul.
>
> But if the watchman see the sword come, and blow not the trumpet, and the people be not warned; if the sword come, and take any person from among them, he is taken away in his iniquity; but his blood will I require at the watchman's hand. (Ezekiel 33:3-6.)

The boy and girl sat still and respectfully. I was not sure if they were comprehending. After their wrong concepts had been bolstered so long and firmly, it was hard for them to change immediately.

They had defiled the beautiful and holy word *love* until it had degenerated to become a bedfellow with *lust*, its antithesis.

As far back as Isaiah, rationalizers were condemned:

> Woe unto them that call evil good, and good evil; that put darkness for light, and light for darkness; that put bitter for sweet, and sweet for bitter!

> Woe unto them that are wise in their own eyes, and prudent in their own sight! (Isaiah 5:20-21.)

As I looked the boy in the eye, I said, "No, my boy, you were not expressing love when you took her virtue." And to her I said, "There was no real love in your heart when you robbed him of his chastity. It was lust that brought you together in this most serious of all practices short of murder. Paul said, 'Love worketh no ill to his neighbour. . . .' " (Romans 13:10.)

I continued, "If one really loves another, one would rather die for that person than injure him. At the hour of indulgence, pure love is pushed out one door while lust sneaks in the other. Your affection has been replaced with biological materialism and uncontrolled passion. You have accepted the doctrine that the devil is so eager to establish—that sex relations are justified on the grounds that it is a pleasurable experience in itself and is beyond moral consideration.

"When the unmarried yield to the lust that induces intimacies and indulgence, they have permitted the body to dominate and have placed the spirit in chains. It is unthinkable that anyone could call this love. You have ignored the fact that all situations or conditions or actions whose pleasures or satisfactions end with the termination of the act will never produce great peoples nor build great kingdoms.

"In order to live with themselves, people who transgress must follow one path or the other of two alternatives. The one is to sear the conscience and dull the sensitivity with mental tranquilizers so that the transgression may be continued; the other is to permit remorse to lead to total conviction, repentance, and eventual forgiveness."

Because of this widespread tolerance toward promiscuity, this world is in grave danger. When evil is decried and forbidden and punished, the world still has a chance. But when toleration for sin increases, the outlook is bleak and Sodom and Gomorrah days are certain to return.

We were in Los Angeles years ago when the news

broke of the illicit affair of a certain movie actress, from which she became pregnant. Because of her popularity, it was big news in heavy headlines in every paper in the land. We were not so surprised at her adultery—it was reported to be common in Hollywood as well as in the world generally. But that such dissoluteness should be approved and accepted by society shocked me. The Los Angeles papers took a poll of the people—club women and ministers, employers and employees, stenographers and teachers and housewives—and almost without exception, as though it were a child's indiscretion, these community members found little fault with her and criticized as "puritanical" and "victorian" those who disapproved. "Let her live her own life," they said. "And why should we interfere with people's personal liberties?" In state and nation and across the seas, such toleration for sin is terrifying.

There is no shame. Isaiah again strikes at the sin:

> The shew of their countenance doth witness against them; and they declare their sin as Sodom, they hide it not. Woe unto their soul! for they have rewarded evil unto themselves. (Isaiah 3:9.)

That the Church's stand on morality may be understood, we declare firmly and unalterably it is not an outworn garment, faded, old-fashioned, and threadbare. God is the same yesterday, today, and forever, and his covenants and doctrines are immutable; and when the sun grows cold and the stars no longer shine, the law of chastity will still be basic in God's world and in the Lord's church. Old values are upheld by the Church not because they are old, but rather because they are right.

Pure sex life in proper marriage is approved. There is a time and an appropriateness for all things that have value. But sexual encounters outside of legalized marriage render the individual a thing to be used, a thing to be exploited, and make him or her exchangeable, exploitable, expendable.

In our mass-production age, "we have witnessed the

reduction of persons to things in a code number, a subscriber, a punched card. Each reduction indicates that the person is expendable, replaceable." This renders men functionaries and destroys their being and loses for them their self, dwarfed by a gigantic universe out there. This is hauntingly true as people are "used" to gratify physical passions in illegitimacy.

We really do not "love" things. We use things like doormats, automobiles, clothing, machines; but we love people by serving them and contributing to their permanent good.

And when we come before the great Judge at the bar of justice, shall we stand before him as a thing or as a person, as a depraved body of flesh and carnal acts or as a son of God standing straight and tall and worthy? And as we answer the vital questions, will we be able to say, "I builded, I did not tear down; I lifted, I did not pull down; I grew, I did not shrivel; I helped others grow, I did not dwarf them; I helped, I did not hinder; I loved intensely and blessed, I did not lust toward exploitation to injure"?

Like some high-pressure salesmen who claim far more for their product than can possibly be delivered, sex exploitation promises what it can never produce nor deliver. So, outside of marriage, improper sex life can bring only disappointment, disgust, and usually rejection "while it propels its participants down the long corridor of repeated encounters which are destined to fail."

Very often the couple—the two people who have been promiscuous, who have been wanton, who have crossed the lines of propriety—become disgusted with one another and discontinue associations altogether. Many come to dislike, if not to hate, the partner in sin.

Illicit sex is a selfish act, a betrayal, and is dishonest. To be unwilling to accept responsibility is cowardly, disloyal. Marriage is for time and eternity. Fornication and all other deviations are for today, for the hour, for the "now." Marriage gives life. Fornication leads to death.

The young man is untrue to his manhood who promises popularity, good times, security, fun, and even love, when all he can give is passion and its diabolical fruits—guilt complexes, disgust, hatred, abhorrence, eventual loathing, and possible pregnancy without legitimacy and honor. He pleads his case in love and all he gives is lust. Likewise, the young lady sells herself cheap. The result is damage to life and canker to the soul.

The Reverend Lawrence Lowell Gruman says:

> It is indeed a quaint morality that belittles sex and shrinks human beings to pleasure-seeking dwarfs, for if sex is good, as eating and sleeping are good, then it, too, has specific limits and an appropriate place and that place is within marriage.

And still these young people talk of love. What a corruption of the most beautiful term! The fruit is bitter because the tree is corrupt. Their lips say, "I love you." Their bodies say, "I want you." Love is kind and wholesome. To love is to give, not to take. To love is to serve, not to exploit.

Dr. Gruman says:

> The sexual encounter ought to be a full and free affirmation of the other person, . . . a total commitment to him, and that spells permanence and permanence is spelled out in marriage. . . . If you love another person fully, wholly, unselfishly, then respect the sexual life of that person by surrounding him with marriage. Using and being used, we fail as human beings and sons of God.

What is love? Many people think of it as mere physical attraction and they casually speak of "falling in love" and "love at first sight." This may be Hollywood's version and the interpretation of those who write love songs and love fiction. True love is not wrapped in such flimsy material. One might become immediately attracted to another individual, but love is far more than physical attraction. It is deep, inclusive, and comprehensive. Physical attraction is only one of the many elements; there must be faith and confidence and understanding and partnership. There must be common ideals and standards. There must be great devotion and companionship. Love is cleanliness and progress and sacrifice and selflessness. This kind of love never tires or wanes, but lives through sickness and sorrow, poverty and privation, accomplishment and disappointment, time and eternity. For the love to continue, there must be an increase constantly of confidence and understanding, of frequent and sincere expression of appreciation and affection. There must be a forgetting of self and a constant concern for the other. Interests, hopes, objectives must be constantly focused into a single channel.

For many years, I saw a strong man carry his tiny, emaciated, arthritic wife to meetings and wherever she could go. There could be no sexual expression. Here was selfless indication of affection. I think that is pure love.

I saw a kindly woman wait on her husband for many years as he deteriorated with muscular dystrophy. She waited on him hand and foot, night and day, when all he could do was blink his eyes in thanks. I believe that was love.

If anyone feels that petting or other deviations are demonstrations of love, let him ask himself: "If this beautiful body that I have misused suddenly became deformed, or paralyzed, would my reactions be the same? If this lovely face were scarred by flames, or this body that I have used were to suddenly become rigid, would there still be love?" Answers to these questions might test one to see if he really is in love or if it is only physical attraction that has encouraged the improper physical contacts.

The young man who protects his sweetheart against all use or abuse, against insult and infamy from himself or others, could be expressing true love. But the young man who uses his companion as a biological toy to give himself temporary satisfaction—that is lust.

A young woman who conducts herself to be attractive spiritually, mentally, and physically but will not by word or dress or act stir or stimulate to physical reactions the companion beside her could be expressing true love. That young woman who must touch and stir and fondle and tempt and use exhibits lust and exploitation.

I have spoken frankly and boldly against the sins of the day. Even though I dislike such a subject, I believe it necessary to warn against the onslaught of the arch tempter who, with his army of emissaries and all the tools at his command, would destroy all the youth of Zion, largely through deception, misrepresentation, and lies.

Do not excuse petting and body intimacies. Remember what the Lord said:

> Ye have heard that it was said by them of old time, Thou shalt not commit adultery:
>
> But I say unto you, That whosoever looketh on a woman to lust after her hath committed adultery with her already in his heart. (Matthew 5:27-28.)

Beware of the devil's trick of making evil seem good by giving it a label that conceals its character. Just such a device is the rationalization that lust is love.

And if there has been lust, repent of it and keep your minds clean, and convict yourself of serious evil if you permit your minds to dwell upon these forbidden things or your hands or bodies to yield to the call of lust.

> Be wise in the days of your probation; strip yourselves of all uncleanness; ask not, that ye may consume it on your lusts, but ask with a firmness unshaken, that ye will yield to no temptation, but that ye will serve the true and living God. (Mormon 9:28.)

# Chapter Fifteen

*Modesty*

# A Style of Our Own

$\mathcal{N}$ations are corrupt and degenerate only as the individuals who make up the people break the divine commandments.

The laws of God are being trampled and God is being mocked in our own world with dishonesty in public and private, with political corruption, almost universal drinking, easy divorces, Sabbath breaking, and sexual sins of every description.

But because we have such faith in our young people, we are certain that if they are advised and warned, they will avoid the pitfalls and retain their virtue and worthiness, for "forewarned is forearmed."

And there is only one path that can keep one from peril, and it is the narrow path marked by the Lord Jesus Christ.

As I study the scriptures, I read of Alma reprimanding and warning his son Corianton, recognizing that his own son was guilty of great sin. Speaking of sexual impurity, Alma reminded his loved but rebellious and defiant son:

Know ye not, my son, that these things are an abomination in the sight of the Lord; yea, most abominable above all sins save it be the shedding of innocent blood or denying the Holy Ghost?

And now, my son, I would to God that ye had not been guilty of so great a crime. I would not dwell upon your crimes, to harrow up your soul, if it were not for your good.

But behold, ye cannot hide your crimes from God; and except ye repent they will stand as a testimony against you at the last day.

Now my son, I would that ye should repent and forsake your sins, and go no more after the lusts of your eyes . . . for except ye do this ye can in nowise inherit the kingdom of God. . . . (Alma 39:5, 7-9.)

The world has drifted a long way from the standard of body and soul cleanliness. Unchastity or sexual impurity has come to be far too common. High school girls and boys and college men and women are falling prey to this insidious sin, which alienates them from their Heavenly Father. I know this to be true. The other brethren and I interview thousands of young people and older ones for advancement in the priesthood, to go on missions and to the temple, and to serve as officers of the Church. And while we find great numbers of our members are clean and virtuous, we do find all too many who have had serious moral problems. We feel certain that there is no people so nearly free from this taint; yet we live in the world, and the world has claimed too great a number.

Unchastity is the great demon of the day. Like an octopus, it fastens its tentacles upon one. There are many paths that lead youth to these defilements. May I mention some approaches that break down moral structures.

Some become casual in their church activity and estrange themselves from the refining and protective influences of the Church. The gospel seems to take second place to their personal interests. They miss their meetings, permitting school work, social life, or business or professions to crowd out the important church activities and the gospel until their feelings toward the Church and its standards are somewhat anesthetized.

Another of the many things that lead to unchastity is immodesty. Today many young women and young men are smug in their knowledge of the facts of life. They think they know all the answers. They talk about sex as freely as they talk about cars and shows and clothes. And a spirit of immodesty has developed until nothing seems to be sacred.

One contributing factor to immodesty and a breakdown of moral values is the modern dress. I am sure that the immodest clothes that are worn by some of our young women, and their mothers, contribute directly and indirectly to the immorality of this age. Even fathers sometimes encourage it. I wonder if our young sisters realize the temptation they are flaunting before young men when they leave their bodies partly uncovered. They frequently wear short skirts and body-revealing blouses and sweaters that seem to be worn to draw attention to the form of the girl and to emphasize sexuality.

The newspapers frequently carry pictures of immodestly dressed people. There has grown up a deplorable exploitation of young women in queen contests. Practically every school, industry, political subdivision, celebration, and class must have a queen. There are queens for every vegetable, fruit, farm product, until it is ludicrous. Surely it can no longer be much of a distinction to be one of the numerous queens. The multiplicity of queens reigning over every act and adventure and project of men reminds us of the gods of Greece and Rome, with a different god for every need and interest. Are any queen contests ever organized for the actual benefit of the young women? Such contests are programs of exploitation whereby business people and other agencies may receive publicity and sell their wares. You may be sure that none of the organizers or promoters have in mind the development of character, the building of faith, or the teaching of cleanliness or chastity for the young women. Because of the publicity, they can offer alluring prizes and give much notoriety to the unsuspecting and popularity-hungry young women.

The flattery of the contest is deceptive and frequently destructive to the queen. Vanity of young women and their families induces and encourages them to enter such contests.

> Woe unto them that draw iniquity with cords of vanity, and sin as it were with a cart rope. (Isaiah 5:18.)

A newspaper described the standards for a queen contest:

> Judging of contestants is based on personality, appearance in an evening gown, appearance in a bathing suit, and talent.

Not a single word is written suggesting character, modesty, worthiness, integrity, or humility as basis for winning.

> Ten finalists in the Miss _____ contest Wednesday night will make their last talent and beauty parade before the eyes of the judges and crowd at the State Fair. . . . Just how good a figure does Miss _____ have? That's a question that may be settled without difficulty Wednesday night. The girl will appear in the pageant opening preliminary contest dressed in a bathing suit.

Why does a girl dress in a bathing suit in a contest? Isn't this a terrific and shameful price for popularity and to be crowned queen? Does she like being exploited? There are eyes of many men, some vulgar and lewd, who want to see that body, too, and judges and crowds appraise it; and so our naive young women dress in very skimpy bathing suits and parade before lustful eyes.

I cannot believe any of our young women would choose to display their sacred bodies to lecherous eyes. I am sure it is the glamour of the contest, the possibility of winning, and lure of the prizes and alleged opportunities that blind their eyes to the reality of the sacrilege. May I quote a few lines from a brother who feels just as I do and just as your prophets seem to feel. After attending one of the games at a western university he wrote:

It was a demonstration of baton twirling. Immediately the atmosphere changed. The girls in glittering drum majorette costumes marched onto the playing field. The costumes were of the briefest, leaving the girls nude from the hips down, with tight and form-revealing clothes scantily covering their torsos. In these garbs, patterned after burlesque show costumes, they came onto the field, and there in the glare of the afternoon sun they gyrated and pirouetted in the eyes of the huge crowd of spectators.

I am sure that the baton twirling of the girls calls for considerable skill, but I am at a loss to see any relationship between it and the exhibitionism that went along with it. The wolf whistles, the other exclamations, which rose from the student bleachers on the east side of the stadium where both cheering sections were seated, were not a tribute to artistic skill. I sat in the public bleachers of the west side, and the experience was acutely embarrassing to me. I am sure that these girls are virtuous, sincere and wholesome, but I cannot think that they would have been either pleased or flattered by the snickers, the suggestive exclamations and the lewd comments which filled the air around me as they performed their act.

We must be different when there is a right and wrong. We need not do anything we do not wish to do. We can create our own styles and standards for costumes. We can also control or influence the patterns in many of our schools and help to develop proper community patterns.

Another quotation from a Seattle paper several years ago: "A scholarly research job at the University of Washington was called off Wednesday because parents objected to the photographing of their daughters in the nude." Thank God for some courageous and sensitive people in that great city. "Scholarly research job!" My, to what extent have we gone! How low we sink to do scholarly work sometimes!

Now, let us consider briefly the wearing of an evening gown. These can be made to fit the body and properly clothe it and can be most beautiful. The Lord gave to our first parents clothes to cover their bodies. We are sure that he is unhappy to see his daughters displaying their sacred bodies in immodest gowns. At least some of the desires fulfilled in the selection of these gowns are not holy ones. Why does a woman wish to wear immodest gowns? Is it to please and allure men? Is it to follow fashion? I am certain that there has not been preconceived evil thought in the minds of most of our young people, but the harm can be done regardless of intent.

There is no reason why women need to wear a low-cut or otherwise revealing gown just because it is the worldly style. We can create a style of our own. I know women who have worn evening gowns through the years and yet have never worn an immodest one, and they have purchased them from the stores. I believe most shops carry in stock the dresses the trade demands.

A woman is most beautiful when her body is clothed and her sweet face is adorned with her lovely hair. She needs no more attractions. Then she is at her best, and men will love her for it. And men will not love her more because her neck or back is bare. Young women, if he is decent and worthy of you he will love you more when you are properly dressed! Of course, if he is a corrupt man, an immodestly dressed woman will please him.

There seems to be a pattern that many young women follow of having their pictures taken with a very low-necked dress, so low, in fact, that bust pictures hardly show any clothing. I see such pictures on pianos and dressers in homes. I have seen them on the tables of missionaries in far-off South America and in Europe. Surely it could be only thoughtlessness that could account for this.

Even newspapers carrying announcements of temple marriages carry also pictures that could hardly be pleasing to our Lord. I quote you from a metropolitan newspaper: "Marriage ceremonies will be solemnized in the Salt Lake Temple, uniting Miss _____ and Mr. _____" From the accompanying bust picture of the young woman, no clothes could be seen!

If the young women are thoughtless in the matter, certainly their elders—the mothers, sisters, and aunts—should give proper guidance.

We knew of one mother who remonstrated with her lovely daughter who intended to buy a modest evening gown. The mother pleaded: "Darling, now is the time to show your pretty shoulders and back and neck. When you are married in the temple that will be time enough to begin wearing conservative clothes." What can be expected of the new generation if the mothers lead their own offspring from the path of right?

Neither is there excuse for young men to bare and expose their bodies. The fellows could show courage and good judgment if they encouraged their young women friends to wear modest clothing. If a young man would not date a young woman who is improperly clothed, the style would change very soon.

I am positive that the immodest clothing worn does have a marked influence upon morals. A police official in an Eastern city remarked: ". . the brutal fact we have to face is that more and more American women are unwittingly inviting sex crimes. . . ." He writes further: "The peculiarly American system of encouraging our girls to be attractive and alluring, of training them to be seductive and then, of course, they must draw an uncrossable line—that system may be carrying the seeds of its own destruction. How many well-meaning mothers send their daughters out, dressed to be tempting eyefuls? How many mothers actually teach their daughters to be 'teasers?' . . . The entire concept of training our young women to lure and repel simultaneously sets up irreconcilable conflicts. . . ."

Why will young women, virtuous in intent, set up in dress and otherwise an appearance of daring sexual willingness? Says this writer: "We pray for a generation of girls who will display their wit, their intelligence, their modest charm, their integrity, their loveliness rather than their bodies and their sexual possibilities."

I am positive that the clothes we wear can be a tremendous factor in the gradual breakdown of our love of virtue, our steadfastness in chastity.

The Lord has promised to the valiant, "All that I have is thine." To reach these lofty heights and limitless blessings, you must take no chances. Keep your lives sweet and clean and pure, so that there will never be any forfeiture. To do this, you will do well to avoid "the very appearance of evil" and "the very approach toward evil."

"He that hath ears to hear, let him hear."

# Chapter Sixteen

# *"Be Ye Clean"*

---

*T*his is a true story. The characters are real.

It was a long-distance call; that was quite apparent, for as I picked up the receiver I could hear the coins dropping in a faraway coin box, then a voice asking, "Brother Kimball?"

I answered, "Yes."

It was a young man's voice. "I have a serious personal problem. Could I bring my girl friend and come to see you?"

"Of course," I said, and a time was arranged.

It was not long until the young couple was announced. The deep, pleasant voice was just what one might expect from the tall, athletic youth who possessed it. He was well-proportioned and, like King David, "ruddy, and withal of a beautiful countenance, and goodly to look to." (1 Samuel 16:12.)

With him at his side was a lovely girl, slight of frame and beautiful of face and form. They were both dressed well, and it was evident that they were from cultured homes. It was obvious that they loved one another, for as they sat together across the desk from me he reached quietly for her hand and there were meaningful glances.

The melodious voice was hesitant and a bit choked with emotion as he introduced his girl friend, and there was pleading in their eyes. "We are in difficulty, Brother Kimball," he said. "We have broken the law of chastity. We prayed and fasted and agonized and finally came to the conclusion that we must try to make adjustments."

I asked them a few questions. It was evident they had been treading deep waters. The girl took over the conversation. "I had convinced myself that I was able to take care of myself, that this was one sin I would never commit. I have always been told that necking was dangerous and petting was sinful in its own right, but I rationalized and would not let myself believe that *I* was in any danger."

I let them tell the story without interruption, feeling it would enable them partially to unload the heavy burden they were carrying.

The boy was now speaking. He was self-accusing. "That Junior Prom date was a turning point. It started out a very special one. But as I see it now it turned out to be a tragic one, the beginning of our troubles. When I saw her coming downstairs that night, I thought no girl was ever so beautiful and so sweet. We danced through the evening; and then when we sat in the car, long and silently afterward, my thoughts became unruly as we became more and more intimate.

"Neither of us dreamed what was happening to us," he continued, "but all the elements were there to break down resistance. We did not notice time—the hours passed. The simple kisses we had often exchanged gradually developed into petting. We stopped at that. But there were other nights—the bars were down. We loved each other so much that we convinced ourselves that it was not so wrong merely to pet since we sort of belonged to one another anyway. Where we ended one night became the starting point for the next night, and we continued on and on, until finally it happened—almost as though we could not control ourselves—we had intercourse. We had even talked about it and agreed that whatever else we did we would not go that far. And then when it was late—so late—so everlastingly late—we woke up to the meaning of what we had done.

"We hated ourselves. We almost hated one another, wanting to become someone else. She suggested we pray, but I told her I felt too unworthy. I wanted to hide from the Lord, from everybody. Oh, Brother Kimball, what can we do? Can things ever be the same? Is there any way we can gain forgiveness?"

His voice broke, and there was a heavy silence.

I sat deep in thought, praying fervently that the Lord would inspire me to assist them.

They seemed to want to talk. It was as though a great flood of emotions and feelings needed release.

"I am so ashamed," she said. "It was as much my responsibility as his. When we reached home, he turned off the engine. It was dark and the street was deserted. We became quiet; the conversation lagged; and the thing began to happen against which we had been warned and rewarned. The kisses became warm, passionate, and long-sustained, and as we lingered longer, we seemed drawn into more intimacy. When I knelt at my bed that night, I asked the Lord to forgive me, and at that moment I honestly intended never to repeat what I had done.

"I felt I loved him as no girl ever loved a man before. That made things between us seem acceptable that I would have criticized in someone else. He was good, but he was human. The necking evolved into petting sooner each night, and a new pattern was being established. I felt unclean when I went to my room. I didn't feel much like praying. Why should I? What use was it to pray when I would likely continue? I wasn't so sure I wanted to quit. I didn't feel it was so bad anyway. We hadn't committed fornication and wouldn't—certainly we wouldn't. That we were sure of.

"We didn't fully realize that each time there were new excesses. Or at least we didn't acknowledge it. And suddenly we awakened to the fact that we had lost our virtue totally—had lost something we had always believed was very important—and that we had committed one of the most serious of all sins. I hated myself. Why hadn't I listened? How could I be so stupid as to trade self-respect for a moment's pleasure? I wanted to scream.

"There was no sleep for me that night. I was unclean. I bathed, scrubbed, washed my hair, put on fresh clothes —and I still felt filthy. I thought about the lepers in the Bible days—how they stood far off and cried to an approaching person, 'Unclean, unclean.' I felt like a leper, like hiding, like avoiding everyone. My soul cried out in agony. Could I keep others from hearing the sobbing of my heart?

"In the nights since then I've often had horrible nightmares. Sometimes I am angry. Other young people had done this same thing and it did not seem to wreck them. Some seemed to pass it off with a shrug of the shoulders, but wanting to live the gospel has always been important to me. I believe the gospel is true, and I get terribly depressed at the big difference between what I've done and what the Lord has wanted me to do.

"Hell? Yes, I think this is what hell is. I always thought of hell as a faraway, mythical, and abstract thing, but we've found it—we've tasted it and it is bitter. We could not say we had not been warned all our lives. Why did we stay in the car late at night after we should have said goodnight?"

She could not stop. It was like a flood of waters escaping from a broken reservoir. "A thousand thoughts ran through my mind," she said, "ugly accusing thoughts—

when I ate, when I walked, when I prayed. The memory haunted me. We talked it over and decided we had to talk to someone to find out where we stand. We still love one another, but this is eating away at us and at our relationship, too."

And now they sat very still, very close, waiting almost breathlessly. "Children of disobedience," I thought. My heart was sobbing for them, "Please, Father, bless me that I may help them."

"Can we be forgiven, Brother Kimball?" they asked plaintively.

"Yes," I replied, "the Lord and his church can and will forgive, but not easily. The way of the transgressor is hard. It always has been and it always will be. The Lord said: 'I tell thee, thou shalt not depart thence, till thou hast paid the very last mite.' " (Luke 12:59.)

But I went on to tell them that in his goodness he provided for us a way to forgiveness. One may do as he pleases, but he cannot evade responsibility. He may break laws, but he cannot avoid penalties. One gets by with nothing. God is just. Paul said: "Be not deceived; God is not mocked: for whatsoever a man soweth, that shall he also reap." (Galatians 6:7.)

Serious as is the sin of fornication, there is forgiveness upon condition of total repentance. The Prophet Amulek quoted the Lord:

> . . . and he hath said that no unclean thing can inherit the kingdom of heaven; therefore, how can ye be saved, except ye inherit the kingdom of heaven? Therefore, ye cannot be saved in your sins. (Alma 11:37.)

And Isaiah:

> Let the wicked forsake his way . . . and let him return unto the Lord . . . for he will abundantly pardon. (Isaiah 55:7.)

Yes, the Lord will forgive. How grateful we all must be for this saving principle!

> Behold, he who has repented of his sins, the same is forgiven, and I, the Lord, remember them no more. (D&C 58:42.)

How glorious this promise!

> . . . though your sins be as scarlet, they shall be as white as snow; though they be red like crimson, they shall be as wool. (Isaiah 1:18.)

The young couple seemed to relax a bit. Hope was returning. "We want to do what is right," said the young man. "Will you tell us what we should do to obtain forgiveness?"

I explained: It is not easy. One must come to a realization of the seriousness of his sin. Since the beginning there has been in the world a wide range of sins. Many of them involve harm to others, but every sin is against ourselves and God, for sins limit our progress, curtail our development, and estrange us from good people, good influences, and from our Lord.

The early apostles and prophets mention numerous sins that were reprehensible to them. Many of them were sexual sins—adultery, being without natural affection, lustfulness, infidelity, incontinence, filthy communications, impurity, inordinate affection, fornication. They included all sexual relations outside of marriage—petting, sex perversion, masturbation, and preoccupation with sex in one's thoughts and talking. Included are every hidden and secret sin and all unholy and impure thoughts and practices.

Conscience tells the individual when he is entering forbidden worlds, and it continues to prick until silenced by the will or by sin's repetition.

Can anyone truthfully say he did not know such things were wrong? These unholy practices, whatever may be their unmentionable names with all their approaches and numerous manifestations, are condemned by the Lord and his church. Some may be more heinous than others, but all are sin, in spite of statements to the contrary of those who falsely pretend to know. The Lord's prophets declare they are not right.

The world may have its norm; the Church has a different one. It may be considered normal by the people of the world to use tobacco; the Church's standard is a higher plane where smoking is not done. The world's norm may permit men and women social drinking; the Lord's church lifts its people to a norm of total abstinence. The world may countenance premarital sex experiences, but the Lord and his church condemn in no uncertain terms any and every sex relationship outside of marriage, and even indecent and uncontrolled ones within marriage. And so, though many self-styled authorities justify these practices as a normal release, the Church condemns them and could not knowingly send such people, unrepentant, into the mission field or give them places of trust or positions of responsibility or temple privileges. Such unholy practices were condemned by ancient prophets and are today condemned by the Church.

Paul lashed out against these unholy evidences of the vulgar mind and of uncontrolled passion and desire:

> Wherefore God also gave them up to uncleanness through the lusts of their own hearts, to dishonour their own bodies between themselves. (Romans 1:24.)

There are those who with vicious tendencies or weak wills say, "The Lord made me this way, gave me these desires and passions, and he will not condemn me." This is untrue.

James said:

> Let no man say when he is tempted, I am tempted of God: for God cannot be tempted with evil, neither tempteth he any man. (James 1:13.)

Let him who has evil tendencies be honest and acknowledge his weakness. I tell you the Lord places no sin in our lives. He has made no man wicked. We are sons and daughters of God, possessing seeds of godhood. We are not limited by instinct as are the beasts. We have godly power to grow and to overcome and become perfect. Sin was permitted in the world, and Satan was permitted to tempt us, but we have our free agency. We may sin or live righteously, but we cannot escape responsibility. To blame our sins upon the Lord, saying they are inherent and cannot be controlled, is cheap and cowardly. To blame our sins upon our parents and our upbringing is the way of the escapist. One's parents may have failed; our own backgrounds may have been frustrating, but as sons and daughters of a living God we have within ourselves the power to rise above our circumstances, to change our lives. Man can change human nature. Man must transform his life. We will be punished for our sins. We must accept responsibility for our sins. We can overcome. We must control and master ourselves.

The lovely girl now said, "While we knew our intimacies were wrong, we did not fully realize the implications."

"I am sure of that," I said. "That is why I elaborate on them."

Since courtship is prelude to marriage and encourages close associations, many have convinced themselves that intimacies are legitimate—a part of the courting process. Many have cast off bridle and harness and have relaxed the restraints. Instead of remaining in the field of simple expressions of affection, some have turned themselves loose to fondling, often called "necking," with its intimate contacts and its passionate kissing. It is an insidious practice leading to other vices. Necking is the younger member of this unholy family. Its bigger sister is called "petting." When the intimacies have reached this stage, they are surely the sins condemned by the Savior:

> Ye have heard that it was said by them of old time, Thou shalt not commit adultery:
>
> But I say unto you, That whosoever looketh on a woman to lust after her hath committed adultery with her already in his heart. (Matthew 5:27-28.)

Who would say that he or she who pets has not become lustful, has not become passionate? Who would say that there has not been mental adultery? Is it not this most abominable practice that God rebuked in his modern reiteration of the Ten Commandments: "Thou shalt not steal; neither commit adultery, nor kill, nor do anything like unto it."

What, may I ask you, is like unto adultery if it is not petting? Did not the Lord recognize that this heinous sin is but the devil's softening process for the final acts of adultery or fornication? Can a person in the light of the Lord's scriptures pursue the path of petting with clear conscience? Can anyone convince himself that this is not deep sin?

The youthful pair now had many questions that carried me on into further explanation. "Are fornication and adultery the same?" they asked.

An older sister in this unholy family, most destructive in her diabolical effects and requiring severe condemnation, is sexual intercourse that is called fornication when committed by the unmarried and adultery when one or both of the couple are married to someone else. The two terms are often interchanged in scripture. Another vicious sister, hiding behind expediency, is the ugly one of illegal abortion. One crime seems to demand another, and sometimes cowardly people, because of possible scandal and social ostracism and not having the courage to meet and solve problems, add to their sexual sin that crime of destroying an unborn child. These twin crimes rate very high in the category of horrible ones, next to murder, according to the scriptures.

When we say that the sexual sins are forgivable, this does not mean they are easily overcome or that forgiveness is to be had simply for the asking. Paul said:

> . . . no whoremonger, nor unclean person . . . hath any inheritance in the kingdom of Christ and of God.

Let no man deceive you with vain words; for because of these things cometh the wrath of God upon the children of disobedience.

Be not ye therefore partakers with them. (Ephesians 5:5-7.)

And Nephi writes:

. . . the kingdom of God is not filthy, and there cannot any unclean thing enter into the kingdom of God; wherefore there must needs be a place of filthiness prepared for that which is filthy. (1 Nephi 15:34.)

The Lord commands:

Thou shalt not commit adultery; and he that committeth adultery, and repenteth not, shall be cast out. (D&C 42:24.)

The young man was agitated now and asked, "Does 'cast out' mean excommunication? And do we have to suffer that penalty?"

And I answered:

The Lord has indicated that the bandage must be the size of the sore; if one has offended many, he must be chastised before many, and if the offense is known to few, then the adjustment involves few. Every unrepentant transgressor should be handled and, if he continues rebellious, should be disfellowshiped or excommunicated. One disfellowshiped is usually forbidden to exercise his priesthood and is denied the blessings of the Church, such as participation in the sacrament, temple privileges, and church activity. Excommunication is a complete severing of all ties. One loses membership, the Holy Ghost, priesthood, sealings, and all church privileges. If the transgression is generally and widely known and is a public scandal, the individual is sometimes permitted to make a public adjustment "not to the members but to the elders" so that all who have heard of the sin may also know of the repentance. This is a clearing privilege that those involved in a publicly known scandal should grasp gladly.

The young woman asked: "Then repentance and publicity are controlling factors?"

"Yes, a transgressor whose sin is secret and has voluntarily confessed and whose repentance is without reservation can be forgiven in secret by proper authorities. But even the Lord could not forgive one without sincere repentance."

> And I say unto you again that he cannot save them in their sins; for I cannot deny his word, and he hath said that no unclean thing can inherit the kingdom of heaven; therefore, how can ye be saved, except ye inherit the kingdom of heaven? Therefore, ye cannot be saved in your sins. (Alma 11:37.)

> For our words will condemn us, yea, all our works will condemn us; we shall not be found spotless; and our thoughts will also condemn us; and in this awful state we shall not dare to look up to our God; and we would fain be glad if we could command the rocks and the mountains to fall upon us to hide us from his presence. (Alma 12:14.)

"That is just the way I feel now," the boy whispered.

Christ said:

> And no unclean thing can enter into his kingdom; therefore nothing entereth into his rest save it be those who have washed their garments in my blood, because of their faith, and the repentance of all their sins, and their faithfulness unto the end. (3 Nephi 27:19.)

The young couple were listening intently, but with growing apprehension, and she finally asked, "How then can we, being so unclean, ever get into the kingdom of heaven?"

I answered, "It is true—no unclean thing can enter the kingdom, but a totally repentant person is no longer unclean; a fully purged and forgiven adulterer is no longer an adulterer. He who has truly 'washed his garments' is free from filth."

This young couple had made their decision. They were ready to comply with any requirements no matter how severe. They drew a little closer to each other and asked, "Brother Kimball, what must we do?"

I continued: "You must repent."

Repentance could well fall into five steps:

1. Conviction of and sorrow for sin

2. Abandonment of sin

3. Confession of sin

4. Restitution for sin

5. Doing the will of the Lord

*1.   Sorrow for Sin*

To be sorry for our sin, we must know something of its serious implications. When fully convicted, we condition our minds to follow such processes as will rid us of the effects of the sin. We are sorry. We are willing to make amends, pay penalties, to suffer even excommunication, if necessary. Paul wrote:

> For godly sorrow worketh repentance to salvation not to be repented of; but the sorrow of the world worketh death. (2 Corinthians 7:10.)

If one is sorry only because his sin was uncovered, his repentance is not complete. Godly sorrow causes one to harness desire and to determine to do right regardless of consequences; this kind of sorrow brings righteousness and will work toward forgiveness.

*2.   Abandonment of Sin*

One discontinues his error when he has a full realization of the gravity of his sin and when he is willing to comply with the laws of God. The thief may abandon his evil in prison, but true repentance would have him forsake it before his arrest and return his booty without enforcement. The sex offender as well as any other transgressor who voluntarily ceases his unholy practices is headed toward forgiveness. Alma said:

> . . . blessed are they who humble themselves without being compelled to be humble. . . . (Alma 32:16.)

And the Lord in our dispensation said:

> By this ye may know if a man repenteth of his sins—behold,
> he will . . . forsake them. (D&C 58:43.)

The discontinuance must be a permanent one. True
repentance does not permit repetition. Peter said:

> For if after they have escaped the pollutions of the world
> . . . they are again entangled therein. . . . it had been better for
> them not to have known the way of righteousness, than, after
> they have known it, to turn from the holy commandment. . . .
> [as the] dog is turned to his own vomit again; and the sow that
> was washed to her wallowing in the mire. (2 Peter 2:20-22.)

Forgiveness is not assured if one reverts to early sins.
The Lord said:

> . . . go your ways and sin no more; but unto that soul
> who sinneth shall the former sins return. . . . (D&C 82:7.)

## 3. Confession of Sin

The confession of sin is an important element in repentance. Many offenders have seemed to feel that a few
prayers to the Lord were sufficient and they have thus
justified themselves in hiding their sins. The Proverbs
tell us:

> He that covereth his sins shall not prosper: but whoso con-
> fesseth and forsaketh them shall have mercy. (Proverbs 28:13.)

> By this ye may know if a man repenteth of his sins—behold,
> he will confess them and forsake them. (D&C 58:43.)

Especially grave errors such as sexual sins shall be
confessed to the bishop as well as to the Lord. There are
two remissions that one might wish to have: first, the forgiveness from the Lord, and second, the forgiveness of the
Lord's church through its leaders. As soon as one has an
inner conviction of his sins, he should go to the Lord in
"mighty prayer," as did Enos, and never cease his supplications until he shall, like Enos, receive the assurance that
his sins have been forgiven by the Lord. It is unthinkable
that God absolves serious sins upon a few requests. He is
likely to wait until there has been long-sustained repentance
as evidenced by a willingness to comply with all his other

requirements. So far as the Church is concerned, no priest nor elder is authorized by virtue of that calling to perform this act for the Church. The Lord has a consistent, orderly plan. Every soul in the organized stakes is given a bishop who, by the very nature of his calling and his ordination, is a "judge in Israel." In the missions a branch president fills that responsibility. The bishop may be one's best earthly friend. He will hear the problems, judge the seriousness thereof, determine the degree of adjustment, and decide if it warrants an eventual forgiveness. He does this as the earthly representative of God, who is the master physician, the master psychologist, the master psychiatrist. If repentance is sufficient, he may waive penalties, which is tantamount to forgiveness so far as the church organization is concerned. The bishop claims no authority to absolve sins, but he does share the burden, waive penalties, relieve tension and strain, and he may assure a continuation of church activity. He will keep the whole matter most confidential.

Some missionaries have foolishly carried with them their secret, unadjusted guilt into the field and have suffered seriously in the effort to get and retain the spirit of the mission. The conflict in the soul is most frustrating. But he who totally repents, voluntarily confesses, and clears his difficulty so far as possible, triumphs in his work and enjoys sweet peace.

### 4.   Restitution for Sin

When one is humble in sorrow, has unconditionally abandoned the evil, and confesses to those assigned by the Lord, he should next restore insofar as possible that which was damaged. If he burglarized, he should return to the rightful owner that which was stolen. Perhaps one reason murder is unforgivable is that having taken a life, the murderer cannot restore it. Restitution in full is not always possible. Virginity is impossible to give back.

However, the truly repentant soul will usually find things that can be done to restore to some extent. The true spirit of repentance demands this. Ezekiel taught:

If the wicked . . . give again that he had robbed, walk in the statutes of life, without committing iniquity; he shall surely live. . . . (Ezekiel 33:15.)

Moses taught:

If a man shall steal an ox, or a sheep . . . he shall restore five oxen for an ox, and four sheep for a sheep. (Exodus 22:1.)

A pleading sinner must also forgive all people of all offenses committed against himself. The Lord is under no obligation to forgive us unless our hearts are fully purged of all hate, bitterness, and accusations against others.

## 5. *Do the Will of the Father*

The Lord in his preface to modern revelations gave us the fifth and one of the most difficult requirements to forgiveness. He says:

For I the Lord cannot look upon sin with the least degree of allowance;

Nevertheless, he that repents and does the commandments of the Lord shall be forgiven. (D&C 1:31-32.)

Under the humiliation of a guilty conscience, with the possibility of detection and consequent scandal and shame, with a striving spirit urging toward adjustment, the first steps of sorrow, abandonment, confession, and restitution must now be followed by the never-ending requirement of doing the commandments. Obviously this can hardly be done in a day, a week, a month, or a year. This is an effort extending through the balance of life. "Unto the end" is an often-used phrase in the scriptures.

If thou wilt do good, yea, and hold out faithful to the end, thou shalt be saved in the kingdom of God. . . . (D&C 6:13.)

. . . he only is saved who endureth unto the end. . . . (D&C 53:7.)

Good works are the evidences and the fruits of repentance. The Redeemer expresses this thought:

Ye shall know them by their fruits. Do men gather grapes of thorns, or figs of thistles?

A good tree cannot bring forth evil fruit, neither can a corrupt tree bring forth good fruit.

> Wherefore by their fruits shall ye know them. (Matthew 7:16, 18, 20.)

## The Lord said:

> But he that has committed adultery and repents with all his heart, and forsaketh it, and doeth it no more, thou shalt forgive. (D&C 42:25.)

Now the phrase "with all his heart" is vital. There can be no reservations. It must be an all-out unconditional surrender. The mere abandonment of the specific sin and even the confession of it are not sufficient to save. The Lord knows, as does the individual, the degree of contrition, and the reward will be according to desserts, for God is just. Feigning repentance or bluffing is futile, for both the transgressor and the Lord can evaluate and recognize insincerity and hypocrisy. One may fool his fellowmen sometimes, but himself and his Lord never. Yet the devout, repenting soul has claim upon the mercy of the Lord.

Doing the commandments includes many activities. General good works and constructive attitudes are supplemented by the bearing of testimony and the saving of souls. The Lord says:

> For I will forgive you of your sins with this commandment —that you remain steadfast in your minds in solemnity and the spirit of prayer, in bearing testimony to all the world. . . . (D&C 84:61.)

> Nevertheless ye are blessed, for the testimony which ye have borne is recorded in heaven for the angels to look upon . . . and your sins are forgiven you. (D&C 62:3.)

And James indicated that each good deed, each testimony, each proselyting effort, each safeguard thrown about others is like a blanket over one's own sins, or like a deposit against an overdraft in the bank.

> Brethren, if any of you do err from the truth, and one convert him;

> Let him know, that he which converteth the sinner from

the error of his way shall save a soul from death, and shall hide a multitude of sins. (James 5:19-20.)

I gave the young couple a copy of the citations to the scriptures I had read to them, and I encouraged them to study the gospel. I recommended particularly the short book of Enos, which records in inspiring detail how a transgressor, after long strugglings and continuous crying mightily unto the Lord through the long hours of the day and then extending into the night, finally obtains forgiveness from the Lord.

And so, my beloved young couple, as you leave my office, do not fail to obtain forgiveness from the Lord and his church and retain for yourselves the blessings. Remember, one must be convicted of sin, bow the knee in monumental humility, forsake the sin, and fortify himself against repetition. He must confess the error to his bishop or other church authority, cleansing and purging himself of all that was vile. He must make restitution by restoring so far as possible that which was damaged and must forgive all who have given him offense. And finally he must live all of the commandments of the Lord, bringing forth fruits meet for repentance. And when he has fasted enough, prayed enough, and suffered enough, and when his heart is right, he may expect that forgiveness will come and with it that glorious peace which passeth understanding.

We knelt and each prayed fervently. The young couple —mellowed, repentant, and determined—thanked me and departed hand in hand.

# Chapter Seventeen

*Forgiveness*

# "*Except Ye Repent...*"

$\mathcal{I}$t is my pleasure to go into the homes of the leaders in the missions, wards, and stakes of Zion, and I am deeply appreciative of the fact that most of our people are trying to live the commandments of the Lord. I find in this church many people who amaze me with their close approach toward perfection, but I do find, as I go about the Church, some who need repentance. I thank the Lord for this glorious principle.

I find parents who have lost the natural affection for their children. I find children who disown and disclaim their parents and evade responsibility concerning them. I find husbands who desert their wives and their children and who use almost every pretext to justify such action. I find wives who are demanding, unworthy, quarrelsome, and who are uncooperative, selfish and worldly, provoking such action. I find those who gossip and bear false witness against their neighbors. I find brethren who hail each other into the courts on trivial matters that could have been settled by themselves. I find blood brothers and sisters who fight over inheritances and bring each other into the courts of the land, dragging before the public the most intimate and personal family secrets, bringing the skeletons out of the closets, leaving nothing sacred, having little regard for one another, but interested only in that which they might acquire by such action.

I saw one family split wide apart, half of the brothers and sisters on one side and half on the other, in a most disgraceful feud. At the funeral half of them sat on one side of the aisle and half on the other. They would not speak to one another. The property involved was worth only a few thousand dollars, and yet they are avowed enemies.

I have seen people in wards and branches who impugn the motives of others and make them "offender for a word." I have seen branches broken wide apart, with the members saying unkind things about one another. They bring into their meetings the spirit of the evil one instead of the spirit of the Christ.

I have seen husbands and wives, living under the same roof, who are selfish, unbending, and unforgiving, who with their misunderstandings have hardened their hearts and poisoned their minds. Then I have seen many people who have become offended at church authorities, their ward, stake, mission, auxiliary, and priesthood leaders, for things that have been said or were imagined to have been said or thought.

To the children who are unkind to their parents the Lord has said: "He that curseth father or mother, let him die the death." (Matthew 15:4.) To the intolerant God has said: "What God hath cleansed, that call not thou common." (Acts 11:9.) To the gossip he has said from Sinai: "Thou shalt not bear false witness. . . ." (Exodus 20:16.) To those who would impugn motives he said: "Judge not, that ye be not judged." (Matthew 7:1.) And to those who would criticize the authorities and use them as stumbling blocks, who would absent themselves from their meetings, who would fail to pay their tithes and other obligations because of fancied offenses, I should like to read the word of the Lord:

Cursed are all those that shall lift up the heel against mine anointed, saith the Lord, and cry they have sinned when they have not sinned before me, saith the Lord. . . .

But those who cry transgression do it because they are the servants of sin, and are the children of disobedience themselves.

And those who swear falsely against my servants. . . .

Their basket shall not be full, their houses and their barns shall perish, and they themselves shall be despised by those that flattered them.

They shall not have right to the priesthood, nor their posterity after them from generation to generation. (D&C 121:16-18, 20-21.)

As I read the scriptures, I find that all the various sins are condemned, and all sinners are called to repentance.

Wherefore, I will that all men shall repent, for all are under sin, except those which I have reserved unto myself, holy men that ye know not of. (D&C 49:8.)

And surely every man must repent or suffer, for I, God, am endless. (D&C 19:4.)

Repentance is a kind and merciful law. It is so far-reaching and all-inclusive. It has many elements and includes a sorrow for sin, a confession of sin, an abandonment of sin, a restitution for sin, and then the living of the commandments of the Lord, and this includes the forgiveness of others, even the forgiving of those who sin against us.

The sinner should make restitution. It is obvious that the murderer cannot give back a life he has taken; the libertine cannot restore the virtue he has violated; the gossip may be unable to nullify and overcome the evils done by a loose tongue; but, so far as is possible, one must restore and make good the damage done.

One of the most important elements in repentance and forgiveness, and really the proof of repentance, is in the living of the commandments of the Lord, or in the continuance of repentance, for certainly one is under a strong condemnation who continues to return to his sin, as a "dog is turned to his own vomit again." (2 Peter 2: 22.)

Now the "doing the commandments" includes many good works, but one of its very important aspects is the purging of our own hearts and forgiving others their trespasses against us.

To obtain forgiveness of our sins we must forgive. Read the scriptures given us on that point: "And be ye kind one to another, tenderhearted, forgiving one another, even as God for Christ's sake hath forgiven you." (Ephesians 4:32.) Then in the Lord's prayer to the people in Jerusalem, he said: "Our Father which art in heaven, . . . forgive us our debts, as we forgive our debtors." (See Matthew 6:9-12.) He made it very clear also to the Nephites:

> For, if ye forgive men their trespasses your heavenly Father will also forgive you;
>
> But if ye forgive not men their trespasses neither will your Father forgive your trespasses. (3 Nephi 13:14-15.)

And again in the Doctrine and Covenants the Lord says:

> My disciples, in days of old, sought occasion against one another and forgave not one another in their hearts; and for this evil they were afflicted and sorely chastened.
>
> Wherefore, I say unto you, that ye ought to forgive one another; for he that forgiveth not his brother his trespasses standeth condemned before the Lord; for there remaineth in him the greater sin. (D&C 64:8-9.)

The Savior recalled to his people the old Mosaic law and then the new and higher law:

> Ye have heard that it hath been said, An eye for an eye, and a tooth for a tooth:
>
> But I say unto you, That ye resist not evil: but whosoever shall smite thee on thy right cheek, turn to him the other also.
>
> And if any man will sue thee at the law, and take away thy coat, let him have thy cloke also.

And whosoever shall compel thee to go a mile, go with him twain.

Ye have heard that it hath been said, Thou shalt love thy neighbour and hate thine enemy.

But I say unto you, Love your enemies, bless them that curse you, do good to them that hate you, and pray for them which despitefully use you, and persecute you. (Matthew 5:38-41, 43-44.)

Why does the Lord ask you to love your enemies and to return good for evil? That you might have the benefit of it. It does not injure the one you hate so much when you hate a person, especially if he is far removed and does not come in contact with you, but the hate and the bitterness canker your unforgiving heart.

One great blessing that comes to those who will forgive, and who love their neighbors and enemies also, is:

That ye may be the children of your Father which is in heaven. . . .

For if ye love them which love you, what reward have ye? do not even the publicans the same?

Be ye therefore perfect, even as your Father which is in heaven is perfect. (Matthew 5:45-46, 48.)

Perhaps Peter had met people who continued to trespass against him, and he asked:

Lord, how oft shall my brother sin against me, and I forgive him? . . .

And the Lord said:

I say not unto thee, Until seven times: but, Until seventy times seven. (Matthew 18:21-22.)

. . .and as oft as thine enemy repenteth of the trespass wherewith he has trespassed against thee, thou shalt forgive him, until seventy times seven. (D&C 98:40.)

That seems very difficult indeed for us mortals, and yet there are still harder things to do. When they have repented and come on their knees to ask forgiveness, most of us can forgive, but the Lord has required that we shall forgive even if they do not repent nor ask forgiveness of us.

In our own dispensation the Lord said:

> And if he trespass against thee and repent not the first time, nevertheless thou shalt forgive him.
>
> And if he trespass against thee the second time, and repent not, nevertheless thou shalt forgive him.
>
> And if he trespass against thee the third time, and repent not, thou shalt also forgive him.
>
> But if he trespass against thee the fourth time thou shalt not forgive him, but shall bring these testimonies before the Lord; and they shall not be blotted out until he repent and reward thee four-fold in all things wherewith he has trespassed against thee.
>
> And if he do this, thou shalt forgive him with all thine heart. . . . (D&C 98:41-45.)

It must be very clear to us, then, that we must still forgive without retaliation or vengeance, for the Lord will do for us such as is necessary. ". . . Vengeance is mine; I will repay, saith the Lord." (Romans 12:19.) Bitterness injures the one who carries it; it hardens and shrivels and cankers.

> Judge not, that ye be not judged.
>
> For with what judgment ye judge, ye shall be judged: and with what measure ye mete, it shall be measured to you again.
>
> And why beholdest thou the mote that is in thy brother's eye, but considerest not the beam that is in thine own eye?
>
> Or how wilt thou say to thy brother, Let me pull out the mote out of thine eye; and, behold a beam is in thine own eye?
>
> Thou hypocrite, first cast out the beam out of thine own eye; and then shalt thou see clearly to cast out the mote out of thy brother's eye. (Matthew 7:1-5.)

Another impressive example of unholy judging comes to us in the Lord's parable of the Unmerciful Servant, who owed to his lord ten thousand talents; since he was unable to pay, his lord commanded that he be sold, and his wife and children and all that he had, and that payment be made. The servant fell down and begged for a moratorium. When the compassionate lord had loosed him and forgiven his debt, this conscienceless person straightway found one of his fellowservants who owed him a hundred pence. Taking him by the throat, he demanded payment in full; and upon failure of the debtor, he cast him into prison. When the lord heard of this rank injustice, he chastised the unmerciful servant:

O thou wicked servant, I forgave thee all that debt, because thou desiredst me:

Shouldest not thou also have had compassion on thy fellow-servant, even as I had pity on thee?

And his lord was wroth, and delivered him to the tormentors, till he should pay all that was due unto him.

So likewise shall my heavenly Father do also unto you, if ye from your hearts forgive not every one his brother their trespasses. (Matthew 18:32-35.)

According to the notes in my Bible, the Roman penny is an eighth of an ounce of silver, while the talent is 750 ounces. This would mean that the talent was equivalent to 6000 pence, and 10,000 talents would be to 100 pence as 600,000 is to one. The unmerciful servant, then, was forgiven 600,000 units, but he would not forgive a single one.

I met a woman once who was demanding and critical. She accused her stake president of harshness and would have displaced him if she could. She had committed adultery, and yet with her comparative debt of sixty million pence, she had the temerity to criticize her leader with a hundred-pence debt. I also knew a young man who complained at his bishop and took offense at the leader's inefficiency and his grammatical errors, yet he himself had in his life sins comparable to the debt of talents and had the effrontery to accuse his bishop of weaknesses comparable only to the pence.

Those of us who have sins, heinous or less serious, would do well to sing frequently the beautiful hymns: "Should You Feel Inclined to Censure," by George H. Durham; "School Thy Feelings, O My Brother," by President Charles W. Penrose; and "Let Each Man Learn to Know Himself," so much sung and loved by President Heber J. Grant.

Remember that we must forgive even if our offender did not repent and ask forgiveness. Stephen, yet in his young life, had mastered this principle. His accusers, unable to find anything against him other than fancied blasphemy, stoned him to death. Not waiting for them to repent, Stephen displayed his saintliness by using his last breath to forgive them, saying: "Lord, lay not this sin to their charge. . . ." (Acts 7:60.) They had taken his very life, and yet he forgave them. The Prophet Joseph moved to his certain death with the same spirit of forgiveness.

The Lord Jesus Christ also gave to us the lesson. Without their asking for forgiveness and without any sign of repentance, and while they were still in their murderous passion, he found it in his heart to forgive them: "Father, forgive them; for they know not what they do." He did not wait till his crucifiers should have a change of heart; but he forgave them while they were yet crimson with his life's blood.

It frequently happens that offenses are committed when the offender is not aware of it. Something he has said or done is misconstrued or misunderstood. The offended one treasures in his heart the offense, adding to it such other things as might give fuel to the fire and justify his conclusions. Perhaps this is one of the reasons why the Lord requires that the offended one should make the overtures toward peace.

> And if thy brother or sister offend thee, thou shalt take him or her between him or her and thee alone; and if he or she confess thou shalt be reconciled. (D&C 42:88.)

He says the same thing to us of this dispensation, to the Nephites on this continent, and to the disciples in Judea:

> . . . if . . . thy brother hath aught against thee—
> Go thy way unto thy brother, and first be reconciled to

thy brother, and then come unto me with full purpose of heart, and I will receive you. (3 Nephi 12:23-24.)

Therefore if thou bring thy gift to the altar, and there rememberest that thy brother hath ought against thee;

Leave there thy gift before the altar, and go thy way; first be reconciled to thy brother, and then come and offer thy gift. (Matthew 5:23-24.)

Do we follow that command or do we sulk in our bitterness, waiting for our offender to learn of it and to kneel to us in remorse?

And this reconciliation suggests also forgetting. Unless you forget, have you forgiven? A woman in a branch in the mission field where there had been friction finally capitulated and said, "Yes, I will forgive the others, but I have an eternal memory." Certainly she had not fulfilled the law of forgiving. She was meeting the letter but not the spirit. Frequently we say we forgive, then permit the grievance to continue to poison and embitter us.

The Lord forgets when he has forgiven, and certainly must we. He inspired Isaiah to say: "I, even I, am he that blotteth out thy transgressions for mine own sake, and will not remember thy sins." (Isaiah 43:25.)

No bitterness of past frictions can be held in memory if we forgive with all our hearts. So long as we are bitter, hold grudges, and are unrepentant ourselves and unforgiving to others, how can we partake of the sacrament? Read again what God said in the matter:

Wherefore whosoever shall eat this bread, and drink this cup of the Lord, unworthily, shall be guilty of the body and blood of the Lord.

But let a man examine himself, and so let him eat of that bread, and drink of that cup.

For he that eateth and drinketh unworthily, eateth and drinketh damnation to himself. . . . (1 Corinthians 11:27-29.)

If we would sue for peace, taking the initiative in settling differences—if we would forgive and forget with all our hearts—if we would cleanse our own souls of sin, bitterness, and guilt before we cast a stone or accusation at others—if we would forgive all real or fancied offenses before we asked forgiveness for our own sins—if we would pay our own debts, large or small, before we pressed our debtors—if we would manage to clear our own eyes of the blinding beams before we magnified the motes in the eyes of others—what a glorious world this would be! Divorce would be reduced to a minimum; courts would be freed from disgusting routines; family life would be heavenly; the building of the kingdom would go forward at an accelerated pace; and that peace which passeth understanding would bring to us all a joy and happiness that has hardly "entered into the heart of man."

# SECTION FOUR

*Righteousness*

# Chapter Eighteen

# "Raise Your Voice to the Heavens"

The Psalmist asks the question: "Who shall ascend into the hill of the Lord?" And answers: "He that hath clean hands, and a pure heart. . . ." (Psalms 24:3-4.)

I ask prospective missionaries how much, how often, how devoutly they pray. The answers have shocked me, for I have difficulty understanding how so many young men and women—personable, able, and eager—would fail to pray consistently.

As I interview older people for important positions, I ask, "Do you have your prayers regularly night and morning?" And many answer that they do have family prayers sometimes. Many try to pray once a day and feel that they are meeting requirements. Others shrug it off by saying they cannot get their families together—life is so demanding.

A certain seminary teacher asked his thirty-five youngsters to answer anonymously the important question: Did your family have its prayer this morning? Of the thirty-five, two had had their prayers; thirty-three families had been too busy, too late, too hurried, or too disinterested.

We do not give ourselves breath, life, or being. We cannot lengthen our days by a single hour. Yet I find that many fail to pray either in gratitude or in supplication, despite the generous offer of blessing if we ask.

> Pray always, and I will pour out my Spirit upon you, and great shall be your blessings—yea, even more than if you should obtain treasures of earth. . . . (D&C 19:38.)

Prayer is not an optional activity; it is basic to our religion. The Lord has given us this solemn commandment: "He that observeth not his prayers before the Lord in the season thereof, let him be had in remembrance before the judge of my people." (D&C 68:33.) The bishop is the judge of the people. It is his responsibility to give blessings and privileges or to withhold them according to the worthiness of the member, which includes establishing a prayer relationship with our Father.

"And they shall also teach their children to pray, and to walk uprightly before the Lord." (D&C 68:28.) ". . . I command thee that thou shalt pray vocally as well as in thy heart; yea, before the world as well as in secret, in public as well as in private." (D&C 19:28.) Yet as we note this requirement of the Lord, we shall emphasize the statement of Alma: ". . . blessed are they who humble themselves without being compelled to be humble. . . ." (Alma 32:16.)

When should we pray? The answer: always. But to be more specific, the Church urges that there be family prayer every night and every morning. It is a kneeling prayer with all or as many members of the family present as possible. Many have found the most effective time is at the breakfast and at the dinner table. Then it is least difficult to get the family members together. These prayers need not be long, especially if little children are on their knees. All of the members of the family, including the little ones, should have opportunity to be mouth in the prayer, in turn, as directed by the one presiding, which will generally be the father who holds the priesthood, but in his absence the mother, and in their absence the oldest child present.

Many young men have stirred their nonpraying families by saying something like this: "In the mission field I will need all the blessings of the Lord, and it would be most helpful to me if I could be assured that every night and every morning as I prepare for my day's proselyting all the members of my family were on their knees, including my needs in their prayers."

Prayers are of many kinds. The prayers in public should always be appropriate to the occasion. A dedication prayer may be longer but an invocation much shorter. It should request the needed things for that particular occasion. The benediction can be still shorter—a prayer of thanks and dismissal. The anointing with oil is a short and specific part of an ordinance and should not overlap the sealing which follows and which may be extended as is appropriate in calling down blessings on the recipient. The blessing on the food need not be long, but should express gratitude for and blessings requested on the food. It should not be repetitious of a family prayer that has just been given.

The family group prayer should be in length and composition appropriate to the need. A prayer of a single couple would be different from one for a family of grown children or for one of small children. Certainly, it should not be long when little children are involved, or they may lose interest and tire of prayer and come to dislike it. When the children pray, it is not likely they will pray overlong. The Lord's Prayer, given as a sample, is only about thirty seconds and certainly one can do much thanking and requesting in one or two or three minutes, though there are obviously times when it might be appropriate to commune longer.

In all our prayers, it is well to use the pronouns *thee, thou, thy,* and *thine* instead of *you, your,* and *yours* inasmuch as they have come to indicate respect. Yet we ought not make too much of form. The Lord ruled against long and hypocritical prayers:

> Woe unto you, scribes and Pharisees, hypocrites! for ye devour widows' houses, and for a pretence make long prayer: therefore ye shall receive the greater damnation. (Matthew 23: 14.)

For whom and what should we pray? We should express gratitude for past blessings. Paul says to Timothy:

> I exhort therefore, that, first of all, supplications, prayers, intercessions, and giving of thanks, be made for all men. (I Timothy 2:1.)

Too often we take blessings for granted, like the sun, the air, health, and opportunity. Or we accept favors, honors, and privileges day after day as did the lepers their newfound health, without a word of thanks. We would thank the person who gives us a seat in the bus, the person who offers a ride, the friend who picks up the check after dinner, the person who does the baby-sitting, or the boy who cuts our lawn, but do we express gratitude to Him who gives us all?

Paul asked that we pray "for kings, and for all that are in authority. . . ." (1 Timothy 2:2.) This will help develop loyalty to community leaders and concern for the Lord's influence on them.

We pray for the poor and needy, and at the same time remember our obligation to do something for them.

> If a brother or sister be naked, and destitute of daily food, And one of you say unto them, Depart in peace, be ye warmed and filled; notwithstanding ye give them not those things which are needful to the body; what doth it profit? (James 2:15-16.)

If we pray we are more likely to pay our fast offerings, contribute to the welfare program, and pay our tithing, for out of these tithes and offerings comes much of the assistance to the poor and needy.

We pray for the missionaries. Children who have petitioned to "bless the missionaries" are most likely to be desirous of filling missions and of being worthy for such service.

We pray for our enemies. This will soften our hearts, and perhaps theirs, and we may better seek good in them. And this prayer should not be confined to national enemies but should extend to neighbors, members of the family, and all with whom we have differences. This is also required of us by the Redeemer, who said:

> . . . Love your enemies, bless them that curse you, do good to them that hate you, and pray for them which despitefully use you, and persecute you;
>
> For if ye love them which love you, what reward have ye?
>
> And if ye salute your brethren only, what do ye more than others? . . . (Matthew 5:44, 46-47.)

We pray for righteousness but do not expect the Lord to *make* us good. He will help us to perfect ourselves, and as we pray for controls and exercise those controls, we grow toward perfection.

We pray for ourselves and our children and all that pertains to us, as Mormon suggests:

> . . . hearken unto the words of the Lord, and ask the Father in the name of Jesus for what things soever ye shall stand in need. . . . (Mormon 9:27.)

We pray for the Church leaders. If children all their days in their turn at family prayers and in their secret prayers remember before the Lord the leaders of the Church, they are quite unlikely to ever fall into apostasy and into the class that Peter mentioned: ". . . Presumptuous are they, selfwilled, they are not afraid to speak evil of dignities." (2 Peter 2:10.) The children who pray for the brethren will grow up loving them, speaking well of them, honoring and emulating them. Those who daily hear the leaders of the Church spoken of in prayer in deep affection will more likely believe the sermons and admonitions they will hear.

When boys speak to the Lord concerning their bishop, they are likely to take very seriously the interviews with the bishop in which priesthood advancements and mission and temple blessings are being discussed. And girls too will have a healthy respect for all church proceedings as they pray for the leaders of the Church. Paul asked the Thessalonian saints to pray for the leaders. "Finally, brethren," he implored, "pray for us, that the word of the Lord may have free course, and be glorified. . . . And that we may be delivered from unreasonable and wicked men. . . ." (2 Thessalonians 3:1-2.) And, to the Colossian saints, he said:

> Continue in prayer, and watch in the same with thanksgiving;
>
> Withal praying also for us, that God would open unto us a door of utterance, to speak the mystery of Christ, for which I also am in bonds:
>
> That I may make it manifest, as I ought to speak. (Colossians 4:2-4.)

What a blessing it would be for the brethren as they approach their stake conferences and general conferences and as they prepare their addresses if all the people were praying for them as Paul requested, and what a blessing to all the Church if all the families were that much interested and concerned. Little or no criticism would find place in their minds and hearts. The brethren pray for the people continually and hope that it is fully reciprocated in every home in the Church.

We pray for our fellow believers. John made it clear how important it is to love the brethren when he said:

> We know that we have passed from death unto life, because we love the brethren. He that loveth not his brother abideth in death. (1 John 3:14.)

We pray for our own family members, their incomings and outgoings, their travels, their work, and all pertaining to them. When children pray audibly for their brothers and sisters, it is likely that quarreling and conflicts and jarrings will be lessened.

We pray for enlightenment, then go to with all our might and our books and our thoughts and righteousness to get the inspiration. We ask for judgment, then use all our powers to act wisely and develop wisdom. We pray for success in our work and then study hard and strive with all our might to help answer our prayers. When we pray for health we must live the laws of health and do all in our power to keep our bodies well and vigorous. We pray for protection and then take reasonable precaution to avoid danger. There must be works with faith. How foolish it would be to ask the Lord to *give* us knowledge, but how wise to ask the Lord's help to acquire knowledge, to study constructively, to think clearly, and to retain things that we have learned. How stupid to ask the Lord to protect us if we unnecessarily drive at excessive speeds, or if we eat or drink destructive elements or try foolhardy stunts.

We pray for forgiveness. I have interviewed numerous prospective missionaries. Too often I find them not praying, even though they have unforgiven follies. "Why don't you pray," I have asked, "when you have such a great obligation to repay? Do you think you can merely write it off and shrug your shoulders and rationalize that it is just a common practice? Are you ashamed to kneel, ashamed of Christ? Is there some disbelief in God? Do you not know he lives and loves, forgives when repentance is forthcoming? Do you know that sins cannot be erased, transgressions cannot be forgiven through evasion and mere forgetfulness?"

Important decisions must be made that affect our lives. The Lord has provided a way for these answers. If the question is which school, what occupation, where to live, whom to marry, or such other vital questions, we should do all that is possible to solve it. Too often, like Oliver Cowdery, we want our answers without effort. The Lord said to him:

> Behold, you have not understood; you have supposed that I would give it unto you, when you took no thought save it was to ask me.

> But, behold, I say unto you, that you must study it out in your mind; then you must ask me if it be right, and if it is right I will cause that your bosom shall burn within you; therefore, you shall feel that it is right.

> But if it be not right you shall have no such feelings, but you shall have a stupor of thought. . . . (D&C 9:7-9.)

We pray for everything that is needed and dignified and proper. I heard a boy about fourteen years of age in family prayer imploring the Lord to protect the family sheep upon the hill. It was snowing and bitterly cold. I heard a family pray for rain when a severe drought was on and conditions were desperate. I heard a young girl praying for help in her examinations that were coming up that day.

Our petitions are also for the sick and afflicted. The Lord will hear our sincere prayers. He may not always heal them, but he may give them peace or courage or strength to bear up. We do not forget in our prayers the folks who need blessings almost more than the physically imperfect—the frustrated and confused people, the tempted, the sinful, the disturbed.

Our prayers are for our children's welfare. Sometimes as children grow up, there comes into their lives a rebellious attitude in spite of all that we can say and do. Alma found his admonitions futile with his sons and he prayed for them, and his prayers were mighty ones. Sometimes that is about all there is left for parents to do. The prayer of a righteous man availeth much, says the scripture, and so it did in this case. The angel said:

> Behold, the Lord hath heard the prayers of his people, and also the prayers of his servant, Alma, who is thy father; for he has prayed with much faith concerning thee . . . therefore, for this purpose have I come to convince thee of the power and authority of God, that the prayers of his servants might be answered according to their faith.

> . . . Alma, go thy way, and seek to destroy the church no more, that their prayers may be answered. . . . (Mosiah 27:14, 16.)

No mother would carelessly send her little children forth to school on a wintry morning without warm clothes to protect against the snow and rain and cold. But there are numerous fathers and mothers who send their children to school without the protective covering available to them through prayer—a protection against exposure to unknown hazards, evil people, and base temptations. The Lord commanded:

> Pray always, that you may come off conqueror; yea, that you may conquer Satan, and that you may escape the hands of the servants of Satan that do uphold his work. Behold, they have sought to destroy you. . . . (D&C 10:5-6.)

We pray for help in carrying out our church callings. The prophet Nephi gave us straight direction in the matter:

> . . . ye must pray always, and not faint; that ye must not perform any thing unto the Lord save in the first place ye shall pray unto the Father in the name of Christ, that he will consecrate thy performance unto thee, that thy performance may be for the welfare of thy soul. (2 Nephi 32:9.)

How should we pray? We should pray in faith, but with awareness that when the Lord answers it may not be with the answer we expect or desire. Our faith must be that God's choice for us is right.

In our prayers, there must be no glossing over, no hypocrisy, since there can here be no deception. The Lord knows our true condition. Do we tell the Lord how good we are, or how weak? We stand naked before him. Do we offer our supplications in modesty, sincerity, and with a "broken heart and a contrite spirit," or like the Pharisee who prided himself on how well he adhered to the law of Moses? Do we offer a few trite words and worn-out phrases, or do we talk intimately to the Lord for as long as the occasion requires? Do we pray occasionally when we should be praying regularly, often, constantly? Do we pay the price to get answers to our prayers? Do we ask for things absurd and not for our good? The Lord promised:

> Draw near unto me and I will draw near unto you; seek me diligently and ye shall find me; ask, and ye shall receive; knock, and it shall be opened unto you.
>
> Whatsoever ye ask the Father in my name it shall be given unto you, that is expedient for you;
>
> And if ye ask anything that is not expedient for you, it shall turn unto your condemnation. (D&C 88:63-65.)

When we pray, do we just speak, or do we also listen? Our Savior said:

> Behold, I stand at the door, and knock: if any man hear my voice, and open the door, I will come in to him, and will sup with him, and he with me. (Revelation 3:20.)

The promise is made to everyone. There is no discrimination, no favored few, but the Lord has not promised to crash the door. He stands and knocks. If we do not listen, he will not sup with us nor give answer to our prayers. We must learn how to listen, grasp, interpret, understand. The Lord stands knocking. He never retreats. But he will never force himself upon us. If our distance from him increases, it is we who have moved and not the Lord. And should we ever fail to get an answer to our prayers, we must look into our lives for a reason. We have failed to do what we should do, or we have done something we should not have done. We have dulled our hearing or impaired our eyesight.

A young man asked me, "Sometimes I feel so close to my Heavenly Father and such a sweet, spiritual influence; why can't I have it all the time?"

I said, "The answer is with you, not with the Lord, for he stands knocking, eager to come in."

If one has lost that spirit of peace and acceptance, then every effort should be made to recapture it and retain it before he reaches the situation of the brothers of Nephi, to whom Nephi said:

> Ye . . . have heard his voice from time to time . . . but ye were past feeling, that ye could not feel his words. (1 Nephi 17:45.)

When we move away from the Lord there seems to grow upon us a film of worldliness, which insulates us from his influence. But when we scrape that film away and humble ourselves with naked soul and sincere supplication and cleansed life, our prayers are answered. We can, as Peter said:

> . . . be partakers of the divine nature, having escaped the corruption that is in the world through lust.
>
> But he that lacketh these things is blind, and cannot see afar off, and hath forgotten that he was purged from his old sins. (2 Peter 1:4, 9.)

If our lives are responsive and clean, if we are reaching and cultivating, the Holy Ghost will come, and we may retain him and have the peace his presence thus affords and the testimony he is sure to bring.

Solitude is rich and profitable. When we pray alone with God, we shed all sham and pretense, all hypocrisy and arrogance. The Savior found his mountains and slipped away to pray. Paul, the great apostle, could not seem to get into the spirit of his new calling until he had found cleansing solitude down in Arabia. He went into solitude a worldly man and came out cleansed, prepared, regenerated. He was born of water in a Damascus river and of the spirit in an Arabian solitude. Enos found his solitary place in the forest. Moriancumer went to the mountain top to ask the Lord to touch the stones to light his people's way. And Nephi learned to build a ship through communication with his Lord on a mountain far from human ears. Joseph Smith found his solitude in the grove with only birds and trees and God to listen to his prayer. In solitude we, too, may pray with greater depth and fervor.

To those of us who would pay pennies toward our unfathomable debt, there is no better example than Enos. Like many sons of good families he strayed; his sins weighed heavily upon him. He wrote:

> And I will tell you of the wrestle which I had before God, before I received a remission of my sins. (Enos 2.)

He speaks graphically. He speaks not of a trite prayer but of an intense striving, a vigorous wrestling and almost interminable struggling.

> Behold, I went to hunt beasts in the forests;

But no animals did he shoot nor capture. He was traveling a path he had never walked before. He was reaching, knocking, asking, pleading; he was being born again. He was seeing the pleasant valleys across the barren wastes. He was searching his soul. He might have lived all his life in a weed patch, but now he envisioned a watered garden. He continues:

> and the words which I had often heard my father speak concerning eternal life, and the joy of the saints, sunk deep into my heart. (Enos 3.)

Memory was both cruel and kind. The pictures his father had painted in sermon and admonition now stirred his soul. He was warmed and inspired. He hungered for the good. Then memory opened the doors to his ugly past. His soul revolted at the reliving of the baser things but yearned now for the better. A rebirth was in process. It was painful but rewarding.

> And my soul hungered;

The spirit of repentance was taking hold. He was self-convicted. He was remorseful for his transgression, eager to bury the old man of sin, to resurrect the new man of faith, of godliness.

> and I kneeled down before my Maker, and I cried unto him in mighty prayer and supplication for mine own soul;

This was no silent, unexpressed wish or hope, but a heart-wrenching, imploring, begging, and pleading. It was vocal and powerful prayer.

He had now come to realize that no one can be saved in his sins, that no unclean thing can enter into the kingdom of God, that there must be a cleansing, that stains must be eliminated, new flesh over wounds. He came to realize that there must be a purging, a new heart in a new man. He knew it was not a small thing to change hearts and minds. He writes:

> and all the day long did I cry unto him;

Here is no casual prayer; no worn phrases; no momentary appeal by silent lips. All the day long, with seconds turning into minutes, and minutes into hours and hours. But when the sun had set, relief had still not come, for repentance is not a single act nor forgiveness an unearned gift. So precious to him was communication with and approval of his Redeemer that his determined soul pressed on without ceasing.

> yea, and when the night came I did still raise my voice high that it reached the heavens. (Enos 4.)

Could the Redeemer resist such determined imploring? How many have thus persisted? How many, with or without serious transgressions, have ever prayed all day and into the night? Have many ever wept and prayed for ten hours? for five hours? for one? for thirty minutes? for ten? Our praying is usually measured in seconds and yet with a heavy debt to pay we still expect forgiveness of our sins. We offer pennies to pay the debt of thousands of dollars.

How much do you pray, my friends? How often? How earnestly? If you have errors in your life, have you really wrestled before the Lord? Have you yet found your deep forest of solitude? How much has your soul hungered? How deeply have your needs impressed your heart? When did you kneel before your Maker in total quiet? For what did you pray—your own soul? How long did you thus plead for recognition—all day long? And when the shadows fell, did you still raise your voice in mighty prayer, or did you satisfy yourself with some hackneyed word and phrase?

If you have not, I sincerely hope that the time will soon come when, as others before you have, you will struggle in the spirit and cry mightily and covenant sincerely, so that the voice of the Lord God will come into your mind, as it did to Enos, saying:

> . . . thy sins are forgiven thee, and thou shalt be blessed.
>
> Because of thy faith in Christ . . . I will grant unto thee according to thy desires. . . . (Enos 5, 8, 12.)

For this is the ultimate object of all prayer, to bring men closer to God, to give them a new birth, to make them heirs of his kingdom.

# Chapter Nineteen

# "Put on the Whole Armour of God"

*F*inally, my brethren, be strong in the Lord, and in the power of his might.

Put on the whole armour of God, that ye may be able to stand against the wiles of the devil.

For we wrestle not against flesh and blood, but against principalities, against powers, against the rulers of the darkness of this world, against spiritual wickedness in high places.

Wherefore take unto you the whole armour of God, that ye may be able to withstand in the evil day, and having done all, to stand.

Stand therefore, having your loins girt about with truth, and having on the breastplate of righteousness;

And your feet shod with the preparation of the gospel of peace;

Above all, taking the shield of faith, wherewith ye shall be able to quench all the fiery darts of the wicked.

And take the helmet of salvation, and the sword of the Spirit, which is the word of God:

Praying always with all prayer and supplication in the Spirit, and watching thereunto with all perseverance and supplication for all saints. (Ephesians 6:10-18.)

The stake conference was over and a returned missionary whom I had known came up to see me. It was apparent that he was unhappy. After our greeting, I asked him if all was well. His reply was not surprising. He said: "I am miserable and unhappy. I do not feel like I used to feel. I am not sure like I used to be sure. I do not believe as I used to believe. I have no testimony. I guess what I used to bear witness to in the mission was not true after all."

"What are you doing?" I asked.

He answered, "I am attending the university."

"What are you studying?"

He named his courses.

I asked him to name the books he had been reading aside from his assigned work.

He named a number of books that related to religion tary, no scripture in two or three years. He was dieting. He was more than dieting; he was starving his spirit, and it should know all sides of religious thought.

I asked, "How many times have you read the Book of Mormon since your mission?"

He shook his head. "Not many times."

"Have you read it once through?"

He shook his head negatively.

"Have you read a single verse?"

He admitted he had not.

"Have you read the New Testament?"

His answer was still negative. No church commentary, no scripture in two or three years. He was dieting. He was more than dieting; he was starving his spirit, and it was in the throes of death.

I asked him about his activity.

He didn't attend church much. He had come to the conference especially to see me.

There was no tithing any more. He used his funds for other needs.

I asked him about his prayers, but I knew what his answer would be. Why should he pray? He had lost his faith. He had removed his helmet of salvation; he had hung up on the wall his sword of the Spirit; he had shuffled off his shoes and was no longer shod with the gospel of peace; he had loosed the girdle with which his loins had been girt with truth; he had removed and stored away his breastplate of positive righteousness and had discarded his whole armor, hidden it away in dark places; and he stood naked to the fiery darts of the enemy. He had forgotten what Paul said about the prevalence of evil, the fiery darts of the enemy, the constant temptations of the devil. He was not prepared to fight—he was being rapidly vanquished. He had fallen. He had done little or nothing, whereas Paul had said, "And having done all, to stand."

In my office sat a young college boy who was in the mission home en route to his mission. He had felt unequal to the spirituality of others about him in the mission home and was led to come to my office to express doubt about the wisdom of his going into the mission field.

He said, "I do not have a testimony."

As we visited I became sure he did have a testimony, though a bit weak. I learned that he had been vigorously pursuing his secular studies at the university for three years, but he had been too busy, he said, to attend the institute of religion. He had found time to belong to and follow the activities of a fraternity. Upon further inquiry, I found that he had given up much of his activity in the Church, attending his Sabbath meetings only rarely. He had done a prodigious amount of reading but none of that reading in the Holy Scriptures. In fact, when I asked about prayer, he confessed he rarely prayed. But, on a sudden spurt of interest or curiosity or for some other reason, he had asked his bishop for a mission.

After our talk I encouraged him to fulfill the calling he had accepted, assuring him that, if he put wholeheartedly into his mission the energies he had devoted to secular education, his testimony would soon grow to match that of others about him.

The powers of darkness to which Paul referred are not dissipated. They are marshaling their forces; they are ready to fight; they have more effective weapons to destroy the souls of men than guns or bombs. In every field of endeavor, in every interest of man, the powers of darkness find their entrenchments and battle against us.

The question rises always, Are we prepared to stand? Have we done all in our power to fortify, immunize, and protect ourselves? Are we on our guard against the enemy's propaganda, his seductive use of words?

The word *new* often attracts our attention and seems to imply that if it is new, it is better, and that it should take the place of the outmoded, the old-fashioned. For example, there is a "new morality" which rationalizes disregard of God's eternal laws of chastity.

There is a "new family life" which makes the bearing and rearing of children unimportant.

There is a "new journalism" which abandons effort at objective reporting and approves an effort to interpret events to fit preconceived views.

Perhaps never in any period of time has it been so necessary to resist as today. Never was it so important to analyze and weigh and measure every supposed new truth and accept only that which stands the test of time, of scripture, of faith, of heart.

Shakespeare in *Macbeth* wrote:

> And ofttimes, to win us to our harm,
> The instruments of darkness tell us truths,
> Win us with honest trifles, to betray us
> In deepest consequence.
>
> (Act I, sc. 3, line 123.)

In the name of "freedom," many offenses occur. It is forgotten that "freedom" for some means deprivations for others. When a riot or insurrection is not only winked at but even justified, and homes are destroyed and innocent people killed, then fetters are placed on some to give "freedom" to others. In the plane and the train and public places, the smoker must have his freedom. He blows his foul smoke into the faces of others without a second thought or apology. And we ask, freedom for whom?

The drunken driver is often handled with a reprimand only and continues to drink and drive and endanger the lives of many innocent ones.

Should people be free to infect society with obscene pictures and vulgar articles and to flaunt corruption before children and others? Why should a few be granted freedom from restraint when many are fettered by the ugliness to which they are exposed?

There is the new freedom of divorce. Some say: "We can try this marriage and if it doesn't work, we can divorce." In the study of a certain area in Utah, the average marriage lasted seven years; and the average age of persons divorced was thirty-two years, and there was an average of nearly two children involved in each case. In the period of this particular survey, there were forty divorces for one hundred marriages. And we ask: freedom for whom? Certainly not for the numerous children whose lives are fettered, whose deprivations are severe. The delinquency quotient, the mental hospitals, the detention homes— these are not so much the product of poverty as of instability.

When I was a boy in Arizona, the big mines in Clifton and Morenci dumped their tailings in the San Francisco River above us. The hard clay came in our irrigation water below and coated our farmlands, our productive acres, with a hard layer of clay almost like cement so that crops could not push their blades out through it. Freedom for whom?

A prominent speaker recently advocated free sex. He said, "The revolution has been won. The new order has come into being. Sex is no longer a case of Shall I? but Can I? And the New Morality has codified the change."

He speaks of the "erotic revolution." Such sex revolutionists would make their own rules and would require acceptance of their erroneous way of life by society, without interference or controls. He leads a school of thought that would give contraceptive devices or birth control pills to everyone who asked for them regardless of age, and would offer free abortions. It is advocated that there be a "switching of wives on weekend parties." He is quoted as saying that the young people are the most deprived, deprived of the right to build their own sexual lives. He says: "Tell your students for me, if they want freedom they are going to have to get it the same way the Negroes get it, by taking it and defying the law by civil disobedience. And every time they go out on a date and have sexual intercourse they are practicing civil disobedience."

There is a defiance today in certain quarters of all that is holy—of all that the Lord has been teaching his offspring for these millennia.

Alexander Pope gave us these oft-quoted words:

> Vice is a monster of so frightful mien,
> As to be hated needs but to be seen;
> Yet seen too oft, familiar with her face,
> We first endure, then pity, then embrace.

They talk of freedom, but it is of freedom to exploit, freedom to deprive others. Freedom, poor freedom, thou seduced and prostituted word! Let us beware of such misuse of words; let us live so that we have power of discernment.

In my experience, few people have ever lost their peace, their spirituality, their testimony when they kept close to the Lord in their prayers, to the Church in their activities, to the people of the Church in their fellowship.

Seldom does one become seriously doubtful or faithless who continues to read the Holy Scriptures and keep his life clean.

"Put on the whole armour of God," as Paul admonished. With this divine influence and protection, we may be able to discern the adversary's deceptions in whatever appealing words and rationalizations and we may be "able to withstand the evil day, and having done all, to stand."

# Chapter Twenty

*Blessings of Righteousness*

# 'Tis Not Vain to Serve the Lord

Some time ago a sister said to me, "Why is it, Brother Kimball, that those who do the least in the building of the kingdom seem to prosper most? We drive a Ford; our neighbors drive a Cadillac. We observe the Sabbath and attend our meetings; they play golf, hunt, fish, and play. We abstain from the forbidden while they eat, drink, and are merry and are unrestrained. We pay tithing and other church donations; they have their entire large income to lavish upon themselves. We are tied home with our large family of small children, often ill; they are totally free for social life—to dine and dance. We wear cottons and woolens, and I wear a three-season coat, but they wear silks and costly apparel, and she wears a mink coat. Our meager income is always strained and never seems adequate for necessities, while their wealth seems enough to allow them every luxury. And yet the Lord promises blessings to the faithful! It seems to me that it does not pay to live the gospel—that the proud and the covenant breakers are the ones who prosper."

Then I said to her, "Yours is an ancient question. Job and Jeremiah made the same complaint." And I quoted for her the Lord's answer through Malachi:

Your words have been stout against me, saith the Lord. . . .

Ye have said, It is vain to serve God: and what profit is it that we have kept his ordinance, and that we have walked mournfully before the Lord of hosts?

And now we call the proud happy; yea, they that work wickedness are set up; yea, they that tempt God are even delivered.

Then they that feared the Lord spake often one to another: and the Lord hearkened, and heard it, and a book of remembrance was written before him for them that feared the Lord, and that thought upon his name.

And they shall be mine, saith the Lord of hosts, in that day when I make up my jewels; and I will spare them, as a man spareth his own son that serveth him.

Then shall ye return, and discern between the righteous and the wicked, between him that serveth God and him that serveth him not. (Malachi 3:13-18.)

For behold, the day cometh, that shall burn as an oven; and all the proud, yea, and all that do wickedly, shall be stubble: and the day that cometh shall burn them up, saith the Lord of hosts, that it shall leave them neither root nor branch.

But unto you that fear my name shall the Sun of righteousness arise with healing in his wings. . . . (Malachi 4:1-2.)

Then I said to the disconsolate sister, "But for many rewards you need not wait until the judgment day. You have many blessings *today*. You have your family of lovely, righteous children. What a rich reward for the so-called sacrifices! The blessings that you enjoy cannot be purchased with all your neighbor's wealth."

No one will escape the reward of his deeds. No one will fail to receive the blessings earned. The parables of the net and the fishes and of the sheep and goats give us assurance that there will be total justice.

Then shall the King say unto them on his right hand, Come, ye blessed of my Father, inherit the kingdom prepared for you from the foundation of the world:

Then shall he say also unto them on the left hand, Depart from me, ye cursed, into everlasting fire, prepared for the devil and his angels. (Matthew 25:34, 41.)

If we can walk now by faith, if we can believe in the rich promises of God, if we can obey and patiently wait, the Lord will fulfill all his rich promises to us:

> Eye hath not seen, nor ear heard, neither have entered into the heart of man, the things which God hath prepared for them that love him. (1 Corinthians 2:9.)

And ponder upon the great promises made for us even in this life:

> Bring ye all the tithes into the storehouse, that there may be meat in mine house, and prove me now herewith, saith the Lord of hosts, if I will not open you the windows of heaven, and pour you out a blessing, that there shall not be room enough to receive it. (Malachi 3:10.)
>
> Then [if you live these commandments] shall thy light break forth as the morning, and thine health shall spring forth speedily: and thy righteousness shall go before thee; the glory of the Lord shall be thy rereward.
>
> Then shalt thou call, and the Lord shall answer; thou shalt cry, and he shall say, Here I am. . . .
>
> . . .then shall thy light rise in obscurity, and thy darkness be as the noonday:
>
> And the Lord shall guide thee continually, and satisfy thy soul in drought, and make fat thy bones: and thou shalt be like a watered garden, and like a spring of water, whose waters fail not. (Isaiah 58:8-11.)

What more could one ask? The companionship of the Lord, light and knowledge, health and vigor, constant guidance by the Lord as an eternal never-failing spring. What more could one desire?

> And [they] shall find wisdom and great treasures of knowledge, even hidden treasures;
>
> And shall run and not be weary, and shall walk and not faint.
>
> And I, the Lord, give unto them a promise, that the destroying angel shall pass by them, as the children of Israel, and not slay them. Amen. (D&C 89:19-21.)

Peace, joy, satisfaction, happiness, growth, contentment—all come with the righteous living of the commandments of God. The one who delights in all of the worldly luxuries of today, at the expense of spirituality, is living but for the moment. His day is coming. Retribution is sure.

The Lord gave us the impressive parable of the Prodigal Son. This squanderer lived but for today. He spent his life in riotous living. He disregarded the commandments of God. His inheritance was expendable, and he spent it. He was never to enjoy it again, as it was irretrievably gone. No quantity of tears or regrets or remorse could bring it back. Even though his father forgave him and dined him and clothed him and kissed him, he could not give back to the profligate son that which had been dissipated. But the other brother, who had been faithful, loyal, righteous, and constant, retained his inheritance, and the father reassured him: "All that I have is thine."

When one realizes the vastness, the richness, the glory of that "all" which the Lord promises to bestow upon his faithful, it is worth whatever it costs in patience, faith, sacrifice, sweat, and tears. The blessings of eternity contemplated in this "all" bring to men immortality and everlasting life, eternal growth, divine leadership, eternal increase, perfection, and with it all—godhood.

# Chapter Twenty-one

# The Mistletoe

This world is full of temptations and snares and booby-traps for youth. They are the same rebellions and temptations of ages past, but today they manifest themselves in new forms. The car with its privacy and mobility has multiplied the possibilities of evil. The revolution on the campus has unleashed new demands for freedom from traditional moral restraint and limitation.

Many youths have exhausted the pleasures that seemed to satisfy their predecessors and now, in their boredom, they demand new experiences, new "kicks," which often involve hazardous, immoral, indecent activities, bringing destruction to body and mind and soul.

The so-called "new morality" is but the old immorality in a new setting, except perhaps less secretive, less restrained, less inhibited. Freedom of sex, freedom to drink and smoke, and freedom to rebel and destroy—all come into the picture. Such evils as psychedelic drugs are taking their toll, and narcotics are introduced by dope pushers to unsuspecting youth. Mugging, brutality, and many other aberrations—all come in turn supposedly to relieve boredom as new "kicks." All these and more first fasten themselves like a leech and later become the tyrannical master. The simple experiment becomes a complex habit, the embryo becomes a giant, the little innovation becomes a dictator, and the person becomes the slave with a ring in his nose. The so-called freedom becomes abject serfdom.

The great majority of our youth are stalwart and splendid, but evil is everywhere present and the devil eager to tempt our finest youth. We are obligated to broadcast a warning to those who will listen.

As an example of the increasing pressures on youth to fall prey to the sins of the world, Wallace Sterling, president of Leland Stanford University, said a few years ago:

> A five-year study of student development at Stanford has shown that for more than three out of four students, drinking is well established . . . even at the time they enter Stanford and is apparently sanctioned by their peers, their parents, and society. (*School and Society,* October 29, 1966.)

Many fine young persons have been trapped by evil, little realizing that they are in danger—like standing on a crumbling ledge.

My good friend, Jim Smith, told me a story something like this:

> Long years ago when I was a little boy and rode the range with the men, tending the cattle and helping with the round-up, I used to look forward to the "rest stop" under the wide spreading branches of a most beautiful tree on Ash Creek.
>
> How we used to enjoy it and admire it with its uniform shape and its thick green foliage! How we came to look forward to it, depend on it, and almost love it as we came to think of it as our very own, having been planted there for our comfort and to satisfy our needs.
>
> Its green coolness was a haven of protection for the birds that made their nests in its branches and perched on the outer twigs for their chorus rehearsals.
>
> The cattle sought out its cool shade and the soft pulverized ground under it for their afternoon relaxation.

And we thirsty cowboys always made a stop to get a cool drink from the canteen and to stretch our tired, cramped limbs for a few moments as we rested from the hot summer Arizona sun.

As we lay on the soft cool earth on our backs and looked up into the tree, we saw high in one of the limbs a little sprig of mistletoe. It stood out in contrast from the grayer leafage of the tree and was not unattractive in its dark green dress with its little whitish berries.

I imagined I could hear the gigantic tree saying to the little mistletoe, "Ha, little friend, you are welcome to stay with me. In my strength, I can easily spare you a little of my sap, which I create from the sun and air and the water under the creek bed. There is plenty for all, and you in your smallness can do me no harm!"

Years later when I was a man, I again came up Ash Creek, again driving cattle. Imagine my consternation and sadness to find the beautiful tree dry and dead, its long jagged branches reaching high like the bony fingers of a skeleton. Not even an uninhabited bird nest graced its forks, no cattle lazed under its branches, no foliage covered its grim nakedness, and no welcome was extended to traveler or cowboy to take shelter under its nude wretchedness; already its limbs were being hacked away by woodcutters.

The infinitely beautiful tree of my youth was now the ugliest tree on Ash Creek.

In seeking for the cause of such devastation, I saw hanging from the limbs of the tree great clusters of mistletoe—the parasite of the tree. The translucent, glutinous berries perhaps had been carried by a bird or the wind. The stickiness of the berry served to attach it to the tree limb or host plant until germination was complete, the little sprout always turning toward the point of attachment.

And as I pondered this story, this thought came to me: How like the little mistletoe is the first cigarette or first drink! How like this predatory plant is the first lie or dishonest act! How like this parasitic growth is the first crime—the first immoral act!

Who would ever dream that a sticky little white mistletoe berry would overpower and kill a huge beautiful tree, a thousand times its size?

A group of youth little dreamed that an insignificant bottle had the power finally to cripple or destroy the soul. It was for "kicks," they said, that they took the liquor with them to the party. The sensations were not all pleasant the first time, but they felt they had proved they were mature and not "chicken." Future parties and associations seemed to be weak without it. It came to be a regular thing, a lift from boredom, an escape from depressions, a hideout from problems.

How could these young people know except through advice and counsel from others that the bottle was a demon; that it would become master; that, like the mistletoe, it would take over and bleed its host and make some of them alcoholics and would convince others that it was constantly needed.

How could these youth know with their first drink that it would become a habit, a part of them? How could they believe the parasite would waste their much-needed money, break up their homes, rob themselves of self-respect, cause accidental deaths, create worlds of unhappiness, and even destroy the mighty soul?

Neither the tree nor the little carrier bird could possibly know the waxy, sticky little mistletoe seed would kill the mighty ash tree. But the youth who begins to drink *can* know, if he listens, that eventual destruction and eternal loss face him if he lets this drinking become a habit that thwarts his spiritual development, for he is a child of God, created in his image, born of royal blood, and an heir to the kingdom if he is able to continue clean and worthy.

I worked with such a person who in his youth laughed at the thought he might become involved beyond his powers. He scoffed at the suggestion that he was losing his power of resistance—was almost insulted at the suggestion that he was fast becoming a slave to a merciless, tyrannical master; but I heard him one day in sober moments curse himself and cry out, "What a waste of everything good! How senseless! How stupid!"

I pondered again: How like the little mistletoe is the abominable practice of cheating, the first little dishonest act! I think of a young man who died in the gas chamber. He had stood tall like the tree on Ash Creek. He had been clean, honorable, and loved but had become barren, desolate, and a menace to society, untrusted, unloved. It had begun with cheating, a little seductive vice no bigger than a mistletoe branch, no stickier than a mistletoe berry. Cheating was done in games and in school lessons. There were little inconsequential misappropriations followed by thefts, small and then larger, which finally ran into armed robberies, to deliberate killing, and to the gas chamber.

Whoever said that sin was not fun? Whoever claimed that Lucifer was not handsome, persuasive, easy, friendly? Sin is attractive and desirable. Transgression wears elegant gowns and sparkling apparel. It is highly perfumed; it has attractive features, a soft voice. It is found in educated circles and sophisticated groups. It provides sweet and comfortable luxuries. Sin is easy and has a big company of pleasant companions. It promises immunity from restrictions, temporary freedoms. It can momentarily satisfy hunger, thirst, desire, urges, passions, wants without immediately paying the price. But, it begins tiny and grows to monumental proportions—drop by drop, inch by inch.

It is doubtful if Cain had murder in his heart when the first jealous thought crossed his mind, when the first hate began to develop, but ounce by ounce, moment by moment, the little parasite developed to rob him of his strength, his balance, and his peace. The evil took over and Cain, like the tree, changed his appearance, his attitudes, his life, and became a world wanderer, vicious and desolate.

How like the first cigarette is the predatory mistletoe plant. Just on a sneaking dare or to avoid a momentary embarrassment, or to be smart or to be accepted by others, or for nebulous other foolish reasons, the first cigarette is often taken.

Certainly the novice has no idea of becoming a chain smoker or dying of lung cancer. Surely he can maintain control. There can be no habit—he assures himself he is master; but time and habit and repetition take a terrible toll.

A bird or the wind or other carrier transports the tiny berry to a tree. It sticks to the limb and grows to suck the life fluid from the tree; and eventually it leaves the giant dead and dry.

The single cigarette multiplies from one to a dozen, to a hundred, yes, to a thousand, to an almost uncontrolable habit.

"Can you quit?" I asked a tobacco addict. "Can you abandon the weed before you are 'hooked'?"

The big man laughed. "Of course," he replied and said, as did the great tree on Ash Creek figuratively say, "Ah, little weed! I am not afraid of you. You are insignificant. I am strong."

And then years after, I heard him say in disgust, "I cannot break the habit. It does me much harm. I am its slave. How stupid of me!"

How like the mistletoe is immorality. The killer plant starts with a sticky, sweet berry. Once rooted, it sticks and grows—a leaf, a branch, a plant. It never starts mature and full grown. It is always transplanted an infant. Nor does immorality begin in adultery or perversion. Those are full grown plants. Little indiscretions are the berries—indiscretions like sex thoughts, sex discussions, passionate kissing. The leaves and little twigs are masturbation and petting and such, growing with every exercise.

The full-grown plant is sex looseness—it confounds, frustrates, and destroys like the parasite if it is not cut out and destroyed, for in time it robs the tree, bleeds its life, and leaves it barren and dry and, strangely enough, the parasite dies with its host.

The small indiscretion seems powerless compared to the sturdy body, the strong mind, the sweet spirit of the youth who gives way to the first temptation. But years later I see him once again and what a change! The strong has become weak; the master, the slave. His spiritual growth curtailed, he has isolated himself from the Church with all its uplifting influences. Has he not suffered a kind of spiritual death, leaving him like the tree, a mere skeleton of what he might have been?

If the first unrighteous act is never given root and the mistletoe never permitted to lodge, the tree will grow to beautiful maturity and the youthful life will grow toward God, our Father.

May our youth and their forebears fortify themselves against the very inception of those insidious evils of the world that can overpower and destroy the soul.

# Chapter Twenty-two

# "*Temptation and a Snare*"

$\mathcal{A}$s I read the papers and follow the doings of people in high and low places, and as I read of the graft in federal, state, and local governments and dishonesty in athletics, colleges, and businesses, I find myself crying out almost in despair for integrity, honesty, and righteousness.

When we speak of righteousness, the image of it varies. To one person, righteousness may be kindness and tolerance; to another, the Word of Wisdom; and to still another, the payment of tithing or attendance at church or observing the Golden Rule.

There are those who would not commit adultery, yet would be unkind to spouse and children. Only recently a well-to-do man was in my office. He lives all the conventional commandments but had struck his faithful wife in his sudden anger and in the presence of some of their children.

The Savior found religionists who would never fail to wash their hands before a meal but who came to the table with their "inward part . . . full of ravening and wickedness." (Luke 11:39.)

Some people are like the Pharisees of whom the Lord said:

> . . . ye tithe mint and rue and all manner of herbs, and pass over judgment and the love of God: these ought ye to have done, and not to leave the other undone. (Luke 11:42.)

Self-justification is the enemy of repentance. God's Spirit continues with the honest in heart to strengthen, to help, and to save, but invariably the Spirit of God ceases to strive with the man who excuses himself in his wrong doing.

Practically all dishonesty owes its existence and growth to this inward distortion we call self-justification. It is the first, the worst, and the most insidious and damaging form of cheating—to cheat oneself.

There is the man who would not drink a cup of coffee but every night would take coal from the open railroad cars. There is the girl who, while attending to all her church duties, stole five hundred dollars from her employer. There was the young man who administered the sacrament on Sunday but on the Saturday night before was involved in sinful petting.

There are numerous ways to falsify and deceive and defraud. There are those who rob homes and banks and businesses; employers untrue to their trusts and employees who soldier on the job, misappropriate money, and waste time. There are the purse snatchers, the meter robbers, the tax evaders, and those who mislabel and misrepresent the products they are selling.

Brigham Young reacted to this subject by saying:

> Be honest. Woe to those who profess to be Saints and are not honest.
>
> Honest hearts produce honest actions—holy desires produce corresponding outward works. Fulfill your contracts and sacredly keep your word.

Some borrow beyond their ability to pay. Others purchase on time and let time run into eternity; some make promises and solemn covenants and disregard and ignore them. There are those who have taken towels from motels and those who have kept overpayment of change. Some succeed in business by sharp practices and close dealing. Then there is the downright pilfering and stealing.

J. P. Senne has said: "Money dishonestly acquired is never worth its cost, while a good conscience never costs as much as it is worth."

Gandhi is reputed to have once said that there are 999 who believe in honesty for every one who practices it. It might be difficult to find one man who did not believe in honesty. We are told that poor old Diogenes went around Athens with a lighted lantern in the middle of the daytime trying to find just one honest man.

Huge quantities of merchandise disappear through shoplifters, enough to build libraries, schools, and churches, and it is sad that allegedly honorable people are sometimes included in the shoplifting.

Sometimes the supposed "best" people boast of traffic violations and outsmarting the police and of crossing international borders with concealed merchandise without paying duty. Often youths pilfer such things as sweaters, ties, jewelry, scarfs, and film, seeing it as a game.

Some businessmen take "all the traffic will bear" in interest or profit, and advertise sales that are fictitious with heavy mark-up so there can be an impressive mark-down, and there are those who overcharge and overweigh and underpay.

At a meeting I held with a group of bishops, I had occasion to read to them that scripture of Paul: "For a bishop must be blameless, as the steward of God . . . not given to filthy lucre." (Titus 1:7.)

I went to the dictionary to see just what Webster would say and found there that lucre itself had a bad connotation, and filthy lucre was even worse. Not all money is lucre; not all money is filthy. There is clean money—

clean money with which to buy food, clothes, and shelter, and with which to make contributions. It is that reasonable pay for faithful service. It is that fair profit from sale of goods, commodities, or services. It is that income received from transactions where all parties profit.

In Proverbs we read: "Better is the poor that walketh in his uprightness, than he that is perverse in his ways, though he be rich." (Proverbs 28:6.)

Filthy lucre is blood money—it is that which is obtained by stealing. Filthy lucre is that which comes through robbery or through gambling. It is that which might be had through sin or sinful operations. Filthy lucre is that which might come from the sale of liquor, wines, and beer. It is that which comes from bribery or from exploitation. I believe that unearned money or compromise money is filthy. Graft money is tainted and that which comes through deceptions, excessive charges, oppression to the poor. Men who accept wages, salaries, or fees who do not give commensurate time, energy, devotion, or service collect money that is not as clean as it should be.

Money is unclean when it is obtained through oppression or misrepresentation. You will remember the prophet Samuel came to his people when the elders of Israel demanded a king, and "he made his sons judges over Israel. And his sons walked not in his ways, but turned aside after lucre, and took bribes, and perverted judgment." (1 Samuel 8:1, 3.)

But Samuel the prophet was clean. He asked:

> Behold, here I am . . . whose ox have I taken? or whose ass have I taken? or whom have I defrauded? whom have I oppressed? or of whose hand have I received any bribe to blind mine eyes therewith? . . .

> And they said, Thou hast not defrauded us, nor oppressed us, neither hast thou taken ought of any man's hand. (1 Samuel 12:3-4.)

Moses said of bribes:

And thou shalt take no gift: for the gift blindeth the wise, and perverteth the words of the righteous. (Exodus 23:8.)

## Much is said about the employer and the employee:

Go to now, ye rich men, weep and howl. . . .

Behold, the hire of the labourers who have reaped down your fields, which is of you kept back by fraud, crieth . . . into the ears of the Lord. . . . (James 5:1, 4.)

The prophet Malachi lists together the sorcerers, the adulterers, the false swearers and those that oppress the hireling in his wages. (See Malachi 3:5.)

Farm help, domestics, unorganized and unprotected people sometimes are oppressed when economic conditions place them in such a position that they must accept what is offered or remain unemployed. And we sometimes justify ourselves in underpaying and even boast about it.

On the other side there are those who accept excessive compensation for services and who fail to give value received and who give no loyalty with their insufficient and inefficient service.

I had an acquaintance, John, who was writing articles for sale. Much of the time he was supposed to be at his regular job he hid away in the furnace room to write and read. And when I asked him about it, he shrugged his shoulders and said, "They all do it." I shamed him out. Now he smiles and gives full service for his wage.

As we look about, we see many who seem greedy for excessive wealth. Paul said:

For we brought nothing into this world, and it is certain we can carry nothing out.

And having food and raiment let us be therewith content.

But they that will be rich fall into temptation and a snare, and into many foolish and hurtful lusts, which drown men in destruction and perdition.

For the love of money is the root of all evil: which while some coveted after, they have erred from the faith, and pierced themselves through with many sorrows. (1 Timothy 6:7-10.)

And this from Proverbs struck me: ". . . he that maketh haste to be rich shall not be innocent." (Proverbs 28:20.)

Are there not many who are hasting to be rich? Is money taken in on the Sabbath, when it is unnecessary, unclean money? Some must work on the Sabbath. If it is not their fault, then of course there is no blame. But men and women who deliberately develop Sunday business programs to increase their holdings, I feel sorry for them. Sometimes consciences are salved over, saying, "We make more so we can do more good with it for worthy causes." Few give more than a small part of the extra income to those worthy causes. Most is spent on themselves. There are those who work primarily for the time and a half or the double pay. It is enticing. But in a stake I visited recently a man whom I interviewed told me he closed his service station on Sunday. I asked him, "Do you not have competition? Can you survive?" He said he lost a little business to his competitor, but the Lord had blessed him and he was doing well.

The Savior knew that the ox falls in the mire, but he knew also that no ox deliberately goes into the mire every week.

In my travels I find faithful people who forgo Sabbath day profits and the handling of forbidden things. I have found cattlemen who have no roundup on the Sabbath; fruit stands along the roadside, generally open day and night through fruit season, closed on the Sabbath; drug stores, eating houses, and wayside stands closed on the Lord's day and the owners seem to get along and at the same time take genuine satisfaction in abiding by the law. And every time I see good folk forgoing these kinds of earnings, I rejoice and feel within my heart to bless them for their faith and steadfastness.

There have been dishonest queen contests and TV quiz frauds, college student cheating, the "fixing" of ball games, the win-at-any-cost attitudes of sports participants and audiences. There are "Robin Hood" thieves who are publicly acclaimed because part of their loot is given to the poor.

A woman embezzled two million dollars from the depositors of a building and loan association, but because she had helped the poor, paid some back rent, and given emergency help with her stolen money, the community would hardly let her be convicted and imprisoned. They were willing to condone the crime and sin of dishonesty.

Many will defraud a corporation or the state or even the Church but would recoil from stealing a dime from a neighbor. Many rob the insurance companies and policy-holders with their fraudulent, unconscionable claims; some are "get-rich-quick" people; some are "get-something-for-nothing" folks.

There are gangsters, extortioners, and other disreputable characters who, through bribery and gifts and contributions, get in high places and influence legislation and court actions.

There are police who assault those they are pledged to protect or appropriate property they are sworn to watch, and there are high officials who rob the public of great amounts.

Some dishonesty is a good deal more subtle. John Ruskin warns to "avoid deception by word or silence."

> . . . the essence of lying is in deception, not in words: a lie may be told by silence, by equivocation, by the accent of a syllable, by a glance of the eye attaching a peculiar significance to a sentence; and all these kinds of lies are worse and baser by many degrees than a lie plainly worded; so that no form of blinded conscience is so far sunk as that which comforts itself for having deceived, because the deception was by gesture or silence, instead of utterance. . . .

There is the person who, seeking a temple recommend, colors the facts, minimizes the errors, exaggerates the virtues; there is the prospective missionary who fails to reveal the whole truth; there is the person who partakes of the sacrament unworthily rather than stir curiosity. Whom do they deceive?

A prayer of a Dallas, Texas, Rotarian is refreshing:

> Teach me that 60 minutes make an hour, 16 ounces one pound, and 100 cents one dollar.

> Help me to live so that I can lie down at night with a clear conscience, without a gun under my pillow and unhaunted by the faces of those to whom I have brought pain.

> Grant, I beseech thee, that I may earn my meal ticket on the square, and in doing thereof that I may not stick the gaff where it does not belong.

> Deafen me to the jingle of tainted money and the rustle of unholy skirts.

> Blind me to the faults of the other fellow, but reveal to me my own.

> Guide me so that each night when I look across the dinner table at my wife, who has been a blessing to me, I shall have nothing to conceal.

> Keep me young enough to laugh with my children and to lose myself in their play.

> And then, when comes the smell of flowers, and the tread of soft steps, and the crunching of the hearse's wheels in the gravel out in front of my place, make the ceremony short and the epitaph simple: "Here Lies a Man." (J. Hugh Campbell, Dallas, Texas, "A Prayer and an Epitaph.")

But not all people are disappointing and dishonorable. For example, in Los Angeles, Douglas William Johnson returned $240,000 that was lost on a street from a Brink's armored car. Ironically, the fickle public condemned him, called him a fool, telephoned him, harassed him, and made life unpleasant for him and for his children at school.

On the train from New York to Baltimore we sat in the dining car opposite a businessman and commented, "It seldom rains like this in Salt Lake City."

The conversation soon led naturally into the golden question: "How much do you know about the Church?"

"I know little about the Church," he said, "but I know one of its people." He was developing subdivisions in New York. "There is a sub-contractor working for me," he continued. "He is so honest and full of integrity that I never ask him to bid on a job. He is the soul of honor. If the Mormon people are like this man, I'd like to know about a church that produces such honorable men." We left him literature and sent the missionaries to teach him.

A magazine article told of a Connecticut grandmother, Hannie Dickinson, who built on the roadside near her home a building a little larger than a child's playhouse on which was the sign "Self-service—Open," and in which were eggs, vegetables, fruits, and flowers. A glass jar was the cash register. She would bring the produce in the early morning and collect at night after her farm operations of the day. She had operated this unusual merchandising business for three summers and reported that not a single person had taken goods without pay nor had they shortchanged her. "It seems that when you trust people, they generally respond with honor," she said.

Alma told the people that a man of integrity "cannot walk in crooked paths; neither doth he vary from that which he hath said; neither hath he a shadow of turning from the right to the left, or from that which is right to that which is wrong. . . ." (Alma 7:20.)

The young Prophet Joseph Smith said: "Be virtuous and pure; be men of integrity and truth; keep the commandments of God."

Sometimes it is easier to explain what integrity is by showing what it is not. I stepped into the Hotel Utah Coffee Shop in Salt Lake City to buy some hard rolls, and as I placed my order with the waitress, a middle-aged woman I knew was sitting at the counter with a cup of coffee at her plate. I am sure she saw me, though she tried not to show it. I could see her physical discomfort as she turned her face from me at a right angle, and there it remained until I had made my purchase and had gone to the cash register. She had her free agency—

she could drink coffee if she wanted to, but what a wallop her character had taken because she was unwilling to face a friend! How she shriveled! At the waters of baptism, in sacrament meetings, and in the temple, she had promised that she would have a broken heart and contrite spirit, repent of all her sins, take upon herself the name of Jesus Christ, and serve him unto the end, manifesting it by her works.

Probably she was certain that I had not seen or recognized her, but the ten stories of the building above her were not enough to keep the angels in heaven from photographing her movements and recording her thoughts of deception. It was a petty thing, but for her it was withering—a weak, mean, cheap, little tricky thing that sent her honor skidding down the incline toward bankruptcy of self-esteem.

John the Revelator "saw the dead, small and great, stand before God; and the books were opened; and another book was opened, which is the book of life: and the dead were judged out of those things which were written in the books, according to their works." (Revelation 20:12.)

Did that woman think she was hiding from God? How wrong she was! No one can conceal thoughts or acts from God, for the photographic cameras are running night and day. So sensitive are they that they record not only sights and sounds but also thought and inclinations. Remember, we are not talking about a cup of coffee; we are talking about the principle of integrity.

Moses failed to realize that the recorder was turned on when he said to the continually complaining children of Israel, crying for the fleshpots of Egypt: "Hear now, ye rebels; must *we* fetch you water out of this rock?" He was reprimanded: "Because ye believed me not, to sanctify me in the eyes of the children of Israel, therefore ye shall not bring this congregation into the land which I have given them." (Numbers 20:10, 12.)

Moses had integrity in great measure, but in that unguarded moment he had presumptuously taken credit for the Lord's miracle and was forbidden to enter the Promised Land.

When Cain's great sin was conceived in his heart and the propitious moment had arrived for the foul deed, undoubtedly he looked to the right and to the left and behind him and was certain there was no eye and no ear; he perpetrated his heinous crime and left his righteous brother lying in his blood. The Lord perceived it all—the sights and sounds and thinking and malice and intents and desires and urges.

Cain was reminded soon, for there came the voice of Majesty saying, "Where is Abel thy brother?" And as though he could hide from Omniscience and Omnipresence, he tried to conceal by saying, "I know not. Am I my brother's keeper?" (Genesis 4:9.)

And the voice of Omnipotence asked in stentorian tones: "What hast thou done? the voice of thy brother's blood crieth unto me from the ground. . . . the earth . . . hath opened her mouth to receive thy brother's blood from thy hand." (Genesis 4:10-11.)

Integrity is not only to be truthful, but it also involves reliability. Periodically every one should review *A Message to Garcia* by Elbert Hubbard:

> In all this Cuban business, there is one man who stands out on the horizon of my memory like Mars at Perihelion.
>
> When war broke out between Spain and the United States, it was very necessary to communicate quickly with the leader of the insurgents. Garcia was somewhere in the fastness of Cuba —no one knew where. No mail or telegraph message could reach him. The President must secure his cooperation quickly.
>
> What to do!
>
> Someone said to the President: "There is a fellow by the name of Rowan who will find Garcia for you if anybody can."
>
> Rowan was sent for and given a letter to be delivered to Garcia. How the fellow by the name of Rowan took the letter,

sealed it up in an oilskin pouch, wrapped it over his heart, in four days landed by night off the coast of Cuba from an open boat, disappeared into the jungle, and in three weeks came out on the other side of the island, having traversed a hostile country on foot, and delivered his letter to Garcia—are things I have no special desire now to tell in detail. The point I wish to make is this: McKinley gave Rowan a letter to be delivered to Garcia. Rowan took the letter and did not ask: "Where is he?" By the eternal! There is a man whose form should be cast in deathless bronze and the statue placed in every college of the land.

General Garcia is now dead, but there are other Garcias. No man has endeavored to carry out an enterprise where many hands were needed but has been well nigh appalled at times at the imbecility of the average man—the inability or unwillingness to concentrate on a thing and do it.

How one's admiration soars for Peter, the number one man in all the world, as he is seen standing at full height and with boldness and strength before those magistrates and rulers who could imprison him, flog him, and perhaps even take his life. We seem to hear those fearless words as he faced his foes and said: "We ought to obey God rather than men." (Acts 5:29.)

Peter looked into the eyes of the crowd and bore his testimony to them of the God they had crucified:

> . . . whom ye delivered up, and denied him in the presence of Pilate, when he was determined to let him go.
>
> But ye denied the Holy One and the Just, and desired a murderer to be granted unto you;
>
> And killed the Prince of life, whom God hath raised from the dead; whereof we are witnesses. (Acts 3:13-15.)

Of those who heard this testimony and charge, 5,000 men saw this courage superior and integrity supreme! And 5,000 men believed.

Turn back to Daniel, a captive and slave but also a prophet of God who was willing to die for his convictions. Was integrity ever placed on a higher plane? The gospel was Daniel's life. The Word of Wisdom was vital to him. In the king's court, he could be little criticized, but even for a ruler he would not drink the king's wine nor gorge himself with meat and rich foods. His moderation and his purity of faith brought him health and wisdom and knowledge and skill and understanding, and his faith linked him closely to his Father in heaven, and revelations came to him as often as required. His revealing of the dreams of the king and the interpretations thereof brought him honor and acclaim and gifts and high position such as many men would sell their souls to get. But when the choice was put to him of ceasing to pray or of being cast into a den of lions, he prayed openly and submitted to the punishment.

We remind ourselves of the integrity of the three Hebrews, Shadrach, Meshach, and Abednego, who like Daniel defied men and rulers, to be true to themselves and to keep faith with their faith. They were required by decree of the emperor to kneel down and worship a monumental image of gold that the king had set up. In addition to losing caste, losing position, and angering the king, they faced the fiery furnace rather than deny their God.

The dedication must have been exciting. Had there ever been such an image? such a spectacle? Ninety feet of gold in the form of a man—what could be more scintillating, more sparkling? There must have been countless people milling in the streets and in the area where the gigantic image stood when the herald announced the procedure and the decree that all must kneel at the sound of the music and all must worship the image. Neither fear of the king nor what he could do to them dissuaded the three courageous young men from their true path of rightness. When the prearranged sounds of the cornet, flute, harp, and other instruments reverberated through the area and the masses of men and women everywhere filled their homes and the streets with kneeling worshipers of the huge golden image, three men refused to insult their true God. They prayed to God, and when confronted by the raging and furious emperor king, they courageously answered in the face of what could be certain death:

> If it be so, our God whom we serve is able to deliver us from the burning fiery furnace, and he will deliver us out of thine hand, O king.
>
> But if not, be it known unto thee, O king, that we will not serve thy gods, nor worship the golden image which thou hast set up. (Daniel 3:17-18.)

Integrity! The promises of eternal life from God supersede all promises of men to greatness, comfort, immunities. These men of courage and integrity were saying, "We do not have to live, but we must be true to ourselves and God." This reminds us of Abraham Lincoln's saying: "I am not bound to win, but I am bound to be true; I am not bound to succeed, but I am bound to live by the light that I have."

There comes from Shakespeare's pen: "There is no terror in your threats: for I am armed so strong in honesty that they pass by me as the idle wind, which I respect not."

Integrity in man should bring inner peace, sureness of purpose, and security in action. Lack of integrity brings disunity, fear, sorrow, unsureness.

Since the Lord said, "Be ye therefore perfect, even as your Father which is in heaven is perfect" (Matthew 5:48), it would be well if all of us would take frequent inventory to see if hidden away under the rugs and in the corners of our lives there might be some vestige of hypocrisy and ugliness or error. Or could there be hidden under the blankets of personal excuse and rationalization some small eccentricities and dishonesties? Are there any cobwebs in ceilings and corners that we think will not be noticed? Are we trying to cover up the small pettinesses and the gratifications we secretly allow ourselves —rationalizing all the while that they are insignificant and inconsequential? Are there areas in our thoughts and actions and attitudes that we would like to hide from those we respect most? Are we certain that all of our innermost secrets are kept confidential? The Lord revealed in 1831: "And the rebellious shall be pierced with much sorrow; for their iniquities shall be spoken upon the housetops, and their secret acts shall be revealed." (D&C 1:3.)

Would a frequent housecleaning be in order for all of us?

I may not be able to eliminate pornographic trash, but my family and I need not buy or view it.

I may not be able to close disreputable businesses, but I can stay away from areas of questioned honor and ill repute.

I may not be able to greatly reduce the divorces of the land or save all broken homes and frustrated children, but I can keep my own home a congenial one, my marriage happy, my home a heaven, and my children well adjusted.

I may not be able to stop the growing claims to freedom from laws based on morals, or change all opinions regarding looseness in sex and growing perversions, but I can guarantee devotion to all high ideals and standards in my own home, and I can work toward giving my own family a happy, interdependent spiritual life.

I may not be able to stop all graft and dishonesty in high places, but I myself can be honest and upright, full of integrity and true honor, and my family will be trained likewise.

I may not be able to insure family prayers, home evening, meeting attendance, and spiritual, well-integrated lives in all my neighbors, but I can be certain that my children will be happy at home. They will grow strong and tall and realize their freedom is found at home, in their faith, in clean living, and in opportunity to serve. As Christ said, "And the truth shall make you free."

No virtues in the perfection we strive for are more important than integrity and honesty. Let us then be complete, unbroken, pure, and sincere, to develop in ourselves that quality of soul we prize so highly in others.

# Chapter Twenty-three

# The Ten Virgins

The ancients looked forward to the coming of the Lord and asked, "When shall all these things be?" The pioneers thought it would be soon and watched for signs; our grandparents watched for the sprouting of the fig tree; our parents watched for the reddening of the sky; and we ourselves have heard all our lives that the Second Coming is near.

Do we lose faith, do we lose patience, do we lose hope, do we get weary in waiting, because the day is long and the event delayed?

The writer of Hebrews warns:

> Cast not away therefore your confidence, which hath great recompence of reward.
>
> For ye have need of patience, that, after ye have done the will of God, ye might receive the promise.
>
> For yet a little while, and he that shall come will come, and will not tarry. (Hebrews 10:35-37.)

I suspect that many people who five years ago had a rich larder, a full pantry, and a year's supply of basic necessities have let their stock dwindle. I suspect that many people have let their insurance lapse. Death seems in the future, for at the moment calamity is absent and hunger is not knocking at the door.

It is difficult to be prepared for an event so long delayed. Many have found it too difficult and they slumber without due preparation. But the day approaches and will finally come. That is sure. It is only the "when" that is unknown.

The apostles of the ancient days were also impatient to know when these events would transpire. To them Jesus said, before he ascended,

> It is not for you to know the times or the seasons, which the Father hath put in his own power. (Acts 1:7.)

And Paul said to the Thessalonians:

> For yourselves know perfectly that the day of the Lord so cometh as a thief in the night.
>
> For when they shall say, Peace and safety; then sudden destruction cometh upon them, as travail upon a woman with child; and they shall not escape.
>
> But ye, brethren, are not in darkness, that that day should overtake you as a thief. (1 Thessalonians 5:2-4.)
>
> But know this, that if the goodman of the house had known in what watch the thief would come, he would have watched, and would not have suffered his house to be broken up.
>
> Therefore be ye also ready: for in such an hour as ye think not the Son of man cometh. (Matthew 24:43-44.)

Many of the Lord's parables and sayings urged men to be prepared for his Second Coming and for the end of this period of the world's existence. He gave the parable of the rich young fool who, in the feeling of temporal security, razed his inadequate barns and built greater ones in which to store his fruits and goods. The man said to himself:

> Soul, thou hast much goods laid up for many years; take thine ease, eat, drink, and be merry.
>
> But God said unto him, Thou fool, this night thy soul shall be required of thee: then whose shall those things be. . .? (Luke 12:19-20.)

And then he gave the parable of the fish and the net:

> Again, the kingdom of heaven is like unto a net, that was cast into the sea, and gathered of every kind:
>
> Which, when it was full, they drew to shore, and sat down, and gathered the good into vessels, but cast the bad away. (Matthew 13:47-48.)

I recall my first trip to Hawaii. The Samoan and Hawaiian Saints were gathered together in a grand celebration. On the morning program was a *hukilau.* I was invited to participate. Wearing some old overalls, I waded with them into the sea. The boats had spread the nets far out, and now we began to pull in the nets. "Heave ho!" they cried, and all together we pulled and strained. As the net load came closer to the shore, it was fuller and heavier and the unruly waves covered us many times. But finally the net was in shallow water and the fish began to jump frantically, trying to escape. Eventually, sweating and straining and puffing, we pulled the catch up on the sand. All kinds of fish were caught, big and little, fat and snakelike. With bulging eyes and gasping mouths they struggled. The initiated who knew fish and were able to judge picked the worthless ones and cast them back into the sea. The edible ones were saved and the catch was brought to the fire for the feast.

> So shall it be at the end of the world: the angels shall come forth, and sever the wicked from among the just. (Matthew 13:49.)

He gave us the parable of the farmer who sowed good seed in his ground but whose enemy planted tares in the field. As both the wheat and the tares grew up in the same field together, the question was asked of the landowner, "Shall we go and gather up the tares?" The householder said:

> Let both grow together until the harvest: and in the time of harvest I will say to the reapers, Gather ye together first the tares, and bind them in bundles to burn them: but gather the wheat into my barn. (Matthew 13:30.)

The time of the reapers is near at hand. Certainly, the fig tree is shooting forth its leaves and the summer is

nigh and the signs of the times presage the harvest with
its separation of the righteous and unrighteous. Certainly,
there are today false Christs and deceivers in the land such
as were spoken of by the Lord from the heights of the
Mount of Olives.

Has there ever been an era when so many nations,
large and small, have been involved in wars? Were there
ever times when there were more rumors of wars and
threats and intrigues? We think of Russia and China, of
Africa and Viet Nam, of the Near East and Ireland. The
places change but the turmoil continues.

Jesus spoke of famines and pestilences and we remember Biafra and Bangladesh. He predicted earthquakes
and other terrestrial disturbances and we think of earthquakes and landslides in California, Chile and Greece,
Japan and Alaska, and unprecedented floods in the United
States. Surely, the end is near as we read the signs of the
times, but when?

> For then shall be great tribulation, such as was not since
> the beginning of the world to this time, no, nor ever shall be.
>
> And except those days should be shortened, there should
> no flesh be saved: but for the elect's sake those days shall be
> shortened. (Matthew 24:21-22.)

We have the general warning that comes from these
world conditions, but we have no precise timetable.

> For as the lightning cometh out of the east, and shineth
> even unto the west; so shall also the coming of the Son of
> man be. (Matthew 24:27.)

The Redeemer stated further:

> Immediately after the tribulation of those days shall the
> sun be darkened, and the moon shall not give her light, and the
> stars shall fall from heaven, and the powers of the heavens
> shall be shaken:
>
> And then shall appear the sign of the Son of man in
> heaven: and then shall all the tribes of the earth mourn, and
> they shall see the Son of man coming in the clouds of heaven
> with power and great glory.

And he shall send his angels with a great sound of a trumpet, and they shall gather together his elect from the four winds, from one end of heaven to the other.

But of that day and hour knoweth no man, no, not the angels of heaven, but my Father only. (Matthew 24:29-31, 36.)

With no warning, no last-minute preparation is possible.

He gave us another parable to try to make clear the importance of being always prepared. It is the parable of the Ten Virgins, a powerful warning to all men.

Then shall the kingdom of heaven be likened unto ten virgins, which took their lamps, and went forth to meet the bridegroom.

And five of them were wise, and five were foolish.

They that were foolish took their lamps, and took no oil with them:

But the wise took oil in their vessels with their lamps.

While the bridegroom tarried, they all slumbered and slept.

And at midnight there was a cry made, Behold, the bridegroom cometh; go ye out to meet him.

Then all those virgins arose, and trimmed their lamps.

And the foolish said unto the wise, Give us of your oil; for our lamps are gone out.

But the wise answered, saying, Not so; lest there be not enough for us and you: but go ye rather to them that sell, and buy for youselves.

And while they went to buy, the bridegroom came; and they that were ready went in with him to the marriage: and the door was shut.

Afterward came also the other virgins, saying, Lord, Lord, open to us.

But he answered and said, Verily I say unto you, I know you not.

Watch therefore, for ye know neither the day nor the hour wherein the Son of man cometh. (Matthew 25:1-13.)

I believe that the Ten Virgins represent the people of the Church of Jesus Christ and not the rank and file of the world. All of the virgins, wise and foolish, had accepted the invitation to the wedding supper; they had knowledge of the program and had been warned of the important day to come. They were not the gentiles or the heathens or the pagans, nor were they necessarily corrupt and reprobate, but they were knowing people who were foolishly unprepared for the vital happenings that were to affect their eternal lives.

They had the saving, exalting gospel, but it had not been made the center of their lives. They knew the way but gave only a small measure of loyalty and devotion. I ask you: What value is a car without an engine, a cup without water, a table without food, a lamp without oil?

Rushing for their lamps to light their way through the blackness, half of them found them empty. They had cheated themselves. They were fools, these five unprepared virgins. Apparently, the bridegroom had tarried for reasons that were sufficient and good. Time had passed, and he had not come. They had heard of his coming for so long, so many times, that the statement seemingly became meaningless to them. Would he ever come? So long had it been since they began expecting him that they were rationalizing that he would never appear. Perhaps it was a myth.

Hundreds of thousands of us today are in this position. Confidence has been dulled and patience worn thin. It is so hard to wait and be prepared always. But we cannot allow ourselves to slumber. The Lord has given us this parable as a special warning.

At midnight, the vital cry was made, "Behold, the bridegroom cometh; go ye out to meet him." Then all the virgins arose and trimmed their lamps.

Even the foolish ones trimmed their lamps, but their oil was used up and they had none to refill the lamps. They hastened to make up for lost time. Now, too late, they were becoming conscious of the tragedy of unpreparedness. They had been taught. They had been warned all their lives.

At midnight! Precisely at the darkest hour, when least expected, the bridegroom came. When the world is full of tribulation and help is needed, but it seems the time must be past and hope is vain, then Christ will come. The midnights of life are the times when heaven comes to offer its joy for man's weariness. But when the cry sounds, there is no time for preparation. The lamps then make patterns of joy on the hillside, and the procession moves on toward the house of banqueting, and those without lamps or oil are left in darkness. When they have belatedly sought to fulfill the requirements and finally reach the hall, the door is shut. In the daytime, wise and unwise seemed alike; midnight is the time of test and judgment—and of offered gladness.

Paul wrote:

> For yourselves know perfectly that the day of the Lord so cometh as a thief in the night.
>
> Therefore let us not sleep, as do others; but let us watch and be sober.
>
> For they that sleep sleep in the night; and they that be drunken are drunken in the night. (1 Thessalonians 5:2, 6-7.)

The foolish asked the others to share their oil, but spiritual preparedness cannot be shared in an instant. The wise had to go, else the bridegroom would have gone unwelcomed. They needed all their oil for themselves; they could not save the foolish. The responsibility was each for himself.

This was not selfishness or unkindness. The kind of oil that is needed to illuminate the way and light up the darkness is not shareable. How can one share obedience to the principle of tithing; a mind at peace from righteous living; an accumulation of knowledge? How can one share faith or testimony? How can one share attitudes or chastity, or the experience of a mission? How can one share temple privileges? Each must obtain that kind of oil for himself.

The foolish virgins were not averse to buying oil. They knew they should have oil. They merely procrastinated, not knowing when the bridegroom would come.

In the parable, oil can be purchased at the market. In our lives the oil of preparedness is accumulated drop by drop in righteous living. Attendance at sacrament meetings adds oil to our lamps, drop by drop over the years. Fasting, family prayer, home teaching, control of bodily appetites, preaching the gospel, studying the scriptures—each act of dedication and obedience is a drop added to our store. Deeds of kindness, payment of offerings and tithes, chaste thoughts and actions, marriage in the covenant for eternity—these, too, contribute importantly to the oil with which we can at midnight refuel our exhausted lamps.

Midnight is so late for those who have procrastinated.

> But behold, your days of probation are past; ye have procrastinated the day of your salvation until it is everlastingly too late, and your destruction is made sure. . . . (Helaman 13:38.)

In Tennyson's poem "Guinevere," the queen, repenting her infidelity, recognizes that the harm she has caused cannot be undone:

> Late, late, so late! and dark the night and chill!
> Late, late, so late! but we can enter still!
> Too late, too late, ye cannot enter now.
>
> No light had we; for that we do repent;
> And learning this the bridegroom will relent.
> Too late, too late! ye cannot enter now.
>
> No light; so late! and dark and chill the night!
> O let us in, that we may find the light!
> Too late, too late: ye cannot enter now.
>
> Have we not heard the bridegroom is so sweet?
> O let us in tho' late, to kiss his feet!
> No, no, too late! ye cannot enter now.

The day of the marriage feast approaches. The coming of the Lord is nigh. And there are many among us who are not ready for the great and glorious event. Of such the Lord said:

> And that servant, which knew his lord's will, and prepared not himself, neither did according to his will, shall be beaten with many stripes.
>
> But he that knew not, and did commit things worthy of stripes, shall be beaten with few stripes. For unto whomsoever much is given, of him shall be much required: and to whom men have committed much, of him they will ask the more. (Luke 12:47-48.)

For those who heed the warning and make their preparations, for those found at midnight with the oil of righteousness in their lamps, for those with patience, long-suffering, and full dedication, the promise is that they shall sit down at the banquet with their Lord.

> And at that day, when I shall come in my glory, shall the parable be fulfilled which I spake concerning the ten virgins.
>
> For they that are wise and have received the truth, and have taken the Holy Spirit for their guide, and have not been deceived—verily I say unto you, they shall not be hewn down and cast into the fire, but shall abide the day.
>
> And the earth shall be given unto them for an inheritance; and they shall multiply and wax strong, and their children shall grow up without sin unto salvation. (D&C 45:56-58.)
>
> . . . and God himself shall be with them, and be their God.
>
> And God shall wipe away all tears from their eyes; and there shall be no more death, neither sorrow, nor crying, neither shall there by any more pain: for the former things are passed away.
>
> And he that sat upon the throne said. . . .
>
> He that overcometh shall inherit all things; and I will be his God, and he shall be my son. (Revelation 21:3-5, 7.)

# Chapter Twenty-four

# *Glimpses of Heaven*

In the temple on the fourth floor is the room of the Council of the Twelve Apostles with large chairs in a semicircle. Here important meetings of that body are held. Around its walls are portraits of the brethren. When I came to this service, I looked upon them with admiration and affection, for these were truly great men with whom I was associated.

Sometime later invitation was given by the First Presidency of the Church for my portrait to be added to the others.

Lee Greene Richards was selected as the artist, and we began immediately. I sat on a chair on an elevated platform in his studio and tried very hard to look handsome, like some of the other brethren. With paints, brushes, and palette ready, the artist scrutinized my features and daubed on the canvas alternately. I returned many times to the studio. After weeks the portrait was exhibited to the First Presidency and to my wife and daughter, but it it did not satisfy them and I was asked to submit to further sittings.

The angle was changed, the hours—many of them—

were spent, and finally the portrait was near completion. This particular day was a busy one like most others. I suppose I was daydreaming, and seemed detached from this world. Apparently he had difficulty translating my far-away gaze onto the canvas. I saw the artist lay down his palette and paints, fold his arms, and look straight at me, and I was shocked out of my dreaming by the abrupt question: "Brother Kimball, have you ever been to heaven?"

My answer seemed to be a shock of equal magnitude to him as I said without hesitation: "Why, yes, Brother Richards, certainly. I had a glimpse of heaven just before coming to your studio." I saw him assume a relaxed position and look intently at me, wondering. I continued:

"Yes. Just an hour ago. It was in the holy temple across the way. The sealing room was shut off from the noisy world by its thick, white-painted walls; the drapes, light and warm; the furniture, neat and dignified; the mirrors on two opposite walls seeming to take one in continuous likenesses on and on into infinity; and the beautiful stained-glass window in front of me giving such a peaceful glow. All the people in the room were dressed in white. Here were peace and harmony and eager anticipation. A well-groomed young man and an exquisitely gowned woman, lovely beyond description, knelt across the altar. Authoritatively, I pronounced the heavenly ceremony which married and sealed them for eternity on earth and in the celestial worlds. The pure in heart were there. Heaven was there.

"When the eternal marriage was solemnized, and as the subdued congratulations were extended, a happy father, radiant in his joy, offered his hand and said, 'Brother Kimball, my wife and I are common people and have never been successful, but we *are* immensely proud of our family.' He continued, 'This is the last of our eight children to come into this holy house for temple marriage. They, with their companions, are here to participate in the marriage of this, the youngest. This is our supremely happy day, with all of our eight children married properly. They are faithful to the Lord in church service, and the older ones are already rearing families in righteousness.'

"I looked at his calloused hands, his rough exterior, and thought to myself, 'Here is a real son of God fulfilling his destiny.'

" 'Success?' I said, as I grasped his hand. 'That is the greatest success story I have heard. You might have accumulated millions in stocks and bonds, bank accounts, lands, industries, and still be quite a failure. You are fulfilling the purpose for which you were sent into this world by keeping your own lives righteous, bearing and rearing this great posterity, and training them in faith and works. Why, my dear folks, you are eminently successful. God bless you.' "

My story was finished. I looked up at the portrait artist. He stood motionless in deep thought, so I continued: "Yes, my brother, I have had many glimpses of heaven.

"Once we were in a distant stake for conference. We came to the unpretentious home of the stake president at mid-day Saturday. We knocked at the door, and it was opened by a sweet mother with a child in her arms. She was the type of mother who did not know there were maids and servants. She was not an artist's model, nor a society woman. Her hair was dressed neatly; her clothes were modest, tastefully selected; her face was smiling; and though young, she showed the rare combination of maturity of experience and the joys of purposeful living.

"The house was small. The all-purpose room into which we were welcomed was crowded and in its center were a long table and many chairs. We freshened up in the small bedroom assigned to us, made available by 'farming out' to the neighbors some of the children, and we returned to this living room. She had been very busy in the kitchen. Her husband, the stake president, soon returned from his day's labors and made us welcome and proudly introduced us to all of the children as they returned from their chores and play.

"Almost like magic the supper was ready, for 'many hands make light work,' and these numerous hands were deft and experienced ones. Every child gave evidence of having been taught responsibility. Each had certain duties. One child had quickly spread a tablecloth; another placed the knives and forks and spoons; and another covered them with the large plates turned upside down. Next came large pitchers of creamy milk, high piles of sliced homemade bread, a bowl at each place, a dish of fruit from storage, and a plate of cheese.

"One child placed the chairs with backs to the table, and without confusion, we all knelt at the chairs facing the table. One young son was called on to lead in family prayer. It was extemporaneous, and he pleaded with the Lord to bless the family and their schoolwork, and the missionaries, and the bishop. He prayed for us who had come to hold conference that we would 'preach good,' for his father in his church responsibilities, for all the children that 'they would be good, and kind to each other,' and for the little cold shivering lambs being born in the lambing sheds on the hill this wintry night.

"A very little one said the blessing on the food, and thirteen plates were turned up and thirteen bowls filled, and supper proceeded. No apologies were offered for the meal, the home, the children, or the general situation. The conversation was constructive and pleasant. The children were well-behaved. These parents met every situation with calm dignity and poise.

"In these days of limited families, or childless ones, when homes often have only one or two selfish and often pampered children, homes of luxury with servants, broken homes where life moves outside the home, it was most refreshing to sit with a large family where interdependence and love and harmony were visible and where children were growing up in unselfishness. So content and comfortable were we in the heart of this sweet simplicity and wholesomeness that we gave no thought to the unmatched chairs, the worn rug, the inexpensive curtains, the numbers of souls that were to occupy the few rooms available."

I paused. "Yes, Brother Richards, I glimpsed heaven that day and many days, in many places." He seemed uninterested in his painting. He stood listening, seemingly eager for more, and almost involuntarily I was telling him of another flight into heavenly situations.

"This time it was on the Indian reservation. While most Navajo women seem to be prolific, this sweet Lamanite wife in their several years of marriage had not been blessed with children of her own. Her husband was well employed. These new converts to the Church were buying their weekend groceries. As we glanced at the purchases in the large, well-filled basket, it was evident that only wholesome food was there—no beer, no coffee, no cigarettes. 'You like Postum, do you?' we asked them, and their reply touched our hearts: 'Yes, we have had coffee and beer all our lives, but since the Mormon missionaries told us about the Word of Wisdom we use Postum, and we know it is better for the children and they like it.'

" 'Children?' we asked. 'We thought you were a childless couple.' This brought from them the explanation that they had filled their home with eighteen Navajo orphans of all ages. Their hogan was large but their hearts even larger. Unselfishness—the milk of human kindness! Love unfeigned! These good Indians could shame many of their contemporaries who live lives of selfishness and smugness."

I said to the artist: "Heaven can be in a hogan or a tent, Brother Richards, for heaven is of our own making." I was ready to return to the picture but apparently he was not so inclined. He stood and listened intently.

"This time I was in Hawaii in the beautiful little temple at Laie. It was a missionary group. The spirit was there; the proselyters could hardly wait their turns to bear testimony of the Lord's gospel. Finally, the little Japanese missionary gained the floor. By the pulpit in her stocking feet she knelt reverently, and with a heart near bursting with gratitude for the gospel and its opportunities, she poured out her soul to heaven.

"Heaven was there, my brother, in that little room, in that sacred spot, in that paradise of the Pacific with those sweet, consecrated young soldiers for Christ."

I continued: "Heaven was in my own home, too, Dr. Richards, when home evening was held. Through the years the room was filled with our children, when each, eager for a turn, sang a song, led a game, recited an Article of Faith, told a story, and listened to faith-promoting incidents and gospel teaching from parents who loved them.

"Again, I found heaven in Europe:

"Elder Vogel was a local convert German boy of great faith. His parents refused to assist him in the mission which he so desired to fill. A kind American member helped with a monthly check to assist with the mission expenses. He enjoyed his work and all went well for a year and a half. One day a letter came from the wife of his sponsor, advising that her husband had been killed in an auto accident and it would be impossible to send any more money.

"Elder Vogel kept his disappointment hidden and prayed earnestly for a solution. As he and his American companion, Elder Smith, passed a hospital one day, a solution to his financial problem was born in his mind. The next day he made an excuse and was gone for a time. When he came back he said little but went to bed early. When asked the reason, he said he was a little extra weary. A few days later Elder Smith noted a small bandage on the arm of the German brother, but his question was passed off lightly.

"Time passed and Elder Smith became suspicious of the periodic bandages until one day, unable to keep his secret longer, Elder Vogel told him: 'You see, my friend in America is dead and can no longer give support to my mission. My parents are still unwilling to help me, so I visit the blood bank at the hospital so I can finish my mission.' Selling his precious blood to save souls! Well, isn't that what the Master did when he gave his every drop in the supreme sacrifice?

"Do you believe in heaven, Brother Artist?" I asked. "Yes, that is it. Heaven is a place, but also a condition; it is home and family. It is understanding and kindness. It is interdependence and selfless activity. It is quiet, sane living; personal sacrifice, genuine hospitality, wholesome concern for others. It is living the commandments of God without ostentation or hypocrisy. It is selflessness. It is all about us. We need only to be able to recognize it as we find it and enjoy it. Yes, my dear brother, I've had many glimpses of heaven."

I straightened up in my chair and posed again. The artist picked up his palette and brushes and paints, did some touching up of the portrait, and sighed contentedly as he said, "It is completed."

The gospel of Jesus Christ teaches men to live righteously, to make the family supreme, the home inviolate. It moves the characters of its adherents toward faultlessness. It is the true way. If lived rightly it will ennoble men toward godhood, and create in their lives heaven while they still live on earth.

# Chapter Twenty-five

# *Honor the Sabbath Day*

$\mathcal{M}$oses came down from the quaking, smoking Mount Sinai and brought to the wandering children of Israel the Ten Commandments, fundamental rules for the conduct of life. These commandments were, however, not new. They had been known to Adam and his posterity, who had been commanded to live them from the beginning, and were merely reiterated by the Lord to Moses. And the commandments even antedated earth life and were part of the test for mortals established in the council in heaven.

The first of the Ten Commandments requires that men worship the Lord; the fourth designates a Sabbath day especially for such worship:

Thou shalt have no other gods before me.

Remember the sabbath day, to keep it holy.

Six days shalt thou labour, and do all thy work:

But the seventh day is the sabbath of the Lord thy God: in it thou shalt not do any work, thou, nor thy son, nor thy daughter, thy manservant, nor thy maidservant, nor thy cattle, nor thy stranger that is within thy gates:

For in six days the Lord made heaven and earth, the sea, and all that in them is, and rested the seventh day: wherefore the Lord blessed the sabbath day, and hallowed it. (Exodus 20:3, 8-11.)

To many, Sabbath-breaking is a matter of little moment, but to our Heavenly Father it is disobedience to one of the principal commandments. It is evidence of man's failure to meet the individual test set for each of us before the creation of the world, "to see if they will do all things whatsoever the Lord their God shall command them." (Abraham 3:25.)

While attending a stake conference in the fall in a predominantly Latter-day Saint community, I was housed in a hotel. Very early Sunday morning I was awakened by considerable noise. I discovered it was caused by a number of men dressed in hunting clothes and carrying rifles. They were en route to the mountains and canyons to get their deer. When the conference day was ended and evening found us on our way home, we passed many a car returning from the hunt with a deer on the fender or on top of the car.

Another Sabbath I drove through an agricultural area and saw many mowing machines and balers and perspiring men in the fields engaged in harvesting the hay crop. Most of them must have been members of the Church.

Still another Sabbath I noticed long lines of people standing and waiting their turn to get into motion picture shows and others obviously on their way to the beach or canyon with picnic baskets and athletic equipment.

The solemn command brought down from the thundering of Mount Sinai was "Remember the sabbath day, to keep it holy." That commandment has never been rescinded nor modified. Instead, it has been reinforced in modern times:

> But remember that on this, the Lord's day, thou shalt offer thine oblations and thy sacraments unto the Most High, confessing thy sins unto thy brethren, and before the Lord.

> And on this day thou shalt do none other thing, only let thy food be prepared with singleness of heart that . . . thy joy may be full. (D&C 59:12-13.)

To hunt and fish on the Lord's day is not keeping it holy. To plant or cultivate or harvest crops on the Sabbath is not keeping holy the Lord's day. To go into the canyons for picnics, to attend games or rodeos or races or shows or other amusements on that day is not to keep it in holy remembrance.

Strange as it may seem, some Latter-day Saints, faithful in all other respects, justify themselves in missing their church meetings on occasion for recreational purposes, feeling that the best fishing will be missed if one is not on the stream on opening day or that the vacation will not be long enough if one does not set off on Sunday or that one will miss a movie he wanted to see if he does not go on the Sabbath. And in their breach of the Sabbath they often take their families with them.

The Savior said:

> Whosoever therefore shall break one of these least commandments, and shall teach men so, he shall be called the least in the kingdom of heaven. . . . (Matthew 5:19.)

There is no criticism of legitimate recreation—sports, picnics, plays, and motion pictures; all have potential for revitalizing life, and the Church as an organization actively sponsors such activities; but there is a proper time and place for all worthwhile things—a time for work, a time for play, a time for worship.

Sometimes Sabbath observance is characterized as a matter of sacrifice and self-denial, but it is not so. It is merely a matter of shifting times and choosing seasons. There is time enough, particularly in our era of the world's history, during the six days of the week in which to do our work and play. Much can be done to organize and encourage weekday activities, avoiding the Sabbath.

A Scout council was accustomed to arranging its summer camp schedule so that the Scouts were moving to the camp on one Sabbath and returning home from camp on the next Sabbath. Latter-day Saint youth were being deprived of religious activities for two successive Sundays. A friendly suggestion to the council authorities brought about a change, so that the camp period ran from Friday to Friday. The Sunday in between was planned so that there was religious observance for the boys who were in the camp.

A seminary group planned a service in the mountains on Sunday. They felt justified in the excursion since they had planned a testimony meeting as part of the day's activities. They did have their meeting and enjoyed a spiritual hour together, but after that hour the day became a day for picnicking, games, hiking, and climbing, with no further thought of the Sabbath. The one hour of devotion did not make of that day a holy day.

The purpose of the commandment is not to deprive man of something. Every commandment that God has given to his servants is for the benefit of those who receive and obey it. It is man who profits by the careful and strict observance; it is man who suffers by the breaking of the laws of God.

The commandment has its negative side, that on the Sabbath "thou shalt not do any work," but it also has its positive aspect. On that day ". . . thou shalt go to the house of prayer and offer up thy sacraments . . . to pay thy devotions unto the Most High . . . with cheerful hearts and countenances. . . ." (D&C 59:9-10, 15.)

The Sabbath is not a day for indolent lounging about the house or puttering around in the garden, but is a day for consistent attendance at meetings for the worship of the Lord, drinking at the fountain of knowledge and instruction, enjoying the family, and finding uplift in music and song.

It is a day for reading the scriptures, visiting the sick, visiting relatives and friends, doing home teaching, working on genealogy records, taking a nap, writing letters to missionaries and servicemen or relatives, preparation for the following week's church lessons, games with the small children, fasting for a purpose, writing devotional poetry, and other worthwhile activities of great variety.

One good but mistaken man I know claimed he could get more out of a good book on Sunday than he could get in attending church services, saying that the sermons were hardly up to his standards. But we do not go to Sabbath meetings to be entertained or even simply to be instructed. We go to worship the Lord. It is an individual responsibility, and regardless of what is said from the pulpit, if one wishes to worship the Lord in spirit and in truth, he may do so by attending his meetings, partaking of the sacrament, and contemplating the beauties of the gospel. If the service is a failure to you, you have failed. No one can worship for you; you must do your own waiting upon the Lord.

With respect to this commandment, among the others, let us follow the prophet Joshua:

> Now therefore fear the Lord, and serve him in sincerity and in truth . . . choose you this day whom ye will serve. . . . but as for me and my house, we will serve the Lord. (Joshua 24:14-15.)

Then we can hope for the blessings promised the children of Israel:

> Ye shall keep my sabbaths, and reverence my sanctuary: I am the Lord.
>
> If ye walk in my statutes, and keep my commandments, and do them;
>
> Then I will give you rain in due season, and the land shall yield her increase, and the trees of the field shall yield their fruit.
>
> And your threshing shall reach unto the vintage, and the vintage shall reach unto the sowing time: and ye shall eat your bread to the full, and dwell in your land safely.
>
> And I will give peace in the land, and ye shall lie down, and none shall make you afraid. . . . (Leviticus 26:2-6.)

Doug Stearns

_____

_____

The Fading of Pharaoh's Curse:
The Decline and Fall of the
Priesthood Ban Against Blacks
In the Mormon Church, Dialogue
14, no. 3 ( Autumn 1981).

Mormonism's Negro Doctrine:
An Historical Overview, Dialogue
8, no. 1 (Spring 1973).

The Latter-Day Saints  Berrett

351, 52, 53.,  368, 69.

# Chapter Twenty-six

# *Hidden Treasures of Knowledge*

*I* sat one day with an attorney friend across the directors' room table of my office in Arizona.

In his slow, pleasant drawl, he said, "I came to congratulate you on your call to the apostleship and to visit with you before you move to Salt Lake City." We talked about what my call entailed, and then he told me one of his experiences when he was a student at George Washington University Law School.

A number of young members of the Church were students there. Since there were no stakes in the East at that time, they held a Sunday School class in a rented residence, and Congressman Don B. Colton from Utah was their teacher.

This particular Sunday morning, they were considering the 89th section of the Doctrine and Covenants, the Lord's law of health.

Brother Colton had made an impressive presentation on the Word of Wisdom, which is "the order and will of God in the temporal salvation of all saints in the last days."

He emphasized also the further statement of the Lord:

> In consequence of evils and designs which do and will exist in the hearts of conspiring men in the last days, I have warned you, and forewarn you, by giving unto you this word of wisdom by revelation. (D&C 89:4.)

The Lord is displeased when his earthly children imbibe "wine and strong drink." He said that "tobacco is not for the body . . . and is not good for man." And, again, ". . . hot drinks are not for the body. . . ."

Brother Colton emphasized the rich promise made by the Lord to those who did observe this law of health:

> And all saints who remember to keep and do these sayings, walking in obedience to the commandments. . . . shall find wisdom and great treasures of knowledge, even hidden treasures; And I, the Lord, give unto them a promise, that the destroying angel shall pass by them, as the children of Israel, and not slay them. Amen. (D&C 89:18-19, 21.)

Then came a question from one of the students: "Brother Colton, the promise is that if one observes these laws, he shall find 'wisdom and great treasures of knowledge, even hidden treasures.' Many of the men in this university use tobacco and liquor and break all commandments including the law of chastity, and yet in some cases excel academically. So far as I can tell, my obedience to the Word of Wisdom has not made me superior intellectually to them. Why is that?"

Brother Colton held this question for the next week.

On Friday, as usual, several of the Congressmen were eating luncheon at the House of Representatives restaurant when Brother Colton joined them. The others began to joke in a friendly fashion, "Hide the cigarettes and coffee cups. Here comes the Mormon Congressman." A Congressman from a western state came to the defense, saying, "Gentlemen, you may joke about Mr. Colton and have your fun at the expense of the Mormon Church, but let me tell you an experience."

He told a story something like this:

"I was back in my home state, building political fences, shaking hands with voters, getting acquainted with my people. Sunday overtook me in a country town.

"I sat in the lobby of the hotel, reading the paper, and through the plate glass window I saw many people going in the same direction. My curiosity was stirred. I followed them to a little church and slid unobtrusively into a back seat and listened and observed.

"This church service was different. I had never seen one like it. A man called the bishop conducted the meeting. The singing was by the congregation, the prayer by a man from the audience, apparently called without previous notice. Soft music was played. All was silent as one young man knelt and said a prayer over bread which he and his companion had broken into small pieces, and then several boys, probably twelve or thirteen years of age, took plates of broken bread and passed it to the congregation. The same was done with the little cups of water. After the choir sang an anthem, I expected a sermon, but the bishop announced, 'Brothers and Sisters, today is our monthly fast and testimony service, and you may proceed to speak as you feel led by the Spirit. This time is not for sermons, but to speak of your own soul and your inner feelings and assurances. The time is yours.'"

The Congressman paused, then continued:

"Never before had I experienced anything like this. From the congregation people arose. One man in a dignified voice said how he loved the Church and the gospel and what it meant in the life of his family.

"From another part of the chapel a woman stood and spoke with deep conviction of a spectacular healing in her family as an answer to prayer and fasting, and closed with what the people called a testimony—that the gospel of Jesus Christ as taught by the Church was true; that it brought great happiness and a deep peace to her.

"Still another woman arose and bore witness of her sureness that Joseph Smith was truly a prophet of God and had been the instrument of the Lord in restoring the true gospel of Christ to the earth.

"A man from the choir, evidently a recent immigrant, seemed sensitive about his language. He was struggling with his v's and his w's, and verbs and sentence construction. Two years ago, two young missionaries in faraway Holland had taught him the restored gospel. He told how happy his family had been since embracing it and what a transformation had come in their lives.

"The old and the middle-aged and the youth responded. Some were farmers and laborers and there were teachers and business and professional men. There was no ostentation, no arrogance, but a quiet dignity, a warm friendliness, a sweet spirituality.

"Then came in succession several children. They spoke less of their knowledge of spiritual things but more of their love for their parents and for the Savior, of whom they had learned much in Primary and Sunday School and at home.

"Finally, the bishop stood and spoke a few appropriate words of commendation, expressing his own sureness. Then he closed the meeting."

The Congressman noted that all around the table were intently listening. He continued:

"Never had time passed so rapidly. I had been entranced. And as each additional speaker had concluded in the name of Jesus Christ, I was moved, deeply stirred, and I pondered: How sincere! How sweet and spiritual! How sure these people seem to be of their Redeemer! How much at peace! What security they have in their spiritual knowledge; what strength and fortitude, and what purposeful lives!"

The Congressman said, "I thought of my own children and grandchildren and their helter-skelter existence, their self-centered activities, their seeming spiritual vacuums, their routine lives in search of wealth and fun and adventure. And I said to myself with an enthusiasm new to me, 'How I wish my own posterity could have this sureness, this faith, this deep conviction. Why, these humble people seem to have a secret that most people do not enjoy, something worth more than all else—a hidden treasure of spiritual wholeness.' "

The luncheon ended. The Congressmen moved back to their offices.

Another Sunday came and Elder Colton was again before his Sunday School class of young college men. He retold the story and said that what the Congressman had observed were the "hidden treasures of knowledge" promised by the revelations. These mysteries of the kingdom related to all truths, not merely scientific accomplishments and legal cases and other secular things. He said "treasures of knowledge" extended far beyond material things, out into the infinite areas not explored by many otherwise brilliant people. He repeated the scriptural statement that has become proverbial among members of the Church: "The glory of God is intelligence, or, in other words, light and truth." (D&C 93:36.)

Knowledge is not merely the equations of algebra, the theorems of geometry, or the miracles of space. It is the knowledge as recorded in Hebrews by which "the worlds were framed by the word of God"; by which "Enoch was translated that he should not see death"; by which Noah, with a knowledge no other human had, built an ark on dry land and saved a race by taking seed through the flood. (See Hebrews 11:3, 5, 7.)

This hidden knowledge is that power which raises one into new and higher worlds and elevates him into new spiritual realms.

The treasures of both secular and spiritual knowledge are hidden ones, but hidden only from those who do not properly search and strive to find them. The knowledge of the spiritual will not come to an individual without effort, any more than will the secular knowledge. Spiritual knowledge gives the power to live eternally and to rise and overcome and develop and finally to create.

Hidden knowledge is not unfindable. It is available to all who really search. The Christ said, "Seek and ye shall find."

But spiritual knowledge is not available merely for the asking. Even prayers are not enough. It takes also persistence and dedication of life.

The knowledge of things in secular life is of time and is limited; the knowledge of the infinite truths is of time *and* eternity.

Of all treasures of knowledge, the most vital is the knowledge of God, his existence, powers, love, and promises.

Christ said:

> He that hath my commandments, and keepeth them, he it is that loveth me: and he that loveth me shall be loved of my Father, and I will love him, and will manifest myself to him. (John 14:21.)

And the prophet Joseph Smith explained that this means that the coming of the Father and the Son to a person is a reality—a personal appearance—and not merely dwelling in his heart. (See D&C 130:3.)

This personal witness is the ultimate treasure.

One may acquire knowledge of space and in a limited degree conquer it. He may explore the moon and other planets, but no man can ever really find God in a university campus laboratory, in the physical test tubes of workshops, nor on the testing fields at Cape Kennedy. God and his program will be found only in deep pondering, appropriate reading, much kneeling in devout humble prayer and in a sincerity born of need and dependence.

These requirements having been fully met, there is no soul between the poles nor from ocean to ocean who may not positively obtain this knowledge, this hidden treasure of knowledge, this saving and exalting knowledge.

President Joseph Fielding Smith, speaking at the Brigham Young University, quoted from latter-day revelation: ". . . man cannot be saved in ignorance," and then asked the question:

> Ignorance of what? By that, do we mean that a man must become proficient in his secular learning—that he must master some branch of education? What does it mean?

> That a man cannot be saved in ignorance of the saving principles of the Gospel. We cannot be saved without faith in God. We cannot be saved in our sins. . . . We must receive the ordinances and the covenants pertaining to the Gospel and be true and faithful to the end. Eventually, if we are faithful and true, we shall gain all knowledge, but that is not required of us in this brief, mortal life for that would be impossible. But here in faith and integrity to the truth, we lay the foundation upon which we build for eternity.

Real intelligence is the creative use of knowledge, not merely an accumulation of facts.

The ultimate and greatest of all knowledge, then, is to know God and his program for our exaltation. We may know him by sight, by sound, by feeling. While relatively few ever *do* really know him, everyone *may* know him, not only prophets—ancient and modern—but, as he said:

> . . . every soul who forsaketh his sins and cometh unto me, and calleth on my name, and obeyeth my voice, and keepeth my commandments, shall see my face and know that I am. (D&C 93:1.)

If men qualify, they have this unalterable promise from their Redeemer.

In one of his prayers, Jesus said:

> I thank thee, O Father, Lord of heaven and earth, because thou hast hid these things from the wise and prudent, and hast revealed them unto babes. (Matthew 11:25.)

Paul said:

But we speak the wisdom of God in a mystery, even the hidden wisdom, which God ordained before the world unto our glory:

Which none of the princes of this world knew. . . .

For what man knoweth the things of a man, save the spirit of man which is in him? even so the things of God knoweth no man, but the Spirit of God. (1 Corinthians 2:7-8, 11.)

To have both the secular and spiritual is the ideal. To have only the secular is, as Jude said:

. . . clouds they are without water, carried about of winds; trees whose fruit withereth. . . . (Jude 12.)

The secular knowledge is to be *desired;* the spiritual knowledge is a *necessity.* We shall need all of the accumulated secular knowledge in order to create worlds and furnish them, but only through the mysteries of God and these hidden treasures of knowledge may we arrive at the place and condition where we may use that knowledge in creation and exaltation.

We must learn to master ourselves, by obedience to the Lord's law of health and his other laws, by control of our physical appetites, and by placing first in our lives the service of God and our fellowmen, so that the hidden things of the spirit may come to us and we attain perfection with the Father and the Son.

# Chapter Twenty-seven

# "*Render . . . Unto God*"

*T*he Pharisees, ever trying to entangle and trick the Savior, again set their traps:

> . . . Is it lawful to give tribute unto Caesar? . . .
>
> But Jesus perceived their wickedness. . . .
>
> . . . Then saith he unto them, Render therefore unto Caesar the things which are Caesar's; and unto God the things that are God's. (Matthew 22:17-18, 21.)

One day a friend wanted me to go with him to his ranch. He opened the door of a new automobile, slid under the wheel, and said, "How do you like my new car?" We rode in luxurious air-conditioned comfort out through the countryside to an elegant landscaped home, and he said with no little pride, "This is my home."

He drove on to a grassy knoll. The sun was retiring behind the distant hills. Pointing to the north, he asked, "Do you see that clump of trees?" I could plainly discern them in the fading day.

He pointed to the east, "Do you see the lake?" It too was visible shimmering in the sunset.

"Now, the bluff that's on the south." We turned about

to scan the distance southward. Then he pointed out the barns, silos, the ranch house to the west. With a wide sweeping gesture, he boasted, "From the clump of trees, to the lake, to the bluff, and to the ranch buildings and all between—all this is mine. And the herd of cattle in the meadow—those are mine, too."

I knew this was a man with great ability as an organizer, intelligent and resourceful, yet he lived in many ways a narrow life. His possessions seemed to own him. He turned away opportunities to serve in the Church because his ranch kept him "too busy," and he contributed little financially because he was always "short of cash because everything is tied up in the ranch."

I could not help thinking of one of the parables of Christ:

> The ground of a certain rich man brought forth plentifully:
>
> And he thought within himself, saying, What shall I do, because I have no room where to bestow my fruits?
>
> And he said, This will I do: I will pull down my barns, and build greater; and there will I bestow all my fruits and my goods.
>
> And I will say to my soul, Soul, thou hast much goods laid up for many years; take thine ease, eat, drink, and be merry.
>
> But God said unto him, Thou fool, this night thy soul shall be required of thee: then whose shall those things be, which thou hast provided?
>
> So is he that layeth up treasure for himself, and is not rich toward God. (Luke 12:16-21.)

The Psalmist said:

> The earth is the Lord's, and the fulness thereof; the world, and they that dwell therein.
>
> For he hath founded it upon the seas, and established it upon the floods. (Psalms 24:1-2.)

My friend was proud that he had developed his ranch from the desert with his own strength and toil, but where had he obtained that strength and where had he obtained the land and the water with which to make it productive, if not from the Lord?

> Thou, O God, didst send a plentiful rain, whereby thou didst confirm thine inheritance, when it was weary. (Psalms 68:9.)

If the earth is the Lord's, then we are merely tenants and owe our landlord an accounting. The scripture says: "Render unto Caesar that which is Caesar's, and to God that which is God's." What percentage of our increase do we pay Caesar? And what percent to God?

The command of the Lord through the prophet Malachi reads:

> Will a man rob God? Yet ye have robbed me. But ye say, Wherein have we robbed thee? In tithes and offerings.
>
> Bring ye all the tithes into the storehouse . . . and prove me now herewith, saith the Lord of hosts, if I will not open you the windows of heaven, and pour you out a blessing, that there shall not be room enough to receive it. (Malachi 3:8, 10.)

And in the latter days, the Lord said again:

> And if ye seek the riches which it is the will of the Father to give unto you, ye shall be the richest of all people, for ye shall have the riches of eternity; and it must needs be that the riches of the earth are mine to give. . . . (D&C 38:39.)

There is no place in holy writ where God has said, "I give you title to this land unconditionally." It is not ours to give, to have, to hold, to sell, despoil, exploit as we see fit.

Modern scripture says that if you live the commandments,

> the fulness of the earth is yours, the beasts of the field and the fowls of the air, . . .
>
> Yea, all things which come of the earth . . . are made for the benefit and the use of man. . . . (D&C 59:16, 18.)

This promise does not seem to convey the earth but only the use and contents that are given to men on condition that they live all of the commandments of God.

That was long years ago. I later saw my friend lying

in death among luxurious furnishings in his palatial home. And I folded his arms upon his breast and drew down the little curtains over his eyes. I spoke at his funeral, and I followed the cortege from the good piece of earth he had claimed to his grave, a tiny, oblong area the length of a tall man, the width of a heavy one.

Recently I saw that same estate, yellow in grain, green in lucerne, white in cotton, seemingly unmindful of him who had claimed it.

Oh, puny man, thou art the busy ant moving the sands of the sea.

It is not only the rancher who is a tenant of the Lord's. I stopped on the highway to buy some fruit from a man I knew. The fruit stand was on the edge of the orchard. And I asked him, "Are these trees yours?"

He said, "From the highway to the hill—all these are mine, and all the fruit we pick and sell."

And I thought to say, "Do you have no partner? You bought the land and the seedlings. But who put chemicals into the soil to make them grow? Who sent the living sap climbing all the limbs? Who made them bloom and scent the air with sweet perfume? Did you make the rain? Can you command the sun? Do you put instructions in the trees to produce buds and blossoms, fruit in ripeness, taste and food value? He who made the land, the trees, and the elements has land-lien on it all. Have you settled your lease payment?

"I am sure you pay to Caesar his full portion, never failing. But do you calculate and pay the part to God?

"Are these trees yours and yours alone? Is there no partner's claim upon the fruit?

"Have you integrity? Would you rob God, your partner, remembering that the earth is the Lord's and the fulness thereof?

"When God had created man and woman he placed

them upon the earth to 'dress it and to keep it and subdue it.' (See Genesis 2:15.) It seems this landlord-tenant relationship is fair—the Lord, the owner, furnishes the land, the air, the water, the sunshine, and all the elements to make it fruitful. The tenant gives his labor."

The Lord promised after the deluge:

> While the earth remaineth, seedtime and harvest, and cold and heat, and summer and winter, and day and night shall not cease. (Genesis 8:22.)

And the psalmist sang again:

> Thou visitest the earth, and waterest it; thou greatly enrichest it with the river of God, . . .

> Thou waterest the ridges thereof abundantly: thou settlest the furrows thereof: thou makest it soft with showers. . . .

> The pastures are clothed with flocks; . . . they shout for joy, they also sing. (Psalms 65:9-10, 13.)

> . . . the earth is full of the goodness of the Lord. (Psalms 33:5.)

A month later, a car accident took the life of this horticulturist. He had not paid his keep, nor did he take his orchard with him. Each spring its trees still bloom; each fall the luscious fruit is picked.

I saw a lovely house upon a beach. The occupant boastfully pointed to it as a thing of beauty, built solid enough to withstand the storms.

One day a warning came. A tidal wave rushed in to shore. All occupants were saved, but as the great sea hurried back to its place, only a concrete floor marked the place where his prized possession had stood. The stones were out at sea, the lumber ground to toothpicks, floating in the water. And I remembered how often the psalmist criticized man for his vanity.

Another day I accompanied a friend to his bank. He checked the contents of his safety deposit box, and, lifting out a handful of stocks and bonds and deeds, he proudly said to me, "All these are mine. These represent the labor of a lifetime."

And I pondered: "How you have prospered! How did you do so well? Where did you get your talents, your abilities? Did you create your sight and voice and memory and ability to think?

"Do you pay tithes? Do you render unto God that which already was his own? I'm sure that Caesar never fails to get his portion. What of God? You accepted your earthly opportunities on condition. You rented his land, his equipment, used his elements, you know.

"Does puny man possess, appropriate, bequeath, and give as though he made the earth and heaven? And this without report or settling accounts?"

I met a man upon the campus of a great university, well-trained and brilliant, holding high degrees. We talked of income. Though his was very large, he felt it all too small to meet his needs.

"Do you pay tithes?"

Why should he pay? He earned it—every cent. I told him of the psalmist's theme:

"The earth is the Lord's, and the fulness thereof; the world, and they that dwell therein."

And he countered, "I claim no earth. I use no elements—I train the minds of men. I owe no debts to anyone. I earn my income."

And then I asked, "By what great power do you earn?"

"My brains," he said.

And then I asked: "Where did your brains find birth? Did you create them? build them in a factory? buy them in a store? Did you add element to element, fashioning them so intricately and giving them such power? Where did you get your strength, your vision, power, and health? Where did you get your breath, your continuity? Do you make brains, build bodies, create souls?"

This man was arrogant and proud. Like the others he needed the admonition given the rebellious Israelites:

> Beware that thou forget not the Lord thy God . . . his commandments . . . and his statutes. . . .
>
> And when thy herds and thy flocks . . . thy silver and thy gold . . . and all that thou hast is multiplied;
>
> Then thine heart be lifted up, and thou forget the Lord thy God, . . .
>
> Who led thee through . . . drought, where there was no water; who brought thee forth water out of the rock of flint; . . .
>
> And thou say in thine heart, My power and the might of mine hand hath gotten me this wealth.
>
> But thou shalt remember the Lord thy God: for it is he that giveth thee power to get wealth. . . . (Deuteronomy 8:11, 13-15, 17-18.)

For long years he had been misusing funds—appropriating the tenth which belonged to his Creator. What right had he to use without permission the Lord's lease funds, and without accounting and without the commensurate worthiness and faithfulness on which his nine-tenths were promised? He had forgotten Malachi's question: "Will a man rob God?" (Malachi 3:8.)

I outlived this man, too. It was a sad affair when his time came. The strong was weak, the powerful inanimate. His brains still encased in his cranium would work no more. He breathed no air; he taught no youth, commanded no more hearers, no more salary; he occupied no apartment but did occupy a little plot of earth on a grassy hillside. But now, I hope he knows that "the earth is the Lord's, and all that therein is."

I asked another man if he paid tithes. He answered with a blush, "We cannot afford to tithe."

"What? Cannot afford integrity? Cannot afford to return to the Great Provider's program that which was already his?"

He said, "My schooling was expensive. Our little ones have cost us much, and there is still another one to come. The doctor and the hospital will take their toll. Our car was wrecked and cost us that much more. Vacation, illness, living costs go up and leave us none to give the Church."

"Do you believe in God?"

"Of course," he said.

"You do?" I asked. "Would God make promises he would not fulfill? You have no confidence in God, else why do you doubt his glorious promises? Your faith is in yourself. God promised he would open heaven's windows and pour you out rich gifts beyond your comprehension, premised on your faithfulness. Do you not need those blessings? For that one-tenth, he'll compensate with blessings little dreamed of. He said: 'Eye hath not seen, nor ear heard, neither have entered into the heart of man, the things which God hath prepared for them that love him.' (1 Corinthians 2:9.)

"And again:

" '. . .seek ye first the kingdom of God, and his righteousness; and all these things shall be added unto you.' (Matthew 6:33.)

"You don't believe that God will measure up? No, you do not trust your Lord. You keep all the funds you have collected and use them according to your own judgment. You fear he would not make good his promises.

"Your very debts, your many troubles show incompetence to handle your affairs. You've partly failed in your rich stewardship. Can you control your business better than the Lord? Would you do well to use this manager in whom you have no trust? We know he will not fail."

Tithing is not for God. It is we who clip the coupons and collect the dividends.

A salaried man complained: "My neighbor has a

farm. His family lives upon it. We buy our living from a store with cash. They kill a beef, a pork, and feed themselves from their deep freeze. Their garden loads the table with vegetables; the field feeds the cows that furnish milk products; their farm grows wheat for the poultry for the table; and the hens furnish meat and eggs. Shouldn't he pay tithes on his farm land production?"

The answer is: Of course, he should pay if he is true to his commitments. No honest man would rob his Lord of tithes and offerings.

We ask again: Do you feel generous when you pay your tithes? Boastful when the amount is large? Has the child been generous to his parents when he washes the car, makes his bed? Are you liberal when you pay your rent, or pay off notes at banks? You are not generous or liberal but merely honest when you pay your tithes.

"I have made the earth, and created man upon it," says the Lord. "I, even my hands, have stretched out the heavens, and all their host have I commanded." (Isaiah 45:12.)

Perhaps your attitudes are the product of your misconceptions.

Would you steal a dollar from your friend? a tire from your neighbor's car? Would you borrow a widow's insurance money with no intent to pay? Do you rob banks? You are shocked at such suggestions. Then, would you rob your God, your Lord, who has made such generous arrangements with you?

Do you have a right to appropriate the funds of your employer with which to pay your debts, to buy a car, to clothe your family, to feed your children, to build your home?

Would you take from your neighbor's funds to send your children to college or on a mission? Would you help relatives or friends with funds not your own? Some people get their standards mixed, their ideals out of line. Would you take tithes to pay your building fund or ward maintenance contribution? Would you supply gifts to the poor with someone else's money? The Lord's money?

The Lord continues to ask: "Will a man rob God? Yet ye have robbed me." (Malachi 3:8.)

And he has said that "today . . . is a day of sacrifice, and a day for the tithing of my people." (D&C 64:23.)

Does not the law of tithing apply to all the children of men, regardless of church or creed? All who believe the Bible really must believe that this is a law of God.

There echo again and again the words of the Master: "Render therefore unto Caesar the things which are Caesar's, and unto God the things that are God's." The Lord will bless all those who love and live this law.

# SECTION FIVE

*The Restored Church*

# Chapter Twenty-eight

# "What God Hath Cleansed"

*A* while ago there came to my desk a letter anonymously written. Generally the wastebasket receives all
such messages written by people who do not have the courage to sign their statements. But this time I saved it. It
reads in part as follows:

> I never dreamed I would live to see the day when the
> Church would invite an Indian buck to talk in the Salt Lake
> Tabernacle—an Indian buck appointed a bishop—an Indian
> squaw to talk in the Ogden Tabernacle—Indians to go through
> the Salt Lake Temple. . . .
>
> The sacred places desecrated by the invasion of everything
> that is forced on the white race. . . .

If Mrs. Anonymous were the only one who felt this
way! However, from many places and different directions
I hear intolerant expressions. While there is an ever-
increasing number of people who are kind and willing to
accept the minority groups as they come into the Church,
there are still many who speak in disparaging terms, who
priest-like and Levite-like pass by on the other side of the
street, disdainful of those who especially need their help.

With ever greater speed the stone that Daniel saw
cut out of the mountain without hands is rolling forth to

fill the whole earth. From a church whose membership was for the first hundred years largely confined to the white nations of America and Europe, we have grown to a worldwide force, embracing men of all colors and cultures. And we must learn the lesson that our fellowship is as universal as God's love for all men.

In the letter quoted there is the suggestion of a superior race. From the dawn of history we have seen so-called races go down from heights to the depths in a long parade of exits. There were the Assyrians, the Egyptians, the Babylonians, the Persians, the Greeks, and the Romans. They, with more modern nations, have been defeated in battle, humiliated and crushed in economic life. Is the implication of Mrs. Anonymous justified that the white race or the American people are superior? John the Baptist, in forceful terms, rebuked a self-styled superior group:

> O generation of vipers, who hath warned you to flee from the wrath to come?
>
> Bring forth therefore fruits meet for repentance:
>
> And think not to say within yourselves, We have Abraham to our father: for I say unto you, that God is able of these stones to raise up children unto Abraham. (Matthew 3:7-9.)

The Lord would have eliminated bigotry and class distinction. He talked to the Samaritan woman at the well, healed the centurion's kin, and blessed the child of the Canaanitish woman. And though he personally came to the "lost sheep of the House of Israel" and sent his apostles first to them rather than to the Samaritans and other gentiles, yet he later sent Paul to bring the gospel to the gentiles and revealed to Peter that the gospel was for all. The prejudices were deep rooted in Peter, and it took a vision from heaven to help him cast off his bias. The voice had commanded: "Rise, Peter; kill, and eat," when the vessel descended from the heaven containing all manner of beasts, reptiles, and fowls. Punctilious Peter expressed his lifelong prejudices and habits in saying, "Not so, Lord; for I have never eaten anything that is common or unclean." Then the heavenly voice made clear that the program was for *all*. "What God hath cleansed," it said, "that call not thou common." Peter's long sustained prejudices finally gave way under the power of the thrice-repeated command. When the devout gentile Cornelius immediately thereafter appealed to him for the gospel, the full meaning of the vision burst upon Peter and he exclaimed, ". . . God hath shewed me that I should not call any man common or unclean." (Acts 10:13-15, 28.)

And when those of the circumcised complained, Peter —now very sure—rehearsed the whole story and concluded with these memorable words:

> Men and brethren, ye know how that a good while ago God made choice among us, that the Gentiles by my mouth should hear the word of the gospel, and believe.
>
> And God, which knoweth the hearts, bare them witness, giving them the Holy Ghost, even as he did unto us;
>
> And put no difference between us and them. . . . (Acts 15:7-9.)

In defense he said, ". . . what was I, that I could withstand God?" (Acts 11:17.)

The gospel had been brought to the Jew or Israel, and now was to be taken to the gentile. It was for *all*.

The Savior instructed his apostles:

> Go ye therefore, and teach all nations, baptizing them in the name of the Father, and of the Son, and of the Holy Ghost. (Matthew 28:19.)

And through the prophet Nephi the Lord—

> inviteth them all to come unto him and partake of his goodness; and he denieth none that come unto him, black and white, bond and free, male and female; and he remembereth the heathen; and all are alike unto God, both Jew and Gentile. (2 Nephi 26:33.)

A special problem exists with respect to blacks because they may not now receive the priesthood. Some members of the Church would justify their own un-Christian discrimination against blacks because of that rule with respect to the priesthood, but while this restriction has been imposed by the Lord, it is not for us to add burdens upon the shoulders of our black brethren. They who have received Christ in faith through authoritative baptism are heirs to the celestial kingdom along with men of all other races. And those who remain faithful to the end may expect that God may finally grant them all blessings they have merited through their righteousness. Such matters are in the Lord's hands. It is for us to extend our love to all.

President Lee's statement, made when he was a counselor in the First Presidency, expresses the proper attitude for us to take:

> We are having come into the Church now many people of various nationalities. . . . These who are members of the Church, regardless of their color, their national origin, are members of the church and kingdom of God. Some of them have told us that they are being shunned. There are snide remarks. We are withdrawing ourselves from them in some cases.
>
> Now we must extend the hand of fellowship to men everywhere, and to all who are truly converted and who wish to join the Church and partake of the many rewarding opportunities to be found therein. To those who may not now have the priesthood, we pray that the blessings of Jesus Christ may be given to them to the full extent that it is possible for us to give them. Meanwhile, we ask the Church members to strive to emulate the example of our Lord and Master Jesus Christ, who gave us the new commandment that we should love one another. (April, 1972.)

The fastest-growing component of Church membership, however, is not black or white, but brown—the Lamanite people of the Americas. There is a sorry history of oppression of them by white men, and, as the letter from Mrs. Anonymous indicates, members of the Church are not immune to the disease of intolerance. Yet it is particularly ironic that Church members who profess to believe the Book of Mormon would hiss and spurn a people to whom such spectacular promises are made by the Lord. Though intolerance is abhorrent anywhere, it is doubly offensive to the Lord when it is directed to those of Israel. We who are gentiles may not, without condemnation, insult and reject our Lamanite brethren.

I would say to Mrs. Anonymous and to all who feel as she does: If the Lord were to acknowledge a superior race, would it not be Israel, the very people whom you would spurn and deprive? Do you carry in your veins Israelitish blood as pure as those whom you criticize? Do you find any scriptures that would show that the Christ would exclude the Lamanite Israelites from the waters of baptism, from the priesthood, from the pulpit, or from the temple? Did not the Lord remove the Amalekites, Midianites, Canaanites to make a place for the chosen Israel?

And centuries later when he saw the impending destruction of Jerusalem and the temple and when it was imminent that Judah and Israel were to be captured and exiled, did not the Lord send a righteous few, under Lehi, to find and colonize this American land, this choicest land under heaven? Did he not lead and teach and punish and forgive this same people through a thousand hectic years of varied experience, and did he not reiterate frequently his willingness to forgive and his eagerness to bless this very people? Did not the Lord show special and preferred interest in his Israel? Did he not reserve for them alone his personal visits and ministrations? And did he not say to them:

> Ye are my disciples. . . .
>
> And behold, this is the land of your inheritance; and the Father hath given it unto you. . . .
>
> And they [the Jews] understood me not that I said they [the Lehites] shall hear my voice; and they understood me not that the Gentiles should not at any time hear my voice—that I should not manifest myself unto them save it were by the Holy Ghost.
>
> But behold, ye have both heard my voice, and seen me; and ye are my sheep, and ye are numbered among those whom the Father hath given me. (3 Nephi 15:12-13, 23-24.)

Oh, intolerance, thou art an ugly creature! What crimes have been committed under thy influence! What injustices under thy satanic spell!

Charlotte Gilman wrote: "I ran into a prejudice that quite cut off my view." ("An Obstacle," stanza 1.)

It was a hypocritical and intolerant group "which trusted in themselves that they were righteous, and despised others," to whom the Lord gave this classic parable:

> Two men went up into the temple to pray; the one a Pharisee, and the other a publican.
>
> The Pharisee stood and prayed thus with himself, God, I thank thee, that I am not as other men are, extortioners, unjust, adulterers, or even as this publican.
>
> I fast twice in the week, I give tithes of all that I possess.
>
> And the publican, standing afar off, would not lift up so much as his eyes unto heaven, but smote upon his breast, saying, God, be merciful to me a sinner.
>
> I tell you, this man went down to his house justified rather than the other: for every one that exalteth himself shall be abased; and he that humbleth himself shall be exalted. (Luke 18:9-14.)

If it be so wrong for fraternization and brotherhood with minority groups and their filling positions and pews and pulpits of the Lord's church, why did the apostle Peter maintain so positively that God "put no difference between us and them . . . "? (Acts 15:9.) And, "What God hath cleansed, that call not thou common." (Acts 11:9.) And, "Of a truth I perceive that God is no respecter of persons: But in every nation he that feareth him, and worketh righteousness, is accepted with him." (Acts 10:34-35.)

Did not the Lord know that in these times there would be many duplicates of Mr. and Mrs. Anonymous who might need the warning that he gave through his prophet Moroni:

> . . . Who will despise the works of the Lord? Who will despise the children of Christ? Behold, all ye who are despisers

of the works of the Lord, for ye shall wonder and perish. (Mormon 9:26.)

## The prophet Mormon wrote:

Yea, wo unto him that shall deny the revelations of the Lord. . . .

Yea, and ye need not any longer hiss, nor spurn, nor make game of the Jews, nor any of the remnant of the house of Israel; for behold, the Lord remembereth his covenant unto them, and he will do unto them according to that which he hath sworn. (3 Nephi 29:6, 8.)

It is most evident that all of the many prejudiced ones fail to catch the spirit of the gospel and the teachings of the Christ as they hiss and spurn and scoff and criticize. The Lord said:

Judge not, that ye be not judged.

For with what judgment ye judge, ye shall be judged. . . .

And why beholdest thou the mote that is in thy brother's eye, but considerest not the beam that is in thine own eye?

Thou hypocrite, first cast out the beam out of thine own eye; and then shalt thou see clearly to cast out the mote out of thy brother's eye. (Matthew 7:1-3, 5.)

## And again, the Lord said through Paul:

Therefore thou art inexcusable, O man, whosoever thou art that judgest: for wherein thou judgest another, thou condemnest thyself. . . .

And thinkest thou this, O man . . . that thou shalt escape the judgment of God? (Romans 2:1, 3.)

## And again through Moroni:

For behold, the same that judgeth rashly shall be judged rashly again . . . he that smiteth shall be smitten again, of the Lord. (Mormon 8:19.)

I remember that the Lord was long-suffering with ancient Israel. For a long time he endured their pettiness, listened to their eternal complaining, revolted at their filthiness, groaned at their idolatries and their adulteries, and wept at their faithlessness, and yet finally forgave them and led the rising generation of them into the promised land. They had been the victims of four centuries of destructive background of servitude, but consistent now with their continued faithfulness, every door was opened to them toward immortality and eternal life.

Here he has the Indian or Lamanite with a background of twenty-five centuries of superstition, degradation, idolatry, and indolence. He has loathed their wickedness, chastised them, brought the gentiles to them for nursing fathers and mothers, and—it would seem—has finally forgiven them. Their sufferings have been sore, their humiliation complete, their punishment severe and long, their heartaches many, and their opportunities reduced. Has he not now forgiven them and accepted them? Can we not now forgive and accept them? Ancient Israel was given forty years. Can we not allow at least forty years of patient and intensive proselyting and organizing among modern Israel before we judge too harshly?

And the same could be said of each person and group that comes into the Church burdened with the unwanted baggage of personal weakness and un-Christian cultural traditions.

What a monster prejudice is! It means prejudging. How many of us are guilty of it? Often we think ourselves free of its destructive force, but we need only to test ourselves. Our expressions, our voice tones, our movements, our thoughts betray us. We are often so willing that others make the contacts, do the proselyting, have the associations. Until we project ourselves into the very situation, we little realize our bias and our prejudice.

Why will we, the prospered, the blessed, hiss? When, oh when, will we cease to spurn? When will we who think we are free of bias purge from our souls the sometimes unconscious prejudice we possess? When will we end our making game of these different from ourselves? When will we cease throwing our pennies disdainfully to them at the gate? When will we follow the example of the Savior?

We who take pride in our own ancestry sometimes

forget the great heritage that belongs to men and groups whom we take lightly. A prime example is the long list of heroes from whom the Indians are descended. The Book of Mormon gives their history.

O ye who hiss and spurn, despise and scoff, who condemn and reject, and who in your haughty pride place yourself above and superior to these Nephite-Lamanites: I pray you do not despise them until you are able to equal their far-away folk who had such faith and fortitude and strength; until you have that faith to burn at the stake with the prophet Abinadi. It is possible that the prophet's children may be among us. Some of them could now be called Lagunas or Shoshones.

I beg of you, do not disparage the Lamanite-Nephite unless you too have the devoutness and strength to abandon public office to do missionary work among a despised people, and this without compensation, as did the four sons of Mosiah; until you too can walk away from the ease and luxury and the emoluments and power of kingship to hunger and thirst, to be persecuted, imprisoned, and beaten for fourteen years of proselyting endeavor as did their people, Ammon and his brothers, and as did the great Nephi. Some of their descendants also could be among us. Their seed could be called Samoans or Maoris.

I ask you, do not scoff and ignore these Nephite-Lamanites unless you can equal their forebears in greatness and until you can kneel with those thousands of Ammonite saints on the field of battle while they sang songs of praise as their very lives were being snuffed out by their enemies. Could you look heavenward smiling and singing while the bloodthirsty demons slashed your body with sword and cimeter? Perhaps the children of the Ammonites are with us. They could be called Zunis or Hopis.

Do not prate your power of speech or your fearlessness unless you too could stand with the prophet Samuel on the city wall, dodging stones and spears and arrows while trying to preach the gospel of salvation. The very descendants of this great prophet are with us. They may be Navajos or Cherokees.

I ask you who sneer, are you better mothers than those of the Ammonites? Those Lamanite women so trained their sons in faith that they fought many battles and came home clean, alive, full of faith. Are you training your sons as did they? Do your sons resist evil, grow to greatness, receive manifestations from the Lord? Do your sons praise your names? The posterity of these unparalleled mothers and these faithful sons may be among us and may be called Mayas or Pimas.

I urge you, do not mock in derision until and unless you too have children loved and fondled by the Lord of creation, children who are encircled about with fire and ministered unto by angels, children who prophesy unutterable things. Their children could be the Piutes or Mohicans among us.

Do not condemn and make game of these good Lamanite-Nephites whose ancestors lived for nearly three centuries in peace and righteousness. Has our own nation ever exceeded a quarter of a century without war and commotion?

Let us not spurn these Nephite-Lamanites until we are assured that we too have the love of the Savior as did their people when the Lord stood in their midst and ordained them with his own hands, blessed them with his own voice, forgave them with his own great heart, broke the bread, poured the wine, and gave the sacrament himself to these upright folk; until we shall have the privilege of feeling the prints of the nails in his hands and feet, and the spear wound in his side.

And in these living descendants are all the seeds of faith and growth and development, of honor and integrity and greatness.

They wait but for opportunity, encouragement, and

brotherliness, and these will be redeemed, will rise, and will become a blessed people. God has said it.

Mr. and Mrs. Anonymous, I present to you a people who, according to prophecies, have been scattered and driven, defrauded and deprived, who are a branch of the tree of Israel—lost from its body, wanderers in a strange land, their own land. I give you nations who have gone through the deep waters of the rivers of sorrow and anguish and pain; a people who have had visited upon their heads the sins of their fathers not unto the third and fourth generations but through a hundred generations. I bring to you a multitude who have asked for bread and have received a stone, and who have asked for fish and have been given a serpent. (See 3 Nephi 14:9-10.) This people ask not for your distant, far-away sympathy, your haughty disdain, your despicable contempt, your supercilious scorn, your turned-up nose, your scathing snobbery, your arrogant scoffing, nor your cold, calculating charity.

It is a people who, unable to raise themselves by their own boot straps, call for assistance from those who can push and lift and open doors. It is a people who pray for mercy, ask forgiveness, beg for membership in the kingdom with its opportunities to learn and to do. It is a good folk who ask for fraternity, a handclasp of friendship, a word of encouragement; it is a group of nations who cry for warm acceptance and sincere brotherhood. I give you a chosen race, an affectionate and warm-hearted people, a responsive but timid and frightened folk, a simple group with childlike faith. I point you to a people in whose veins flows the blood of prophets and martyrs; a people who have intelligence and capacity to climb to former heights but who need the vision and the opportunity and the assistance of the nursing parents.

These people can rise to the loftiness of their fathers when opportunity has knocked at their door a few generations. If we fully help them, they can eventually soar to greatness. The ungerminated seeds are waiting for the rains of kindness and opportunity, the sunshine of gospel's truth, the cultivation through the Church program of training and activity, and the seeds will come to life and the harvest will be fabulous. For the Lord has promised it!

# Chapter Twenty-nine

# "To Kick Against the Pricks"

On the road to Damascus the Lord appeared to Saul of Tarsus and said, "I am Jesus whom thou persecutest: it is hard for thee to kick against the pricks." (Acts 9:5.)

In this figure of speech is captured the essence of rebellion against God; we can only hurt ourselves. If one is pricked by a goad and angered by the pain, he may foolishly strike out at the source of irritation, only to suffer even more.

In my youth a neighbor moved about for many days on crutches. He was a bit evasive when asked the cause of his misfortune, but an ear witness chuckled as he told me, "John stubbed his toe on a rocking chair in the night, and in his quick anger he kicked the chair and broke his toe."

Another Saul, the first king of Israel, kicked against the pricks, to his eternal sorrow. He disobeyed the commands of God and rebelled against the limitations imposed by his Lord. His stubbornness cost him his kingdom and brought forth the caustic denunciation from the prophet Samuel:

For rebellion is as the sin of witchcraft, and stubbornness is as iniquity and idolatry. Because thou hast rejected the word of the Lord, he hath also rejected thee from being king.

. . . When thou wast little in thine own sight, wast thou not made the head of the tribes of Israel, and the Lord anointed thee king over Israel? (1 Samuel 15:23, 17.)

O foolish king! Given power, wealth, and opportunity, you threw them all away because of your arrogance, self-will, and conceit.

There was a man who rebelled against the call of Brigham Young to go to southern valleys, saying, "Nobody can tell me what I must do." Through his personal rebellion he took his entire family out of the Church. How little he retarded the Church in its great colonization program! The valleys were settled in spite of him. How little his disaffection injured the Church! It has grown steadily without him. But how he has suffered in his eternal progression! In contrast, there are those who pulled up stakes, obeyed the call, colonized new areas, established themselves, and reared families of faith and devotion.

To satisfy his own egotism, to feed his pride, to justify vain ambition, a man took a stand against the authorities of the Church. He followed the usual pattern— no apostasy at first, only superiority of knowledge with mild criticism of the brethren. He loved the brethren, he said, but they had failed to see things he saw. He was sure his interpretation was correct. He would still love the Church, he maintained, but his criticism grew and developed into ever-widening areas. He could not yield in good conscience; he had his pride. He spoke of it among his associates; he talked of it at home. His children did not accept his philosophy wholly, but their confidence was shaken in the brethren and the Church. They were frustrated and became inactive. They married out of the Church and he lost them. He later realized the folly of his position and returned to humbleness and activity, but he had lost his children.

There is a man who, released from high position in the Church, resisted his release. He knew positions were temporary trusts, but he turned his venom to the presiding leader who had released him, complaining of the way it had been done. Proper recognition had not been given, the time had not been propitious, it was a reflection upon his effectiveness. He built up a case for himself, became bitter, absented himself from his meetings, justified himself in his deficiencies, and estranged himself from the work of the Lord. His children came along and partook of his frustrations. His grandchildren grew up without spirituality. In later life he "came to himself," and on the brink of the grave he made an "about face." But he found his family would not effect the transformation that now he would give his life to have them make.

Often children suffer for their parents' errors. I know a man and woman who became angry at the bishop when he denied them a recommend to the temple. Eight lovely children had blessed their temple marriage. They would not be so dealt with by this young bishop. Why should they be deprived and humiliated? Were they less worthy than others? Surely this boy-bishop was too strict, over-orthodox. Never would they be active nor put their foot inside the door of that church so long as that bishop presided. They would show him! This family history is tragic. The four younger children were never baptized. The four older ones were never ordained, endowed, or sealed. No missions were filled by this family. The parents are today ill at ease, still defiant. They had covered themselves with a cloud, and righteous prayers could not pass through.

The individual who fights the designs and purposes of the Lord finds disillusionment, disappointment, and misery. The Lord says: "And the rebellious shall be pierced with much sorrow. . . ." (D&C 1:3.) He outlines the fate of those who kick against the pricks, who fight against him, who decry his program.

> . . . As well might man stretch forth his puny arm to stop the Missouri river in its decreed course, or to turn it up

stream, as to hinder the Almighty from pouring down knowledge from heaven upon the heads of the Latter-day Saints.

Behold, there are many called, but few are chosen. And why are they not chosen?

Because their hearts are set so much upon the things of this world, and aspire to the honors of men, that they do not learn this one lesson—

That the rights of the priesthood are inseparably connected with the powers of heaven, and that the powers of heaven cannot be controlled nor handled only upon the principles of righteousness.

That they may be conferred upon us, it is true; but when we undertake to cover our sins, or to gratify our pride, our vain ambition, or to exercise control or dominion or compulsion u)on the souls of the children of men, in any degree of unri ;hteousness, behold, the heavens withdraw themselves; the S) irit of the Lord is grieved; and when it is withdrawn, Amen to the priesthood or the authority of that man.

Behold, ere he is aware, he is left unto himself, to kick against the pricks, to persecute the saints and to fight against God. (D&C 121:33-38.)

The Caesars burned the early saints as torches, subjected them to the claws of wild beasts in the coliseums, drove them underground into the catacombs, confiscated their property, and snuffed out their lives to destroy the program of the Lord, but all to no avail, for the fires of devotion and sacrifice were only intensified thereby.

The persecutors decapitated John the Baptist and martyred the apostles, all to destroy the works of God. They failed. Where relatively few contemporaries ever heard them, hundreds of millions have since been enlightened by their doctrines, lifted by their example, and inspired by their testimonies.

"Mormonism will fail if we dispose of their prophet," persecutors of the Church said a century ago as they murdered Joseph Smith in cold blood. Undoubtedly their fiendish grins of satisfaction at such a foul deed changed to perturbed grimaces when they came to realize that they had been but kicking against prickly points, injuring only themselves. Mormonism was not destroyed by the cruel martyrdom. Rather the bullet-torn flesh seeded the soil, the blood they shed moistened the seed, and the spirit they sent heavenward will testify against them throughout eternities. The cause they sought to destroy persists and grows.

Gamaliel, the noted Pharisee doctor of the law and teacher of Saul of Tarsus, understood the futility of fighting against God. When the chief priests would have slain the apostles, this wise man warned them:

> . . . take heed to yourselves what ye intend to do as touching these men.
>
> . . . Refrain from these men, and let them alone; for if this counsel or this work be of men, it will come to nought:
>
> But if it be of God, ye cannot overthrow it: lest haply ye be found even to fight against God. (Acts 5:35, 38-39.)

This thing of which we speak is not a vice of strangers; rebellion is a sin of those who belong to us.

The antediluvians were a law unto themselves and locked doors against themselves. Jonah, in his egotism, took offense when the repentance of Ninevah rendered unnecessary the fulfillment of his prophecy. Judas fought against God and suffered the buffetings of Satan. Sherem, with his learning, his eloquence, and his flattery, sought to turn away people from the simple faith, and he died in remorse and humiliation. Nehor tried to advance his own cause, increase his popularity, and lead a following with his criticisms and flatteries, and he came to an ignominious death. Korihor, with his teachings of intellectual liberty and his rationalizations, followed his temporary popularity with begging in the streets. Paul and Saul and Alma, and many another in our day, have undertaken to cover their sins, gratify their pride and vain ambition, grieve the Spirit of the Lord, withdraw from holy places and righteous influences. In the words of the Savior:

> Behold, ere he is aware, he is left unto himself, to kick against the pricks, to persecute the saints, and to fight against God. (D&C 121:38.)

A page in the journal of the Prophet Joseph Smith records:

> Write to Oliver Cowdery and ask him if he has not eaten husks long enough? If he is not almost ready to return, be clothed with robes of righteousness, and go up to Jerusalem? Orson Hyde hath need of him. (*History of the Church,* vol. 5, p. 366.)

This alludes to the Prodigal Son whose sad fate brought him low to the eating of husks with the swine after he had wasted his inheritance. Like him, Oliver Cowdery, man of rare opportunity, fought against his conscience, stifled his best impulses; and finally when the earthly powers were nearly at an end, his influence in the world largely terminated, he came to himself and came back to the program he had resisted. His brother-in-law, David Whitmer, said of him as he was restored to the Church late in life: "Oliver died the happiest man I ever saw. After shaking hands with his family and kissing his wife and daughter, he said: 'Now I lay me down for the last time!' . . . and he died with a smile on his face." Peace, sweet peace finally comes to men when they humbly yield to the gentle pressure of the Spirit.

Alma the younger was also to learn what it meant to kick against the pricks. The story of his transformation is not unlike that of Paul. With his companions, he set about to "steady the ark," to set straight the leaders of the church, and to take over the minds of people. These were brilliant young men, eloquent, impressive. And like Saul of Tarsus, they went about to destroy the church. Wicked they were, and idolatrous, and their power and influence lay in their erudition and "great swelling words" and flattery.

The angel of the Lord appeared unto them in a cloud. His voice was "as it were with a voice of thunder which caused the earth to shake." The astonished men fell to the earth, Alma becoming dumb and lifeless. Carried helpless to his father, he recovered after long fasting and prayers by those who loved him.

It took great courage to admit they were wrong, but these young men did so and went about "zealously striving to repair all the injuries which they had done to the church." They had kicked against the pricks as did Paul, but once convinced of errors, they returned to battle for the Lord all the balance of their days.

And be it said here to their everlasting glory that numerous good people have tasted of and recovered from offense, having come to realize that so long as we live upon the earth, we shall live and work with imperfect people and there will be misunderstandings, offenses, and injuries to sensitive feelings. The best of motives are often misunderstood. It is gratifying to find numbers of good people who, in their bigness of soul, have straightened out their thinking, swallowed their pride, forgiven what they felt were personal slights, and who have returned to good feeling for the sakes of themselves and their posterity. Numerous others who have walked critical, lonely, thorny paths in abject misery have accepted correction, acknowledged errors, cleansed their hearts of bitterness, and come again to peace, that coveted peace which is so conspicuous in its absence.

It is best of all if we so conform our lives to the Lord's commandments that we never feel the pricks, but if we do suffer the pains of conscience and just rebuke, let us follow the example of Paul and after our repentance be as energetic in the works of righteousness as we were in opposition. So will we hope, too, for the commendation that the Lord has for his worthy children.

# Chapter Thirty

# The Need for a Prophet

$\mathcal{I}$t is Sunday morning, January 18, 1970. A great heart stops beating and an aged body relaxes and slumbers. Like an earthquake sends a tidal wave around the earth, communications now cover the earth and millions of serious-minded people in even faraway places stop to pay saddened tribute to a mighty man of God who has passed from mortality.

For days, long lines of loving followers inch their way along the street, even in the rain, to see once more the visage of their departed leader.

The Tabernacle is crowded with those who loved him, and sweet tributes are paid.

The earthly body of the prophet, David O. McKay, is laid to rest in dignified reverence.

In our feeling of emptiness, it hardly seems that we could go on without him; but as one star sinks behind the horizon, another rises in the sky, and death spawns life.

The work of the Lord is endless. Even when a powerful leader dies, not for a single instant is the Church without leadership, thanks to the kind Providence who gave his kingdom continuity and perpetuity. As it already had happened eight times before in this dispensation, a people reverently close a grave, dry their tears, and turn their faces to the future.

The moment life passes from a President of the Church, a body of men become the composite leader—these men already seasoned with experience and training. The appointments have long been made, the authority given, the keys delivered. For five days, the kingdom moves forward under this already authorized council. No "running" for position, no electioneering, no stump speeches. What a divine plan! How wise our Lord, to organize so perfectly beyond the weakness of frail, grasping humans!

Then dawns a notable day (January 23, 1970), and fourteen serious men walk reverently into the temple of God—this, the Quorum of the Twelve Apostles, the governing body of The Church of Jesus Christ of Latter-day Saints, several of whom have experienced this solemn change before.

When these fourteen men emerge from the holy edifice later in the morning, a transcendently vital event has occurred—a short interregnum ends, and the government of the kingdom shifts back again from the Quorum of the Twelve Apostles to a new prophet, an individual leader, the Lord's earthly representative, who has unostentatiously been moving toward this lofty calling for sixty years. The man is Joseph Fielding Smith.

Not because of his name, however, did he ascend to this high place, but because when he was a very young man he was called of the Lord, through the then-living prophet, to be an apostle—a member of the Quorum—and was given the precious, vital keys to hold in suspension pending a time when he might become the senior apostle and the President.

In that eventful temple meeting, when he has been "ordained and set apart" as the President of the Church by his brethren, the Twelve, he chooses his counselors—two mighty men of valor: Elder Harold B. Lee and Elder Nathan Eldon Tanner, with their rich background as teachers, businessmen, public officials, and especially Church leaders.

And a presidency of three and a newly constituted Council of Twelve walk humbly to their offices without fanfare or ostentation, and a new administration moves into a new period with promise of great development and unprecedented growth.

Two years pass. Again it is a Sunday, now July 2, 1972, and another prophet goes to his rest. For a second time in three years the faithful acknowledge their debt to a great man for his leadership and to the Lord for giving guidance through such a man. The decision as to succession is repeated as each time before. Again the Quorum of the Twelve under inspiration designate their senior member as the man called of God to be President of the Church. President Harold B. Lee takes his place at the head as prophet.

It was a very young man who introduced the restored program to this new world. Joseph Smith (December 23, 1805-June 27, 1844) was but 24 years of age when the Church was organized.

When he was martyred at 38, the second President, Brigham Young (June 1, 1801-August 28, 1877), became senior apostle and then the President of the Church (December 27, 1847) at 46 years of age. He presided thirty years (until he was 76).

John Taylor (November 1, 1808-July 25, 1887) was 71 when he became President of the Church (October 10, 1880); when he died at 78, Wilford Woodruff (March 1, 1807-September 2, 1898) became the senior apostle (July 25, 1887). Two years later (April 7, 1889), he was sustained President of the Church at 82 years of age. He died at 91, whereupon President Lorenzo Snow (April 3, 1814-October 10, 1901) became the senior apostle. He was 84 years of age when eleven days later (September 13, 1898) he became the President of the Church. His presidency was short-lived. He served three years (until October 10, 1901).

President Joseph F. Smith (November 13, 1838-November 19, 1918) was senior apostle seven days; he became the President of the Church October 17, 1901, at 62 years of age; he died at 80.

President Heber J. Grant (November 22, 1856-May 14, 1945) was senior apostle less than a week when he became the President of the Church (on November 23, 1918) at 62; he died at 88.

President George Albert Smith (April 4, 1870-April 4, 1951) was the senior apostle for seven days and became President of the Church (May 21, 1945) at 75; he died at the age of 81.

President David O. McKay, the ninth President (September 8, 1873-January 18, 1970) was senior apostle five days and was sustained as President of the Church (April 9, 1951) at 77; he died at the age of 96.

President Joseph Fielding Smith (July 19, 1876-July 2, 1972) became the senior apostle January 18, 1970, and President of the Church five days later, at the age of 93. He died at 95.

President Harold B. Lee, born March 28, 1899, was senior apostle five days and became President on July 7, 1972, at age 73.

The Presidents from John Taylor to Joseph Fielding Smith, inclusive, became President at ages ranging from 62 to 92 and died at ages from 79 to 96.

It is interesting to note that these eight Church Presidents assumed their presiding responsibility at an average of 76 years and relinquished it by death at 87 years. They served an average of eleven years; consequently, after Brigham Young the average age of the living President of the Church has been about 81 years.

We may expect the Church President will always be an older man: young men have action, vigor, initiative; older men have stability and strength and wisdom through experience and long communion with God.

In President McKay's declining days, speculation ran high among the curious and the concerned and the less knowledgeable and continued as a major topic of discussion through the interregnum.

More than a million members had never known any other President than David O. McKay; consequently, it was natural for some to be confused.

They talked about age. The old patriarchs were not young. Adam was very old as he presided over his posterity, which spread over many generations. Abraham, Isaac, Joseph, and Moses presided over the people, dying at 175, 180, 110, and 120 years, respectively. They were old in years, but from their accumulated experience came massive wisdom and security.

The precedent of succession by the senior apostle has been repeated from the beginning. Brigham Young was the senior apostle, holding all the keys and authorities, and in each case, the President has been the senior apostle. This is the pattern the Lord has followed and he retains the leadership in his divine hands.

When the first succession took place, the restored church was an infant only fourteen years old. There had been no prophet nor "open vision" for numerous centuries. Little wonder, then, that the people should be full of questions when the bullets at Carthage terminated the life of the one in whom all these priceless blessings—the church, revelation, prophecy—seemed to be centered. When the apostles had returned from their missions, buried their dead prophet, and considered the future, all doubt was dissipated when the senior apostle, already holding all the keys, stood forth like Moses and led the way.

The editorial in *Times and Seasons* of September 2, 1844, on the succession said:

Great excitement prevails throughout to know "who shall be the successor of Joseph Smith!"

In reply we say, be patient, be patient a little till the proper time comes, and we will tell you all. "Great wheels move slow." At present, we can say that a special conference of the church was held in Nauvoo on the 8th, ult., and it was carried without a dissenting voice, that the "Twelve" should preside over the whole church, and when any alteration in the presidency shall be required, seasonable notice will be given; and the elders abroad, will best exhibit their wisdom to all men, by remaining silent on those things they are ignorant of. . . . (*Times and Seasons,* vol. 5, September 2, 1844, p. 632.)

As we tighten our tugs and strain our weight against the collar, with each change we move forward on a new journey with a strong will under our inspired leaders, led by our prophet.

President Joseph Fielding Smith was venerable and worthy of respect by reason of his character, dignity, age, position. He was one who had "clean hands and a pure heart, who has not lifted up his soul unto vanity, nor sworn deceitfully." He was a true son of his Maker and a clean and holy man of God. He carried for sixty years the keys of the kingdom, gradually moving toward the day of his presidency. For six decades he was sustained by the Church as a prophet. Finally he was sustained as the prophet, the one who alone holds the keys in total use under the Lord Jesus Christ, who is the chief cornerstone and head of the Church.

President Lee is the youngest President in more than forty years. He brings to the position rich experience, life-long dedication, and personal integrity beyond question. Longer than any man living he has served as an apostle of the Lord, faithfully and spiritually.

To be a prophet of the Lord, one does not need to "be everything to all men." He does not need to be youthful and athletic, an industrialist, a financier, or an agriculturist; he does not need to be a musician, a poet, an entertainer, a banker, a physician, a college president, a military general, or a scientist.

He does not need to be a linguist and speak French and Japanese, German and Spanish, but he must understand the divine language and be able to receive messages from heaven.

He need not be an orator, for God can make his own. The Lord can present his divine messages through weak men made strong. He substituted a strong voice for the quiet, timid one of Moses, and he gave to the young man Enoch power that made men tremble in his presence, for Enoch walked with God as Moses walked with God.

The Lord said: ". . . whether by mine own voice or by the voice of my servants, it is the same." (D&C 1:38.)

What the world needs is a prophet-leader who gives example—clean, full of faith, godlike in his attributes with an untarnished name, a beloved husband, a true father.

A prophet needs to be more than a priest or a minister or an elder. His voice becomes the voice of God to reveal new programs, new truths, new solutions. I make no claim of personal infallibility for him, but he does need to be recognized of God, to be an authoritative person. He is no pretender, as numerous persons are who presumptuously assume position without appointment and authority. He must speak like his Lord: "as one having authority, and not as the scribes." (Matthew 7:29.)

He must be bold enough to speak truth even against popular clamor for lessening restrictions. He must be certain of his divine appointment, of his celestial ordination, and of his authority to call to service, to ordain, to pass keys that fit eternal locks.

He must have commanding power like prophets of old: ". . . to seal both on earth and in heaven, the unbelieving and rebellious . . . unto the day when the wrath of God shall be poured out upon the wicked without measure" (D&C 1:8-9), and rare powers: ". . . that whatsoever you seal on earth shall be sealed in heaven; and whatsoever you bind on earth, in my name and by my word, saith the Lord, it shall be eternally bound in the heavens; and whosesoever sins you remit on earth shall be remitted eternally in the heavens; and whosesoever sins you retain on earth shall be retained in heaven" (D&C 132:46).

What is needed is more a Moses than a Pharaoh; an Elijah than a Belshazzar; a Paul than a Pontius Pilate.

He need not be an architect to construct houses and schools and high-rise buildings, but he will be one who builds structures to span time and eternity and to bridge the gap between man and his Maker.

When the world has followed prophets, it has moved forward; when it has ignored them, the results have been stagnation, servitude, death.

Every moment of every day, there are numerous programs on the air. We hear very few, relatively, for we are engrossed in our day's duties, but with powerful-beaming broadcasting stations, we could hear any of the programs if we were tuned in.

For thousands of years there have been constant broadcasts from heaven of vital messages of guidance and timely warnings, and there has been a certain constancy in the broadcasts from the most powerful station. Throughout all those centuries there have been times when there were prophets who tuned in and rebroadcast to the people. The messages have never ceased.

One such message came to Daniel in the presence of others, and he who was on the proper frequency said: "And I Daniel alone saw the vision: for the men that were with me saw not the vision. . . ." (Daniel 10:7.)

On the road to Damascus, a company of men traveled together. A spectacular event came from the heavens, but only one man was in tune to receive it. That which was but static to all the other ears was an awesome call to duty to Saul of Tarsus; it changed his life and contributed toward the transformation of millions of lives, but he was the only one who was attuned.

It is said that certain Russian fliers reported that as they penetrated the far outer space, they saw no God or angels. Our prediction to any unbelieving, godless spacemen is that though they could go a thousand times farther and a thousand times higher, they will be still far from God and eternal things, for the spiritual is not understood by the finite.

Abraham found God on a tower in Mesopotamia, on a mount in Palestine, and in royal quarters in Egypt. Moses found him on a backside desert, at the Red Sea, on a mount called Sinai, and in a "burning bush." Joseph Smith found him in the cool freshness of a primeval forest. Peter found him at the Sea of Galilee and on the Mount of Transfiguration.

May the Lord our God sustain each newly appointed prophet that he may continue to serve the Lord's "bread of life" and "living water" to us, and that he will "light the lamps of Israel" and verily become the mouthpiece of God. Our prayer is that the Lord will speak to him as he did to Joshua:

> This day will I begin to magnify thee in the sight of all Israel, that they may know that, as I was with Moses, so I will be with thee. (Joshua 3:7.)

And may the Lord bless us, his servants, who have raised our hands in sustaining vote, that from this time forth we may, like the children of Israel, uphold the prophet's hands and shout as did the children of Israel in one voice:

> All that thou commandest us we will do, and whithersoever thou sendest us, we will go.

> According as we hearkened unto Moses in all things, so will we hearken unto thee: only the Lord thy God be with thee, as he was with Moses. (Joshua 1:16-17.)

"To your tents, O Israel," stand firm and loyal and immovable in support of the prophets of God.

# Chapter Thirty-one

# They Named Him Joseph

About sixty years ago, F. M. Bareham wrote the following:

> A century ago [in 1809] men were following with bated breath the march of Napoleon and waiting with feverish impatience for news of the wars. And all the while in their homes babies were being born. But who could think about babies? Everybody was thinking about battles.
>
> In one year between Trafalgar and Waterloo there stole into the world a host of heroes: Gladstone was born in Liverpool; Tennyson at the Somersby Rectory; and Oliver Wendell Holmes in Massachusetts. Abraham Lincoln was born in Kentucky, and music was enriched by the advent of Felix Mendelssohn in Hamburg.

Quoting Bareham further:

> But nobody thought of babies, everybody was thinking of battles. Yet which of the battles of 1809 mattered more than the babies of 1809? We fancy God can manage His world only with great battalions, when all the time he is doing it with beautiful babies.
>
> When a wrong wants righting, or a truth wants preaching, or a continent wants discovering, God sends a baby into the world to do it.

While most of the thousands of precious infants born every hour will never be known outside their own neighborhoods, there are great souls being born who will rise above their surroundings. We see, with Abraham,

> the intelligences that were organized before the world was; and among all these there were many of the noble and great ones;

and we hear the Lord saying:

> These I will make my rulers . . . Abraham, thou art one of them; thou wast chosen before thou wast born. (Abraham 3:22-23.)

He commanded Adam:

> Be fruitful, and multiply, and replenish the earth, and subdue it. . . . (Genesis 1:28.)

And the Psalmist sang:

> Lo, children are an heritage of the Lord. . . .
>
> Happy is the man that hath his quiver full of them. . . . (Psalms 127:3, 5.)

Regarding these "men of the hour," Carlyle said:

> The most precious gift that heaven can give to the earth; a man of genius, as we call it; the soul of a man actually sent down from the skies with God's message to us.

What mother, looking down with tenderness upon her chubby infant, does not envision her child as the President of the Church or the leader of her nation! As he is nestled in her arms, she sees him a statesman, a leader, a prophet. Some dreams do come true! One mother gives us a Shakespeare, another a Michelangelo, and another an Abraham Lincoln, and still another a Joseph Smith.

When theologians are reeling and stumbling, when lips are pretending and hearts are wandering, and people are "running to and fro, seeking the word of the Lord and cannot find it"—when clouds of error need dissipating and spiritual darkness needs penetrating and heavens need opening, a little infant is born. Just a few scattered neighbors in a hilly region in the backwoods even know that

Lucy is expecting. There is no prenatal care or nurses; no hospital, no ambulance, no delivery room. Babies live and die in this rough environment and few know about it.

Another child for Lucy! No trumpets are sounded; no hourly bulletins posted; no pictures taken; no notice is given; just a few friendly community folk pass a word along. It's a boy! Little do the brothers and sisters dream that a prophet is born to their family; even his proud parents can little suspect his spectacular destiny. No countryside farmers or loungers at the country store, no village gossips even surmise how much they could discuss, did they but have the power of prophetic vision.

"They are naming him Joseph," it is reported. But no one knows, not even his parents, at this time, that this infant and his father have been named in the scriptures for 3,500 years, named for and known to their ancestor, Joseph, the savior of Egypt and Israel. Not even his adoring mother realizes, even in her most ambitious dreaming and her silent musings, that this one of her children, like his ancestor, will be the chief sheaf of grain to which all others will lean and the one star to which the sun and moon and other stars will make obeisance.

He will inspire hatred and admiration; he will build an empire and restore a church—the Church of Jesus Christ. Millions will follow him; monuments will be built to him; poets will sing of him; authors will write libraries of books about him.

No living soul can guess that this little pinkish infant will become the peer of Moses in spiritual power and greater than many prophets before him. He will talk with God, the Eternal Father, and Jesus Christ, his Son; and angels will be his guest instructors.

His Vermont contemporaries know not that this little one just born will live as few men have lived, accomplish what few men have accomplished, and die as few have ever died, in his own sacred blood in a prison at the hands of assassins as a martyr to everlasting truth.

All expectations are understated. Destiny outdistances all imagination and dreams!

> God moves in a mysterious way
> His wonders to perform;
> He plants his footsteps in the sea
> And rides upon the storm.
>
> Deep in unfathomable mines
> Of never-failing skill,
> He treasures up his bright designs
> And works his sovereign will.
> —William Cowper

During the unfolding of this Smith-flower; during the brief ripening years of this fruit of the loins of that other Joseph of Israel, the world is preparing for the greatest event since the meridian of time. The triplet infants, Liberty, Freedom, and Justice, are contending for life; a small colonial nation is struggling to its feet; the people from many lands, squirming in the "melting-pot," are firming up, suffering labor pains toward the birth of a divine new program, "a marvelous work and a wonder," the restoration of the gospel in all its far-reaching detail.

"We fancy," said Bareham, "God can manage His world only with great battalions, when all the time He is doing it with beautiful babies."

O foolish men who think to protect the world with armaments, battleships, and space equipment, when only righteousness is needed!

Having read the pages of history, six thousand years of it, can we not see that God sent his babies to become the teachers and prophets to warn us of our threatening fate? Cannot we read the handwriting on the wall? History repeats itself.

O mortal men, deaf and blind! Can we not read the past? For thousands of years have plowshares been beaten into swords and pruning hooks into spears, yet war persists.

Ever since Belshazzar saw the finger writing upon the wall of his palace, the warning reappears. It seems to restate with great forcefulness Daniel's indictment of an unhumble people:

> . . . God hath numbered thy kingdom, and finished it.
>
> Thou art weighed in the balances, and art found wanting.
>
> And thou his son, O Belshazzar, hast not humbled thine heart, though thou knewest all this;
>
> . . . and thou hast praised the gods of silver, and gold, of brass, iron, wood, and stone, which see not, nor hear, nor know: and the God in whose hand thy breath is, and whose are all thy ways, hast thou not glorified.
>
> . . . Blessed be the name of God . . . he removeth kings, and setteth up kings. . . . (Daniel 5:26-27, 22-23; 2:20-21.)

The answer to all of our problems—personal, national, and international—has been given to us many times by many prophets, ancient to modern. Why must we grovel in the earth when we could be climbing toward heaven? The path is not obscure. Perhaps it is too simple for us to see. We look to foreign programs, summit conferences, land bases. We depend on fortifications, our gods of stone; upon ships and planes and projectiles, our gods of iron—gods that have no ears, no eyes, no hearts. We pray to them for deliverance and depend upon them for protection. Like the gods of Baal, they could be "talking or pursuing or on a journey or peradventure sleeping" when they are needed most. And like Elijah, we might cry out to our world:

> How long halt ye between two opinions? if the Lord be God, follow him. . . . (1 Kings 18:21.)

My testimony to you is, the Lord *is* God. He has charted the way, but we do not follow. He personally visited Joseph Smith in our world, in our century. He outlined the way of peace in this world and eternal worlds. That path is righteousness. The Prophet Joseph with all the successor prophets proclaimed the ripening of this world in iniquity and the solution of all vexing problems. The Book of Mormon, which he translated, relates the story of 200 years of peace in the old days, which was the greatest era of happiness of which we have any complete record.

God lives, as does his Son, Jesus Christ; and they will not indefinitely be mocked. May we hearken and repent, "for the day of the Lord is near in the valley of decision . . . the Lord will be the hope of his people. . . ." (Joel 3:14, 16.)

Joseph Smith is a true prophet of the living God and his successors likewise. The mantle of authority and prophecy and revelation and power lies in his choice servant who now leads us, and he is God's prophet not only to Latter-day Saints, but to every living soul in all the world. This is my testimony.

# Chapter Thirty-two

*Book of Mormon*

# A Book of Vital Messages

---

$\mathcal{T}$here is a book I have read many times, yet each time I read it I find it engages my interest the more.

It is a story of courage, faith, and fortitude; of perseverance, sacrifice, and super-human accomplishments; of intrigue, of revenge, of disaster, of war, murder, and rapine; of idolatry and of cannibalism; of miracles, visions, and manifestations; of prophecies and their fulfillment.

Across the stage of this drama of life through the ages marched actors in exotic, colorful costumes, from the blood-painted nudity of the warrior to the lavish, ornamented pageantry of royal courts—some actors loathsome and degraded, others so near perfection that they conversed with angels and with God. There are the sowers and reapers, the artisans, the engineers, the traders, the toilers; the rake in his debachery; the alcoholic with his liquor; the pervert rotting in his sex; the warrior in his armor; the missionary on his knees.

It is a fast-moving story of total life; of opposing ideologies; of monarchies and judgeships and mobocracies. Its scenes carry the reader across oceans and continents. It promises to tell of the "last days of God," but instead

it records the last days of whole peoples and the triumph
of God. Class distinction is there with its ugliness; race
prejudice with its hatefulness; multiplicity of creeds with
their bitter conflicts.

Since this "best seller" left its first press, it has been
printed in nearly two dozen languages, more than a half-
million copies a year; millions of copies are in libraries,
public and private, and in numerous hotels and motels
along with the Bible. Even the blind may read it in three
thick books of braille. Can anyone be considered to be
well-read who is not familiar with this book?

Its story has a vital message to all people. The gentiles will find the history of their past and the potential
of their destiny. The Jewish people will find the blueprint
of their future. The covenants of God to the Jews are un-
folded, as are the promises regarding Jerusalem, their
ancient city, and their lands. And it reveals how the Jews,
so long persecuted, scattered, and tortured since their
dispersion, may come into their own. The gentiles are
warned that they must "no longer hiss, nor spurn nor
make game of the Jews, nor any of the remnant of the
House of Israel," for the Lord will remember his covenant
to them when they respond. The book is also the story
of the ancestors of the American Indians and accounts
for their dark skins.

Archaeologists may be excited as they read of ruins of
ancient cities, highways, and buildings, and there may
yet be hidden buried art treasures and priceless records.

Those interested in exploration and travel will learn
of unprecedented land treks and ocean crossings fraught
with all the dangers of storms, hidden reefs, hurricanes,
and even mutiny. The first recorded ocean crossing was
about forty centuries ago, made in eight seaworthy barges
as long as a tree and tight as a dish, peaked at the end like
a gravy boat, corked at top and bottom, illuminated by
luminous stones. This fleet of barges was driven by winds
and ocean currents, landing at a common point in the
Americas, probably on the west shores.

There were other crossings of the ocean. One great migration and voyage, perhaps the greatest in all of history, involved a group of people who abandoned Jerusalem on the eve of its destruction by Nebuchadnezzar. They probably landed on the west coast of South America, where the ocean currents drove them. They traveled in a ship constructed by a young builder who may never have seen an ocean-going vessel.

This remarkable book tells again of movement of 5,400 people in one group, sailing northward on the Pacific coast in very large ships, seeking for new worlds to conquer; some of them were likely drawn into the strong westward ocean currents to find the isles of the sea and to become the progenitors of the Polynesians.

The student of society will find in this unusual book the disintegration of nations through pride, soft living, and luxuries, terminating finally in hunger and fetters. He will see unified peoples fighting for liberty and then internecine wars destroying those freedoms. He will see the land waving with ripening grain, the silkworm spinning, flocks and herds grazing, vineyards and orchards bearing, and a people wearing rich adornments. He will see stone quarries and lumber mills and mines and craftshops; and then devastated landscapes, burned homes, parched earth, warring antagonists, and deserted lands. He will see towers and temples and kingly courts and palaces of the rich and their luxury, and dissipation, immorality, and debauchery, comparable to that in Babylon, Jerusalem, and Rome.

He will see people sometimes thriving in communal living; he will see them taxed fifty percent or more and see them again in slavery and bondage. He will see power-greedy, paternalistic, centralized governments move toward the inevitable revolution that finally impoverishes but frees the people to begin again from ashes.

The astronomer and geologist herein may see signs in the heavens and new stars come into focus; night without darkness, bright "as the midday sun"; three days without sun or any reflected light, and a vapor of darkness so impenetrable that no candles, nor torches, nor fire could give any light. "There arose a great storm, such an one as never had been known in all the land," and terrible tempests, thunder and sharp lightnings, whirlwinds of tornadic and hurricane proportions—swift enough to carry away people never to be heard of again—twistings, foldings, whirlings, slidings, and faultings, causing great landslides and burying great cities. Tidal waves swallow entire communities, and fire consumes many cities and human bodies. The labors of centuries are broken, burned, buried, and washed away; and earth convulsions of such intensity and prolongation occur that "the face of the whole earth" is deformed, these earth spasms being a revolt by the created earth against the crucifixion of its Creator.

Engineers will learn from this great book that those many centuries ago men erected buildings, temples, and highways with cement; that paved roads connected city to city and land to land; that when forests had been denuded, a reforestation program was initiated for the future.

The psychologists may find studies in human behavior, the workings of the human mind, and the rationalizing processes by which men convince themselves that "good is bad, and that bad is good." Here they will watch history unfold for thousands of years and see not only episodes in the lives of individuals, but also causes and effects in a total history of races.

This comprehensive book should be studied by politicians and government leaders to see the rise and fall of empires and the differences between statesmanship and demogoguery. They will see nations born in war, live in war, deteriorate in war, and die in war through the centuries. They may find answers to problems of capital and labor, of dishonesty, confiscatory taxes, graft, and fraud; of dissensions, internal rupture, and civil wars. They will see a chief judge, frustrated by growing corruption, resign from the judgment seat to proselyte for righteousness; princes who prefer to teach men rather than to rule over them; a king who tilled the earth to provide his own living rather than become burdensome to the people he served.

Scientists will read of stones that provided light; at least 1500 years before Columbus this people knew that the earth was round and revolved about the sun; they had a special instrument like a round ball, made of brass, curious in workmanship, with two spindles, so sensitive that it would give guidance regardless of direction and would record the feelings, emotions, and inner rebellions of men so much that it would not function properly where there was discord. This instrument, which would point the way to wild game, was operated by faith, and on it from time to time writing would appear, plain to be read, increasing the understanding of those who read it.

Military men may learn much in strategy and intrigue, in movements, in morale. Guerrilla warfare, sieges, and the scorched-earth policy were not originated in Civil War days nor in Russia, but were programs of survival long centuries before Columbus.

They will learn that great cultures stagnate in war shadows and cease to survive when continuous wars make people migrants and when fields are abandoned and livestock is appropriated for nonproducing soldiers; when in wartime forests are destroyed without replanting and farmers and builders become warriors. Men cannot plant, cultivate, and harvest when in camps, nor build when on the run. Long and bloody wars mean sacked, burned, ruined cities, confiscatory taxes, degenerated peoples, and decayed cultures.

Victory and defeat alike leave countries devastated and the conqueror and the conquered reduced. Wickedness brings war and war vomits destruction and suffering, hate, and bloodshed upon the guilty and the innocent alike.

This book should convince of the futility of war and the hazards of unrighteousness. A few prophets swimming in a sea of barbarism find it difficult to prevent the crumbling and final collapse of corrupt peoples. There is a great but conditional promise:

> And this land shall be a land of liberty unto the Gentiles, and there shall be no kings upon the land. . . .
> And I will fortify this land against all other nations.
> . . . I, the Lord, the king of heaven, will be their king, and I will be a light unto them forever, that hear my words. (2 Nephi 10:11-12, 14.)

In this book ministers and priests can find texts for sermons and men generally can find final and authoritative answers to difficult questions. Is there life after death? Will the body be literally resurrected? Where do the spirits of men go between death and the resurrection? Can one be saved in unchastity? What is the correct organization of Christ's church? Can one be saved without baptism? Is it wrong to baptize infants? Is specific authority essential to administer ordinances? Is continuous revelation necessary and a reality? Is Jesus the actual Son of God?

Here is recorded the glorious coming of the Savior to his temple in America. He blessed the little children and wept as angels descended out of heaven and encircled them. He organized his church with twelve apostles, called disciples, to whom were given the same priesthood, authority, and keys that their contemporaries, Peter, James, and John held in the other land.

The coming of the resurrected Redeemer to this land was spectacular—the small piercing voice from heaven heard at Jordan and Transfiguration's Mount awed them as it announced: "Behold, my Beloved Son, in whom I am well pleased, in whom I have glorified my name— hear ye him." (3 Nephi 11:7.)

And then they saw a man descending out of heaven in white robes and he stood in their midst, saying: "Behold, I am Jesus Christ. . . . I am the God of Israel and the God of the whole earth and have been slain for the sins of the world." And the multitude thrust their hands into his side and felt the prints of the nails and knew of a surety that this was the very Christ so recently crucified across the sea, and so recently ascended into heaven, and now among them to teach them his saving gospel.

This historical book tells of three men who, like John the Revelator, are still on earth though it is nearly two thousand years since their mortal birth—men who have not suffered the pains of death, but who have control over the elements, who make themselves known at will and go any place on the globe when needed, and who cannot be imprisoned, burned in the furnace, buried in pits, or destroyed by beasts.

This narrative tells of one group of people with such faith they buried their weapons and died victims of their enemies rather than take their enemies' lives; of a group of boys who had inherited great faith from their mothers and were trained to trust that God would protect them. It tells of the fulfillment of that faith when 2,060 of them fought in battles. Men all around them died and many of them were sorely wounded, but because of the faith of these young men and their mothers, not one of the 2,060 suffered death.

But after all, the interest for archaeologists, historians, political scientists, and so on is not the book's major value to man. Rather, it is the book's power to transform men into Christ-like beings worthy of exaltation.

It is the word of God. It is a powerful second witness of Christ. And, certainly, all true believers who love the Redeemer will welcome additional evidence of his divinity.

This inspiring book was never tampered with by unauthorized translators or biased theologians, but comes to the world pure from the historians and authorized abridgers through an inspired translation. The book is not on trial—its readers are.

Here is a scripture as old as creation and as new and vibrant as tomorrow; it bridges time and eternity; it is a book of revelations and is a companion to the Bible brought from Europe by immigrants. It agrees closely with that Bible in tradition, history, doctrine, and prophecy even though the two were written simultaneously on two hemispheres under diverse conditions. It even foretells the reaction of people to be expected when this hidden record should be presented to them:

> A Bible! A Bible! We have got a Bible, and there cannot be any more Bible.
>
> But thus saith the Lord God: O fools, they shall have a Bible; and it shall proceed forth from the Jews. . . .
>
> Thou fool, that shall say: A Bible, we have got a Bible, and we need no more Bible. . . .
>
> Know ye not that . . . I rule in the heavens above and in the earth beneath; and I bring forth my word unto the children of men, yea, even upon all the nations of the earth?
>
> Wherefore murmur ye, because that ye shall receive more of my word? Know ye not that the testimony of two nations is a witness unto you that I am God, that I remember one nation like unto another? . . .
>
> And I do this that I may prove unto many that I am the same yesterday, today, and forever. . . . And because that I have spoken one word ye need not suppose that I cannot speak another; for my work is not yet finished. . . . (2 Nephi 29:3-4, 6-9.)

Then he says he will eventually gather the scattered faithful into one fold and he will be their shepherd. And the records of the Ten Tribes are still to be recovered.

> And it shall come to pass that the Jews shall have the words of the Nephites, and the Nephites shall have the words of the Jews; and the Nephites and the Jews shall have the words of the lost tribes of Israel; and the lost tribes of Israel shall have the words of the Nephites and the Jews. (2 Nephi 29:13.)

We seem to hear Almighty warn: "Fools mock and they shall mourn," and "Woe be unto him that rejecteth the word of God." One prophet wrote: "And if ye shall believe in Christ, ye shall believe in these words for they are the words of Christ."

In the final chapter of the book is the never-failing promise that every person who will read the book with a sincere, prayerful desire to know of its divinity shall have the assurance. Aside from all other interest that the Book of Mormon holds, this reason for our prayerfully studying it remains prominent: through it we can obtain true knowledge of God and what he wishes of us.

# Chapter Thirty-three

# *The Lamanite and the Gospel*

The history of the American Indian over the past 400 years is one of oppression and exploitation. In the eastern United States the Indians were "used" by the colonists as pawns, as guides, and they were induced to fight on one side or the other of numerous conflicts between colonial powers.

They were pushed and driven and evicted and exiled. They fought the "Battle of America," a continuing battle with some conquests and temporary wins but with infinitely more losses, each one resulting in a further move westward reminiscent of the continuing flight northward by their Nephite victims more than a thousand years earlier. In the eighteenth and nineteenth centuries, the retreat was across the length of the land.

They fought back. Of course, they fought back. This was their homeland—these, their forests; these, their mountains; these, their plains; these, their buffalo and deer and wild turkey; these, their burial grounds. They did not have cannons or guns at first, and they learned to defend themselves and to fight their battles with bows and arrows and spears and fire, their own weapons.

The history of the Indians has been a checkered one, and disturbing and unpleasant, but it has been said "the darkest hour is just before the dawn." And, the dawn has come and the full day approaches.

The greatest and choicest land of all the world had been given by the Lord to the descendants of Lehi as their inheritance forever. Never would they have lost it had they lived the commandments of the Lord, carried forward their culture, and grown and developed as they could and as they did in certain times in their ancient history. But they forgot their benefactor, lost their written language and culture, and degenerated until they were no match for the wily and subtle Europeans.

Not long ago, I clipped an advertisement from a magazine. On it is a picture of a sad-faced Indian woman with her blanket wrapped around herself and her little child whom she hugs close to her. The title is "Bad Deal at the Trading Post":

> More than 50% of America's farm products today consists of plants used by the Indians before Columbus planted his flag. They include beans, chocolate, corn, cotton, peanuts, potatoes, pumpkins, tobacco and tomatoes. To combat illness, the Indian has given us arnica, cascara, cocaine, ipecac, oil of wintergreen, petroleum jelly, quinine and witch hazel. Botanists have yet to discover, in 400 years, any medicinal herb that was not used by the Indian.
>
> That's what *they* gave *us*. Here's what *we* have *given* them: High infant mortality rate, short life expectancy. Dependency on handouts. Loss of pride. Much illness. Unemployment as high as 80% in some tribes. The 600,000 remaining American Indians are struggling to hang on to the lowest health, education and economic rungs in American life. Somebody better do *something* before those rungs collapse. Remember, you're up there somewhere on that ladder yourself.

This was not the kind of a deal where two peoples jockey back and forth and finally arrive at an amicable arrangement wherein each benefits about equally. This was a deal where power ruled; where the white party of the first part took nearly everything of value—the lands, the water, the mountains, the rivers, the buffalo and the fish, and the homeland and security. The red party of the second part received nearly nothing—limited reservations of stark and barren "badlands," which had been theirs from the first. The white conquerors even took much of that. It was a bad deal.

That bad deal began soon after the pivotal year of 1492 and has never yet ended. It was an unfair one, an unequal one, a treacherous one. Why didn't the Indians rise and demand fair treatment? The answer is, they did. But unorganized, with limited war materiel and uncountable defeats behind them, they could not cope with the situation.

Perhaps of all prophecies ever made, none have been fulfilled more literally and more intensely and more devastatingly than this one from Mormon:

> But behold, it shall come to pass that they shall be driven and scattered by the Gentiles. . . . (Mormon 5:20.)

And what a tragic and literal fulfillment those scriptures had.

Go to the rounded hill standing above the Big Horn and Little Big Horn rivers in Montana. Ride up the hill on a paved road to a government building constructed to memorialize Custer's last fight. Look about you and see the monuments—small marble monuments.

The encyclopedia says:

> Custer rode for the heart of the Indian line. A rise across the stream masked the enemy and as Custer swept down, the *savages* rode against him and swarmed around to his rear. Outnumbered twenty to one, the heroic band [that was the white man] still fought their way up to the ridge and a small number with their general reached it. Then a fresh band of one thousand Cheyennes rose up under Rain-in-the-face and not a soul was left. . . . The bodies of the slain division were left as they lay. . . . Forty-two Indians were killed; the battle field has been marked with a small marble monument where each *white* man fell. (*Encyclopedia Americana* 8:336-337; italics added.)

The account reads "not a soul was left alive" from the battle, again fulfilling the scriptures, "They shall be considered as naught." The thousands of Redmen who rode away—this time triumphantly—were not considered souls by the historians.

Another instance: The story of the Cherokees would melt the stoniest heart—driven at the point of a bayonet from their homes and lands, evicted from their country and sent to the swampy, mosquito-ridden area of Indian Territory. The prejudiced historian again said that the Indians were the culprits. Their suffering and death means little; their homes and gardens and farms were expropriated. The "white heroes" evicted and expropriated for their own use (at the point of bayonets) the lands of the "red demons."

We follow the Navajos from their exquisitely beautiful red sandstone lands of northeastern Arizona in their long, pitiful, painful march to central New Mexico, to Bosque Redondo on the Pecos River. We suffer and starve and freeze with them in the lonely four years, and then walk with them back to their homeland after signing their treaties.

In recent times our attention was arrested by a double-page picture in *Life* magazine. It is the dead of winter. Plodding across the thousands of square miles of deep snow and the wind-scoured stubbly plain, two Indian women on their horses make a new deep trail through the snow. It is good that their horses can break trail; it is good that their warm skirts are long to their ankles; it is good that their blankets cover them well and their scarves cover their heads and faces, for the wind is bitter and the cold intense, and the way is long. Thank goodness they have a sense of direction, for if the horses failed, never would they be found alive. They have left in their hogans their children, so they might find food for their families. Their wagon is under a tree, a solitary tree; frozen sheep are here and there half covered in the snow. That frozen one that the boy is dragging is one of over

half a million sheep, goats, and cattle that were stranded
with no food save that from a lucky drop. They will
have food for a few days but soon the carcasses will be
spoiled beyond eating.

Why do I return to a rehearsal of the indignities
against the Indian? The answer is that we have a debt
to pay. We are deeply indebted and we shall never have
liquidated that debt until we shall have done all in our
power to rebuild the Indian and give him back the opportunities that are possible for us to give him.

The glider without an engine lies helpless on the
ground until a motorized plane tows it high into the air
with a tow line. When the glider is aloft, it is on its own
and flies about at the will of its pilot, hundreds of miles
in either direction—up and down, even to high altitudes.
The pilot finds the updrafts and increases his altitude.
He sails from updraft to updraft like a great bird in the
air. He remains aloft until he chooses to descend.

Remember that the glider would remain on the
ground until it rotted unless some power lifted it. The
sailplane is the Indian. The tow line is the Indian program
and the gospel of Christ. The members of the Church
are the power plane and must do the lifting and the tow-
ing. The updrafts are the gospel principles.

And this, of course, reminds us of Paul's statement
to Rome:

> For whosoever shall call upon the name of the Lord shall
> be saved.
> How then shall they call on him in whom they have not
> believed? and how shall they believe in him of whom they
> have not heard? and how shall they hear without a preacher?
> (Romans 10:13-14.)

*We* must be the preachers.

As we see the Indians pushed from pillar to post;
from the eastern seaboard to the west; from their free,
open country to their narrow, limited reservations; from

their carefree, open world to their limited lands supposed worthless, we remember Jacob's lament:

> . . . the time passed away with us, and also our lives passed away like as it were unto us a dream, we being a lonesome and a solemn people, wanderers, cast out from Jerusalem, born in tribulation, in a wilderness, and hated of our brethren, which caused wars and contentions; wherefore, we did mourn out our days. (Jacob 7:26.)

In our own dispensation, the Indian was vanishing. In the Cherokees' "Trail of Tears," 4,600 died within a very short time on that merciless march from Georgia to Indian Territory. There were no marked graves. Herded like cattle, they traveled ten miles a day.

We were told that 450 years ago, nearly a million American Indians inhabited what is now the United States. By the close of the nineteenth century, sometimes referred to as a "Century of Shame," only 235,000 remained.

I have seen changes myself. On October 23, 1927, the Arizona Temple at Mesa, Arizona, was dedicated by President Heber J. Grant. At that time, I was stake clerk of the St. Joseph Stake and was secretary of the temple fund and collected the tens of thousands of dollars that the people of our stake contributed for the erection of this temple.

In the dedication services, President Grant made reference to the part which the Lamanites would play in this particular temple.

> We beseech thee, O Lord, that thou wilt stay the hand of the destroyer among the descendants of Lehi who reside in this land and give unto them increasing virility and more abundant health, that they may not perish as a people but that from this time forth they may increase in numbers and in strength and in influence, that all the great and glorious promises made concerning the descendants of Lehi may be fulfilled in them; that they may grow in vigor of body and of mind, and above all love for thee and thy son, and increase in diligence and in faithfulness in keeping the commandments which have

come to them with the gospel of Jesus Christ, and that many
of them may have the privilege of entering this holy house
and receiving ordinances for themselves and their departed
ancestors. (*Temples of the Most High,* p. 173.)

It is remembered that the Indian was called, for long
years, "the Vanishing American," and disease and hardships and hunger and war had, through the years, taken
their heavy toll.

Wilford Woodruff, the President of the Church, in
an oft-quoted statement said:

> I am looking for the fulfillment of all things that the Lord
> has spoken, and they will come to pass as the Lord God lives.
> Zion is bound to rise and flourish. The Lamanites will blossom
> as the rose on the mountains. I am willing to say here that,
> although I believe this, when I see the power of the nation
> destroying them from the face of the earth, the fulfillment of
> that prophecy is perhaps harder for me to believe than any
> revelation of God that I ever read. It looks as though there
> would not be enough [Indians] left to receive the Gospel; but
> notwithstanding this dark picture, every word that God has
> ever said of them will have its fulfillment, and they, by and
> by, will receive the Gospel. It will be a day of God's power
> among them, and a nation will be born in a day. Their chiefs
> will be filled with the power of God and receive the Gospel,
> and they will go forth and build the new Jerusalem, and we
> shall help them. They are branches of the house of Israel. . . .
> (*Journal of Discourses* 15:282.)

The Lamanite population of the Americas, at the
greatest number, must have run into many millions, for
in certain periods of Book of Mormon history, wars continued almost unabated and the soil was covered with the
bodies of the slain. Mormon says:

> . . . and there had been thousands slain on both sides,
> both the Nephites and the Lamanites. (Mormon 4:9.)

> And it is impossible for the tongue to describe, or for man
> to write a perfect description of the horrible scene of the blood
> and carnage. . . . (Mormon 4:11.)

There were the peoples of the Mulekites, all of whom
were slain. There were the people of the Jaredites who in-

habited the land for centuries and who must have grown
to great numbers. Coriantumr, you remember, saw—

> that there had been slain by the sword already nearly two
> millions of his people [Was it ever heard of before or since, two
> million in a battle?] . . . yea, there had been slain two millions
> of mighty men, and also their wives and their children. (Ether
> 15:2.)

As Mormon tells of the last great battle, he tells of his
his own ten thousand who were hewn down and the ten
thousand of Moroni. Then twenty-one other men with
their ten thousand each—

> and their flesh, and bones, and blood lay upon the face of the
> earth . . . to molder upon the land, and to crumble and to return
> to their mother earth. (Mormon 6:15.)

The remnants of Israel broke up into numerous tribes
and families and the civil war battles continued. It is
estimated by some that when Columbus came, there were
only about 233,000 of the scores of millions who had been
on this continent. They were almost gone and were still
vanishing by war and pestilence.

In 1927, when President Grant offered this prayer,
they were losing their children, as Mormon said. "They
were considered as naught" before the oncoming settlers,
and when the smoke of battles dissipated, the dead white
men were lauded, numbered, buried, but the Indians were,
in fact, uncounted. They had been dying by war and now,
after their subjugation in 1868, they were dying from germs
and viruses, starvation and freezing. Their health level was
at perhaps an all-time low. The infant mortality was ter-
rifyingly high. How could little babes survive? The inci-
dence of tuberculosis and other diseases was unbelievable.
The Indians' water supply was contaminated generally,
and potentially dangerous; and without waste disposal
facilities, viral infections and pneumonia and malnutrition were common and devastating.

> Since 1900, the American Indians have climbed back to
> over 600,000 in number. By 1975, they will have reached their
> original force; in fact today, Indians comprise the fastest

growing ethnic group in America. There is now a significant number of them in every state of the Union. (Gordon H. Fraser, *Moody*, p. 23.)

There are probably nearly as many actual members of the Church today who are Lamanites and Mestizos (people of mixed blood partly Lamanite) as there were total Indians in the United States when the tide turned and the vanishing American began to increase, in line with the prayers and prophecies of the leaders of the Church.

Today they are coming into the Church in large numbers. There are several stakes largely Lamanite, with ward, quorum, and auxiliary leadership from the Lamanites. There are many missions devoted to teaching Lehi's children.

There are some many thousands of youngsters in the Indian seminary program, thousands of Indians in United States universities and a larger number in the Pacific schools and BYU. There are many thousands in schools in Mexico and Chile and in the Pacific and in the Indian placement program.

Many young people have filled missions and thousands are now preparing for them. Numerous Lamanites are receiving their endowments and sealings.

Some of my most happy moments have been when I have been performing marriage ceremonies in the holy temple with two wonderful Indians across the altar.

The Twelve Apostles in their "Proclamation to the World" in 1845 stated:

> Thy sons and daughters of Zion will soon be required to devote a portion of their time in instructing the children of the forest, for they must be educated and instructed in all the arts of civil life, as well as in the gospel.
>
> They must be clothed, fed, and instructed in the principles and practice of virtue, modesty, temperance, cleanliness, industry, mechanical arts, manners, customs, dress, music and all other things which are calculated in their nature to REFINE, PURIFY, EXALT, and GLORIFY them as sons and daughters of the

royal house of Israel and of Joseph, who are making ready for the coming of the bridegroom.

And so as the sons and daughters of Zion we will soon be required to give a portion of our time, the Lord says through his prophets, to the training and teaching of these Lamanites, who have been deprived so long and who now are beginning to stretch and yawn and awaken from their sleep and come into their own.

As Elder Boyd K. Packer returned from Peru, he told me of his experience in a branch sacrament meeting in Cuzco in the lofty Andes. The chapel was still, the opening exercises finished, and the sacrament in preparation.

A little Lamanite ragamuffin entered from the street. Calloused and chappy were the little feet that brought him in the open door, up the aisle, and to the sacrament table. Here was dark and dirty testimony of deprivation, want, unsatisfied hungers—spiritual as well as physical. Almost unobserved, he slyly came to the sacrament table and, with a seeming spiritual hunger, leaned against the table and lovingly rubbed his unwashed face against the cool, smooth-white linen.

A woman in the front seat, seemingly outraged by the intrusion, caught his eye, and with motion and frown, sent the little ragamuffin scampering down the aisle out into his world, the street.

A bit later the little urchin, seemingly compelled by some inner urge, overcame his timidity and came stealthily, cautiously down the aisle again, fearful, ready to escape if necessary, but impelled as though directed by inaudible voices with "a familiar spirit" and as though memories long and faded were reviving, as though some intangible force were crowding him on to seek something for which he yearned but could not identify.

From his seat on the stand, Elder Packer caught his eye, beckoned to him, and stretched out big welcoming arms. After a moment's hesitation, the little Lamanite ragamuffin was nestled comfortably on his lap, in his arms, the tousled head against the great warm heart—a heart sympathetic to waifs, and especially to little Lamanite ones.

Later, Elder Packer with a subdued voice recalled this incident to me. As he sat forward on his chair, his eyes glistening, emotion in his voice, he said: "As this little one relaxed in my arms, it seemed it was not a single little Lamanite I held. It was a nation, indeed a multitude of nations of deprived, hungering souls, wanting something deep, good and warm they could not explain—a humble people yearning to revive memories all but faded out, of ancestors standing wide-eyed, open-mouthed, expectant and excited. A people reaching for truths they seemed to remember only vaguely; for prophecies which surely would some day be fulfilled; looking up and seeing an holy glorified Being descend from celestial areas and hearing a voice say: 'Behold, I am Jesus Christ, the Son of God . . . and in me, hath the Father glorified his name . . . I am the light and the life of the world.' "

The day of the Lamanite is surely here and we are God's instrument in helping to bring to pass the prophecies of renewed vitality, acceptance of the gospel, and resumption of a favored place as part of God's chosen people. The promises of the Lord will all come to pass; we could not thwart them if we would. But we do have it in our power to hasten or delay the process by our energetic or neglectful fulfillment of our responsibilities.

# Chapter Thirty-four

# A Changing World for Barry Begay

*T*here he is, running like the wind, barefoot, hatless, long hair in flight, worn overalls and ragged shirt, his face brown from the Arizona sun and wind and from his brown-skinned parents. Barry and his little brothers and sisters are a lively group, playing around the rock, pole, and dirt hogan.

The Begays, sitting on the dirt floor, are eating their meal. There is a leg of mutton. There is fry bread. There are no spoons, no forks. There is no milk. They have no cow. There is no salad. They have no garden. The fare is scant.

Barry is seven. His youngest brother has no clothes on his little brown body. The sisters have long full skirts, like their mother's, with some silver coins sewn to their blouses.

The mother's worn purple velveteen skirt reaches near her ankles; her waist is of greenish hue, her shoes high laced, her hair in a bob at the back of her neck and tied with white wool yarn. The father is thin and tall. He wears his curled-up hat even while he eats. They are not demonstrative but it is evident that pride and affection are in these humble quarters.

A few days pass. It is bright and summery. In Navajo land Barry Begay is herding sheep. The pasture, overgrazed, is dry and dusty. The scraggly dog also shows malnutrition. But as he barks and bites hind legs, the woolly animals heed direction. The little boy has a man's responsibility, for there are coyotes and other predatory animals also starving in this barren valley, and the sheep are precious. The sheep furnish meat for the table; the pelts cover the cold ground in their hogan, being at once rug, chair, bed, cover. The fleece is sold at the trading post or saved to card and spin and weave into rugs to exchange for flour and cloth and food.

Under the shade of the lone cedar tree, Mother Begay, an expert weaver, sits on the ground and laboriously works into an intricate design the yarns she has dyed in brilliant colors.

Two years have passed. Nine-year-old Barry may now go to the new government school only three miles away. Little Susie can herd the sheep and drive away the predators. For Barry it will be a long walk, and at times, the wind will be merciless; the sun will beat down like a blow torch, and the snow will be wet and freezing; but loving parents, anxious to give their children what they themselves never had, are determined that he make the effort.

Another summer day and the wind in whirling cones picks up tumbleweeds and dances across the valley. Two fair and well-groomed young men approach the hogan. Father Begay is fixing his wagon, and Mother Begay sits under the gnarled, weathered cedar weaving her blanket.

"*Yatehee,*" they say in greeting as they wipe the sweat from their brows and introduce themselves as missionaries for The Church of Jesus Christ of Latter-day Saints. The Begays have heard about the elders. In spite of the language barrier, John and Mary Begay seem to understand that the book about which the elders speak is a history of their "old people" back for ages. It seems that the spirit that accompanies the strange mixture of words and signs is that of a "familiar spirit." Genuine interest in the message and attraction to the pleasing personality of the teen-age ministers brings about many hours of learning, and then one day the Begays are baptized in the little pond some distance away. They are now members of the far-away Salt Lake City church in which they have confidence and a warm feeling of belonging.

Barry is ten years old now, husky, laughing, running, and joking. He is summer-herding the sheep. The missionaries who have taught Barry in the trailer house Indian seminary now announce a fantastic new program. Barry may go to a far-away city and live in a good home, attend a superior school, and be given other advantages not afforded on the reservation. Unthinkable, they feel at first, to send their little boy so far away for so long a time. But, convinced it is for Barry's good, the parents agree.

All the family goes in the wagon to the point of assembly, a day's journey away, and with few tears but pounding hearts place their loved boy on the big bus with about thirty other little Indians. Stoically they stand like statues until the bus disappears over the horizon. The hogan is a little empty without Barry, but opportunity will come to him.

A few days later, the Begays receive a fat letter from the Smiths, the foster family where Barry has become a loved member, telling how the bus has been met by interested case workers who love the Indian people, how Barry has had a haircut by a kindly volunteer barber, has been bathed and shampooed by other friendly volunteer men, and then has been examined by dentists and doctors and nurses, all of whom freely give of their time without compensation. The letter also tells of Barry's timidity and silence at first and then of his blossoming out when he feels the warmth in his new home and family.

In summers Barry is back with the sheep—back in the hogan where there are now beds and a table and chairs. He is helping the Begay family to get into the regular habit of family prayers on their knees, "the Lord's way." They are speaking better English now that Barry teaches them. On Sundays the Begays drive to the distant branch and Barry helps with the sacrament and speaks in the meeting, telling about his experiences in the northern land.

Another summer is over. Again, the family is at the gathering point and three instead of one climb out of the Begay wagon and board the big bus for the north. The two sisters have mixed feelings of fear and eagerness. With near-empty arms and hearts, the Begay parents return with their smaller ones to the hogan. Their personal sacrifices for their children are calculated ones.

Arriving in Utah, there are happy renewals of friendships. Barry is enrolled in seminary and in MIA. He takes part in dramatic skits, music groups, and athletics. Now he is a priest. He may teach, baptize with authority, bless the sacrament emblems. No privilege available to any boy is denied this fast-growing young brave.

Eventful years have passed. It is graduation night, and Barry in cap and gown receives his high school diploma. Barry has been president of his class. He was swift and strong and accurate on the ward basketball team.

At home, the faithful lives of his parents have brought them prosperity. They spend nothing on tobacco or liquor. All goes into their progressive living. Barry is surprised to find this time a two-room frame house out in front of the hogan. There are curtains at the windows and rugs on the lumber floors, and a cupboard with dishes and pots and pans. The gospel and the church associations are working miracles with the Begay family.

Another year is history. Two young nineteen-year-olds, one brown and one white, are driving a Rambler and approach a cluster of hogans. Barry, the Indian elder, takes the lead, for he can speak two languages fluently. He knows the people's thinking processes, their idioms and expressions, their reactions. Other families are converted. Coffee is thrown away and milk substituted. No more liquor for these good people—that money will go into fixing up the home. At the river, twenty men and women and children are baptized into the fold of Christ's church. A little branch is organized and Elder Begay is its first president, soon to be replaced by the Indian converts as they are trained. He speaks feelingly to his people: "I am proud to be a Mormon. I am proud to be an Indian. I will attend BYU and obtain training through which to serve my people."

The two years of his mission have flown as if by magic. Elder Begay says farewell to his fellow missionaries, stops a few days at the Begay home to ruffle his hair, put on his old overalls, run with the dog, tend the sheep, and tell his loved folks more about the glorious message he has learned. He also tells them of the beautiful, talented Indian girl he met at the university and of his growing romantic interest in her. As he returns to college, the wise and generous tribe gives him a scholarship, making his further education a certainty.

"Time flies on wings of lightning." We are now in the beautiful temple dedicated in "Holiness to the Lord." The room is large, and the furnishings exquisite. The tan rug helps keep a sacred quietness. Many Indian and non-Indian people are here, including the four parents: the real parents and the foster parents, so kind and gracious and generous. The years and the associations have made some changes in John and Mary Begay. His long bobbed hair of years ago is short now. He wears a suit; his shoes have been shined and his clothes pressed. There he sits today, tall and dark and handsome in his white temple clothes. Mary still loves her beads and turquoise, her silver and her velveteen, but she now modernizes and stylizes her hair and dresses. Happy beyond expression, she wants to be sealed for all eternity to this stalwart husband with whom she has shared joy and pain, hardship and privilege, wind and weather.

What a beautiful couple they are as Barry and his bright-eyed sweetheart, Gladys, stand admiring one another, then kneel and are sealed for all eternity! She wipes a tear and his eyes are glistening.

And now, John and Mary kneel across the altar. The faces, which were near expressionless that first time we saw them, are now beaming. There is a new light in those eyes. In their white temple clothing they look heavenly. And through the impressive priesthood ceremony, Mary becomes the wife of John for all eternity. There are, you know, tears of ecstasy and joy, and these are of that holy kind.

Today is gone. Tomorrow dawns. On the university campus, the organ is playing a staccato march. The graduates in dark gowns and tasseled caps march from the gathering field to the auditorium. Yes, there they are on the sixth row, and the Begay parents are beaming, as is Gladys with two little ones by her side and a baby in her arms. In the marching lines are many Indian graduates. And there is Barry. How handsome and poised he is! And now the president of the university is awarding the doctoral degrees. When the name Barry Begay is spoken, my heart leaps. Barry Begay with a doctor's degree! Our Barry Begay with a Ph.D! *Our* Barry Begay! All our efforts, our disappointments, our worries, our battles with contending forces; all our waiting and striving and praying seem nothing. Our dreams are coming true! John, Mary, and Gladys modestly wait their turn to express pride and affection to their Dr. Barry Begay.

The scene changes to Windowrock. Several years have passed. At his desk in a most vital position as tribal councilman, Barry Begay wields a powerful influence among his people. Because of him and his fellow workers, the Indians now ride in better cars on safer highways to better homes. There are lights and water and telephones and radio and TV. Their sick are treated in modern, well-equipped hospitals, and Indian nurses attend the patients for whom Indian doctors prescribe and on whom they operate. Tribal funds derived from gas, oil, coal, and timber guarantee every Indian child schooling through college. The Indians are experts on the farm, on the grazing lands, in the silversmith shop. Indian teachers train the little ones; Indian lawyers look after legal matters. Trained Indians are prominent in office, industry, business, government, and on college faculties. There are Indian governors, senators, and impressive and influential laymen.

The scene changes and more years pass. It is the Sabbath. This stake conference congregation is mostly Indian. The one-hundred-voice choir is a dark-skinned folk, though they are now much lighter. They have long been delightsome. General Authorities from Salt Lake City are here. The high council and bishoprics, largely Indian, sit on the stand of the newly completed stake and ward building. Here is dignity. Three thousand eyes and ears are focused on the impressive man who rises to the pulpit. It is President Barry Begay, former bishop, who preaches such a profound sermon to his people. His children are all being well trained. His son, Barry, Jr., serves on a mission in Bolivia.

It is President Begay, Doctor Begay, Brother Begay, Elder Begay who administers to the sick in the hospital, preaches funeral sermons, assists people with their marital, moral, financial problems. It is *our* Barry Begay, the little boy who is now a great man.

There are thousands of Barrys in all stages of that life story. They are of many tribes from New York to Santiago, from Anchorage to Montevideo and the isles of the sea. They talk many languages and dialects. They are coming from Cardston and Bemidji, from Blackfoot and Hopi land, from South America and Mexico. Great numbers are coming to training in schools and church, growing in wisdom and stature, learning the best of the white man's culture and retaining the best of their own.

The Lord chose to call them Lamanites. They are fulfilling prophecies. They are a chosen people with noble blood in their veins. They are casting off the fetters of superstition, fear, ignorance, prejudice, and are clothing themselves with knowledge, good works, and righteousness.

Yesterday they were deprived, weak, and vanishing; today thousands are benefitting in the Indian seminaries, in regular ones, and in college institutes of religion as they become involved in the placement program and in church work within the stakes and missions. Many are receiving secular as well as spiritual training in Mexico, South America, and Hawaii, and the isles of the sea. Many are now in college and large numbers in full-time mission service. Tens of thousands are in church organizations in all the Americas and in the Pacific. Lamanite-Nephite leaders are now standing forth to direct and inspire their people.

The day of the Lamanite is here and the gospel brings opportunity. Millions farm the steep hillsides of Andean ranges and market their produce with llamas and burros. They must have the emancipating gospel. Millions in Ecuador, Chile, and Bolivia serve in menial labor, eking out bare subsistence from soil and toil. They must hear the compelling truths. Millions through North America are deprived, untrained, and achieving less than their potential. They must have the enlightening gospel. It will break their fetters, stir their ambition, increase their vision, and open new worlds of opportunity to them. Their captivity will be at an end—the captivity of misconceptions, illiteracy, superstition, fear. "The clouds of error disappear before the rays of truth divine."

The brighter day has dawned. The scattering has been accomplished—the gathering is in process. May the Lord bless us all as we become nursing parents unto our Lamanite brethren and hasten the fulfillment of the great promises made to them.

# Index

Abandonment of sin, 180
Abinadi, 99
Abraham, 23, 49-51, 89
Adultery, 133, 138-39, 143, 174, 176-77, 230, 233
Ages of Church Presidents, 316
Allredge, Ida, 106
Alma, 161, 206
Alma the Younger, 310
Anonymous woman, letter from, 293
Apostasy, 62
Apostles, 34, 38, 43, 314
Archaeology, 330
Argentina, 137
Arizona Temple, 344
"Armour of God," 213, 219
Arrogance, 287
Astronomy, 49, 331
Authority, 328

Baal, worship of, 9
Babies, 323
Ballard, Melvin J., 40, 43, 100
Baptism, 17
Bareham, F. M., 323
Baton twirling, 165
Begay, Barry, 351-57
Begay, Barry, Jr., 357
Begay, Gladys, 356
Begay, John, 352, 355-56
Begay, Mary, 352, 355-56
Begay, Susie, 352

Belshazzar, 55
Benediction, 201
Bible, 336
Bigotry, 294
Birth, 323
Bishop, confession to, 181
Bleak, James C., 44
Blessing on food, 201
Blessings, 222, 224, 271
Blood, missionary who sold, 264-65
Book of Mormon, 80, 329-37
Borrowing, 234
Bribes, 236
Brigham Young (movie), 29
Brotherhood, 298
Brotherly love, 303
Budgeting, 129; for tithing, 288
Businessman, impressed by honest Mormon, 240-41

Cain, sin of, 243
Calling of General Authorities, 33-34, 38, 43
Calling of stake presidency, 35
Cannon, David H., 44
Cannon, George Q., 21, 35, 37, 39, 42, 46
Careers for women, 128
Carthage Jail, 100
Celestial life, 85
Character, 242
Chastity, 151-59, 162, 169-74, 216
Cheating, 229

Cherokees, 342, 344

Children, 117-18, 119, 132, 187-88, 206, 262, 263, 307, 324

Christ, Jesus, appears to Abraham, 89; appears to Enoch, 71-72; appears to Joseph Smith, 79-81, 93; appears to Nephites, 73, 78-79; appears to Saul of Tarsus, 89-90; bears witness to Adam and Eve, 71; birth of, 56, 73; calls apostles, 75; childhood of, 74; coming to America, 334; concept of, 69-81; created earth, 70-71; crucifixion of, 77; in vision of Orson F. Whitney, 26-27; is omnipotent, 96; love of for Lamanites, 302; miracles of, 75-76; raises the dead, 76; Redeemer of the world, 70; resurrection of, 56, 77; second coming of, 249-57; serving, 221-24; Son of God, 85; taught forgiveness, 194; taught tolerance, 294; testimony of, 69-81; transfiguration of, 23, 91; travels of, 74-75; witness of Nicodemus concerning, 14-19; worlds created by, 50

Church callings, 207

Church membership, 112

Church programs for Indians, 347

Cigarettes, 229, 274

Civilizations, rise and fall of, 51

Colonization of West, 28, 29, 306

Colton, Don B., 273

Columbus, Christopher, 46

Commandments, 184, 189, 223-24, 274, 283, 311

Communication, 137-40

Communion with God, 4

Compliance, 305-11

Confession of sin, 181

Consecration, 3

Council in heaven, 70-71, 87

Council of the Twelve, 259, 314, 347

Courage, 15, 311

Courtship, 176

Coveting, 145

Cowdery, Oliver, 5, 31, 80, 205, 310

Creation of worlds, 50, 53, 70-71

Criticism, 188, 193, 306

Custer, George, 341

Daniel, 90, 244-45

Davis Stake, 35

Death, 43, 95-106, 287

Deceit, 240

Decisions, 205

Declaration of Independence, 44

Dedication, 259-65

Dedication prayer, 201

Desert, living on, 109

Destiny, 105

Diamonds, analogy of, 83

Dickinson, Hannie, 241

Disfellowshiping, 178

Dishonesty, 229, 234, 237, 239, 247

Disobedience, 268, 305

Divine language, 319

Divorce, 217, 247

Dreams, 24

Drinking, 228, 274

Embezzlement, 239

Employment, 130

Endowment House, 45, 46

Engineering, 332

Enoch, 23, 31, 54, 71, 90

Enos, 24, 112, 181, 209-10

Eternal life, 14, 16, 97, 246

Evening gown, 165, 167

Evil, 213-19, 226

Exaltation, 279

Example, 319

Excommunication, 178

Extra-terrestrial civilizations, 48

Faith, 3-12, 205, 223, 245; of Adam, 4; of Abraham, 6-7; of children of Israel, 7-9; of Elijah, 9-10; of Joshua, 9; of Noah, 5-6; of Sarah, 6; reservoirs of, 110; to live commandments, 11

False Christ, 252

False witness, 187

Family cooperation, 262

Family home evening, 112, 123, 247, 264

Family planning, 132

Family prayer, 112, 199-201, 247

Fast offerings, 202

Fasting, 4

Fellowship, 296

Fidelity, 133-34, 141-48

Filthy lucre, 236

Forgiveness, 173, 187-96, 205

Fornication, 173, 174, 177

Free agency, 96, 97

Freedom, 217, 225

Fruit grower, example of, 284

Fruit stand, example of, 241

Funeral of BYU student, 101

Gamaliel, 309

Garden of Eden, 71

Genealogy, 41

General Authorities, calling of, 33-34, 38, 43

Geology, 331

George Washington University Law School, 273

Glider, analogy of, 343

God, appears to Joseph Smith, 93; appears to Moses, 86; creed concerning, 63; how to know, 67, 86; knowledge of, 84; manifestation of, 83-93; one of three Gods, 85; search for, 60; source of blessings, 287; stealing from, 289; theologian viewpoints of, 61-62; trust in, 106, 288; visits of, 57

Godhead, 85

Good works, 183

Government in Book of Mormon, 332

Grant, Heber J., 32, 34, 37, 43, 316, 344

Grant, Jedediah M., 25

Gratitude, 202

Greed, 237

Grudges, holding, 195

Gruman, Lawrence Lowell, 157


Habit, 228

Happiness, 126, 196

Hawaii, hukilau in, 251

Health, laws of, 205

Hezekiah, 104

History of Jews and gentiles, 330

Hollywood actress, 155

Home, 247

Home-breaking, 144

Homemaking, career of, 128

Honesty, 235, 241, 247, 289

Hotel Utah, 241

House on beach, example of, 285

Hubbard, Elbert, 243

Humility, 185

Hyde, Orson, 30, 36, 41

Hypocrisy, 184, 246, 298


Idleness of youth, 120-22

Ignorance, 279

Immodesty, 146, 163-68, 169-74

Immorality, 230

Incompatibility, 144

Indian boy, story of, 348-49

Indian programs in Church, 347

Indian seminaries, 358

Indian student placement program, 353-54

Indians, 263, 301, 339-49

Infidelity, 133-34, 138-39, 141-48, 174

Insincerity, 184

Integrity, 233-48, 284, 287

Intolerance, 188

Isaac, sacrifice of, 6-7

Israelites, promises to, 297

Jacob, 111

Jaredites, 72

John the Baptist, 5, 57, 308

Johnson, Luke, 41

Johnson, Lyman, 41

Joseph, vision of, 26

Judge's comments on youth, 120-22

Judging others, 299

Justice, 222

Juvenile delinquency, 116, 120-22


Kimball, David Patten, 104

Kimball, Heber C., 25, 36, 46, 105

Kindness, 233

King Ahab, 10

King Follett address, 66

Kingdom, building, 221

Knowledge, of God, 59-67, 278; reservoirs of, 110; secular, 280; spiritual, 278, 280

Kolob, 50


Lamanites, 296, 300, 303, 339-49, 351-57

Language, prayer, 201

Laws of health, 205

Lee, Harold B., 296, 315, 316, 318

Lehi, 340, 342

Liahona, 47

Life on other planets, 54

Liquor, 228, 274

Logan Temple, 40

Lord's Prayer, 190

Love, 130-31, 147, 153, 154, 157-58, 191, 203

Low-necked fashions, 166

Loyalty, 137-40

Lucifer (see SATAN)

Lust, 133, 153, 159, 174, 176-77


Manifesto, 42

Mantle of authority, 328

Mantle of leadership, 42

Maoris, 301

Marital problems, 138-39

Marriage, 125-35, 138-39, 141-48, 155

Marriage covenant, 144

Materialism, 19

Matthias, 18

McAllister, J.D.T., 44, 45

McClellan, William E., 41

McKay, David O., 32, 39, 122, 313, 316

Melchizedek Priesthood, 57

Merrill, Marriner W., 41, 43

*Message to Garcia*, 243

Messages from other worlds, 55

Messengers, divine, 56-57

Migrations, in Book of Mormon, 331

Military strategy, 333
Minority groups, 298
Miracles, 3-12
Missionaries, 31, 199, 202, 205, 213-15, 264, 352-53
Mistletoe, story of, 226-27
Modesty, 161-68
Morality, 143, 155, 218, 225, 230, 249
Mosaic law, 190
Moses, 23, 86-88, 267
Mothers, 115-19, 261
Motives, 311
Mount of Transfiguration, 23
Mulekites, 345
Musser, Elder, 27

Navajo, 342, 352
Nebuchadnezzar, 10
Necking, 176
Negroes, 295-96
Nephi, 111, 208, 209
Nephites, 78, 335
New morality, 218, 225
Nicodemus, 14-19
Noah, 5-6

Obedience, 223, 280
Oppression, 237
Organization of Church, 35

Packer, Boyd K., 348-49
Parable of Good Sower, 251
Parable of Pharisee and Publican, 298
Parable of Prodigal Son, 225, 310
Parable of Rich Man, 282
Parable of Ten Virgins, 253-55
Parable of Unmerciful Servant, 192-93
Parent-child relationships, 123
Parents, 111, 112, 115-23, 128, 132, 176, 187-88, 206, 262, 263, 307
*Parents* magazine, 118
Paul, 18, 23, 99, 209
Peter, 91, 244
Peter, James, and John, 5, 23, 26, 57, 91
Peterson, Ziba, 31
Petting, 158, 159, 170, 174, 176
Pharaoh, 49
Physical handicaps, 158
Pioneers, 28-29, 306
Polynesians, 331
Pornography, 152, 247
Portrait painted for temple room, 259
Prayer, 4, 97, 122, 131, 134, 171, 199-212, 213, 215
"Prayer and an Epitaph," 240
Prayer language, 201
Predictions of disasters, 252

Prejudice, 293-304
Premarital sex, 151-59
Preparedness, 249-57
Presidency of the Church, 313-21
President of the United States, 44
Priesthood, 99, 102, 131, 204, 295
Principles, 139
Proclamation on Lamanites, 347
Procrastination, 256
Prophecy, 341
Prophets, 327
Psychology, in Book of Mormon, 332

Qualifications for prophet, 319
Quarreling, 134, 144, 187
Queen contests, 163-64

Race, 294
Ranching, example of, 281
Rationalizing, 18
Rebellion against God, 305, 309
Release from office, 307
Repentance, 146, 159, 169-85, 187, 189, 210, 234
Reservoirs, 110
Restitution for sin, 182, 189
Restoration, 323-28
Revelation, 21-46, 319; comes in dreams, 24; concerning other worlds, 52; continuation of, 21, 22; discussed by George Q. Cannon, 21-23; for individual needs, 30; of Heber C. Kimball, 46; of signers of Declaration of Independence, 44; of soldiers in Europe, 30; of Wilford Woodruff, 24, 30-31; present-day, 43; sermon by Wilford Woodruff on, 41-42; to build temples, 32; to call apostles, 34
Rewards of living commandments, 283
Richards, Lee Greene, 259
Richards, George F., 39
Rigdon, Sidney, 5
Righteous living, 223, 256, 261
Righteousness, 109-14, 113, 233, 327
Rioting by teenagers, 116
Russell, Brother, 36

Sabbath day, 238, 267-71
Sacrament, 275
Sacrament meeting in Andes, 348-49
*Salt Lake Herald,* 26
Salt Lake Valley, 32
Samaritan woman, 294
Samoans, 301
Samuel the prophet, 236
Santa Claus, 69
Satan (Lucifer), 87-88, 92, 141

Saul, king of Israel, 305
Scout camp on Sabbath, 270
Sealing power, 319
Second coming of Christ, 249-57
Self, forgetting, 131
Self-control, 176
Self-esteem, 242
Self-justification, 234
Self-mastery, 280
Self-restraint, 225-31
Seminary outing on Sabbath, 270
Sermons in Book of Mormon, 334
Service, 221-24; Church, 282
Seventies, quorum of, 34
Sex exploitation, 156
Sexual impurity, 161
Shadrach, Meshach, and Abednego, 245
Shoplifting, 235
Sick, healing of, 103
Sin, sorrow for, 180, 229
Smith, Elder, 264
Smith family, 353
Smith, George A., 25, 36
Smith, George Albert, 32, 316
Smith, Hyrum, 36, 100
Smith, Jim, 226
Smith, Joseph, 12, 23, 25, 31, 32, 36, 37, 38, 42, 44, 52, 56, 66, 79-81, 84, 92-93, 100, 103, 194, 209, 242, 278, 308, 310, 315, 317, 324-25
Smith, Joseph F., 26, 32, 33, 38, 39, 42, 43, 101, 316
Smith, Joseph Fielding, 32, 279, 314, 316, 318
Smith, Lucy Mack, 325
Snow, Lorenzo, 315
Soldier in Italy, 30
Solitude, 209
Solomon's Temple, 32
Sorrow for sin, 180
Space, 47-58, 321, 330
Space communities, 51
Spafford, Belle S., 119
Spirit world, 104
Spiritual darkness, 84
Spiritual growth, 231
Spiritual life, 247
Spiritual preparedness, 255
St. George Temple, 44, 45
Stake organizations, 35-36
Stake presidency, how called, 35
Standards of Church, 175
Success, 261
Succession in the Presidency, 313-21
Suffering, 98
Sustaining those in authority, 306

Tabernacles, 32
Talmage, James E., 98
Tanner, Nathan Eldon, 315
Taylor, John, 34, 42, 315
Teasdale, George, 34
Teenagers, 116, 120-22
Telephone lines, analogy of, 137-40
Television, 53
Temple marriage, 127, 135, 260-61, 355
Temple work, 46, 263
Temples, 32, 33
Temptation, 139, 225
Ten Commandments, 267
Ten Tribes, 336
Testimony, 13-20, 69-81, 214, 215, 244
Testimony meeting, 275-76
Three Nephites, 335
*Time,* professor quoted in, 69
Tithing, 139, 202, 281
Tolerance, 293-304
Traffic violations, 235
Transgression, 229

Unchastity, 162, 169-74
Unselfishness, 263
Urim and Thummim, 47, 49, 50, 53

Visions, 23; of Abraham, 89; of Daniel, 90; of George F. Richards, 39-40; of Heber C. Kimball, 36; of Heber J. Grant, 37; of Joseph Smith, 56, 92; of Joseph F. Smith, 43-44, 101-102; of Marriner W. Merrill, 43; of Melvin J. Ballard, 40-41; of modern-day apostles, 36; of Moses, 86; of mothers, 324; of Old Testament prophets, 26; of Orson F. Whitney, 26-28; of Wilford Woodruff, 37
Voegel, Elder, 264

War, 334
Ward organizations, 35-36
Washington, George, 44
Wealth, earthly, 17
Wedding reception, 127
Welfare program, 110, 202
Wells, Bishop, 39
Wesley, John, 46
Whitmer, David, 310
Whitmer, Peter, 31
Whitney, Orson F., 26
Williams, Brother, 30
Witness, 4; of Christ, 18
Woodruff, Wilford, 24-25, 30-31, 32, 36, 37, 41, 44-46, 315, 345
Word of Wisdom, 242, 263, 273-80, 354

Work, 121-22
Working mothers, 116
Working on Sunday, 268
Working wife, 129
Worldliness, 209
Worship, way to, 271

Young, Brigham, 25, 28, 29, 32, 33, 35, 41,
   42, 44, 45, 119, 315, 317, 334
Young, Brigham, Jr., 37
Young, Richard W., 43
Young, Seymour B., 34
Youth, pressures on, 226